Foreign Affairs
Who Benefits From Trade?

Foreign Affairs September 2016

TABLE OF CONTENTS

TODAY AND TOMORROW

Introduction

Gideon Rose

REUTERS

Trade policy is one of the hottest issues of the 2016 election, but throughout the campaign, the level of discussion about it has been abysmally low. This collection is designed to correct that, offering readers everything they need to understand the relevant facts and arguments and make informed decisions for themselves about what should be done in this crucial arena.

The central political fact about trade is that its benefits are generally indirect and diffuse while its costs are often direct and concentrated. All told, the material gains outweigh the material costs, especially over time. But it is hard to realize those gains because the policies required to do so are often blocked by those who stand to lose. Battles over trade policy, therefore, often follow the "double movement" that economic historian Karl Polanyi ascribed to capitalism more generally: the operations of unfettered markets produce economic dynamism and social disruption, which in turn produce a political backlash aimed at stopping or reversing the process.

During the second half of the twentieth century, the advanced industrial world resolved this dialectic through a sort of synthesis, for both trade and capitalism at large: markets would be allowed to spread, domestically and internationally, but they would be checked and regulated by political actors in order to limit or offset their costs. The result was decades of growth and progress.

In recent years, however, opposition to trade has risen once again, to the point where both the Republican and the Democratic candidates for president have now openly declared their opposition to the Trans-Pacific Partnership (TPP)—the Barack Obama administration's flagship trade deal, which has been years in the making and still awaits confirmation. And it is now an article of faith for most supporters of Donald Trump and Bernie Sanders that preventing further global trade liberalization is crucial to restoring U.S. jobs and prosperity.

We at Foreign Affairs have been covering these debates closely for almost a century, and so we're delighted to offer this volume to inform and provide context for the crucial decisions that need to be made. In the pages that follow, readers will find a broad range of pieces from a star-studded lineup of trade supporters and critics, including Nobel Prize–winning economists, labor leaders, U.S. trade representatives from both sides of the aisle, and many others.

The first section, "We Didn't Start the Fire," gives some historical background: the basic case for the benefits from trade, stated just as the Depression's beggar-thy-neighbor policies led to a giant contraction of international commerce, followed by an update on the postwar policy consensus about the virtues of gradual, managed trade liberalization.

The second section, "Who, Whom?"—titled after the old Bolshevik adage that politics revolves around who wins and who loses—showcases the revival of U.S. trade debates in the 1980s and 1990s, when deindustrialization spurred fresh concerns that increasingly liberalized trade was hurting U.S. workers, particularly in the manufacturing sector. From Robert Reich to Paul Krugman, unemployment to wage stagnation to economic inequality, many of the authors and issues represented could be ripped from today's headlines.

The third section, "New Millennium, New Era?" continues the story into the twenty-first century, as the spread of the digital economy and rise of China and other developing nations gave a new twist to old disputes. Does the traditional calculus of comparative advantage still hold. Are any jobs safe from outsourcing? And how did the TPP become the centerpiece of the global trade agenda?

The final section, "Today and Tomorrow," takes stock of the current state of knowledge and policy, offering authoritative assessments of what has actually been learned over the years and putting the tussle over the TPP in its proper intellectual context. Just as war is too important to be left to the generals, so trade is too important to be left solely to the economists—or to demagogues and the uninformed. So read and decide for yourself!

GIDEON ROSE is Editor of *Foreign Affairs.*

Foreign Trade or Isolation?

G. B. Roorbach

REUTERS

ONE of the remarkable phenomena of the world's economic life in the past few decades has been the way in which international commerce has grown by leaps and bounds. A hundred years ago the aggregate value of world trade was less than $2,000,000,000 or only $2.34 per capita; by 1900 it had increased tenfold, to over $20,000,000,000, or $13.00 per capita. With the dawn of the twentieth century, however, the rate of increase became even more rapid, and in the interval between 1900 and the outbreak of the World War it doubled, reaching a value of $40,000,000,000 or $24.50 per capita.[i] By 1929 the value of world trade had reached a total of over 67 billion dollars -- more than $35.00 for every person on the face of the globe.[ii]

This rapid increase in international commerce was, of course, a corollary of the industrial revolution. The increase in factory production in favored industrial sections, at first predominantly in Great Britain, created a demand for materials far beyond the ability of the local region to supply; and at the same time the magnitude of machine output required a market much larger than the local area had capacity to consume. This meant that to the trade in articles of skill and refinement, in goods of high value and small bulk, which for centuries had dominated international exchange, there was added the enormous volume of bulky foods and raw materials characteristic of present-day trade. The limited local economy of days before the industrial revolution was transformed with startling rapidity into a world economy in which the economic machine of each country was dependent more and more upon the smooth operation of the economic organization of every other country. The industrial countries grew and prospered under this division of economic activity, as did also the countries producing the foods and raw materials which were exchanged for the factory-made goods. Standards of living increased along with rapid increases in populations.

In the United States, the growth of foreign trade has followed in general the trend of the trade of the rest of the world. There was a gradual but not rapid growth of American exports following 1830; a more rapid expansion from 1850 to 1873, when American cotton, foodstuffs, forest products and mineral exports came into increasing demand in industrialized Europe; a much less rapid growth from the depression of 1873 down to the end of the nineties; and then at the opening of the century a burst of exports which was still further stimulated by the war and, after a lull in 1920, carried on upward during the post-war boom. In 1929 exports from the United States were in value more than twice the value of pre-war exports and, after eliminating price changes, 70 percent greater in volume. The United States became the greatest exporter of all the nations in absolute amounts, although in per capita importance it was still behind the small industrial nations of Europe or sparsely populated agricultural nations such as Australia. The great advance in American foreign trade during the post-war period was in manufactured products. Although crude material exports had increased markedly in absolute amounts, and foodstuff exports also were larger, the great advances were in manufactured goods. In 1929 manufactured products made up 63 percent of the vastly expanded American exports as compared to 32 percent of our much smaller trade in 1900.

This period of expanding exports in the United States was, of course, also a period of tremendous increase in domestic trade. In fact, the growth of exports as a whole did not quite keep pace with the growth of production. This was due especially to the fact that farm products exported did not keep pace with the tremendous increase in farm production during the period. In the export of manufactured goods other than foodstuffs, however, a larger percentage of production was exported in 1929 (9.1 percent) than in 1900 (7.8 percent). In a country as large as the United States and with such diverse resources it of course is inevitable that the domestic market should absorb a large part of the total production. What is foreign trade to the small countries of Europe is domestic inter-state trade in the United States. But the fact that foreign trade takes so large a proportion as 10 percent of the tremendous production of the country is a factor of the very first importance to our industries and to our general economic prosperity.

Following the great depression that began in 1929, foreign trade of all countries suffered a great decline. The exports of the United States in 1931 were less than half those of 1929 in value although the marked decline in prices materially exaggerates the decline when value figures are used. For the first quarter of 1932, exports were 35 percent less than for the corresponding quarter of 1931 and 60 percent less than the five-year average, 1927-31. No other important trading country has had so great a falling off in its foreign trade, although the decrease is universally large.

The great slump in international trade during the last two and a half years raises the question as to the actual importance of foreign trade in the modern world and especially its future significance to the United States. Certain it is that the economic conditions favoring the flow of trade have grown steadily more and more adverse in recent years; and political action has made the barriers more and more insurmountable or impenetrable.

It has been suggested that the era of large foreign trade development characteristic of the past one hundred years has come to an end. The spread of industrialization and the growth of agricultural production in many parts of the world, the intense nationalism that seeks for each country economic as well as political independence, the multiplication of trade barriers through tariffs and other means until trade in some regions is all but eliminated -- all these factors are pointed to as indicating a permanent growth of local economic self-sufficiency and a corresponding decline in international trade. The first phase of the industrial revolution, it is said, was one in which certain nations, having become highly industrialized largely as a result of an early start, of necessity traded heavily with those nations which remained producers of foods and raw materials; but now the world has become, or is in process of becoming, commercially equalized. There has been, so to speak, an economic "evening-up." As more and more nations develop efficiency in local production the reasons for international trade, namely the advantages of an international division of labor and the comparative gains growing out of the exchange of goods, become less important, particularly under the economic and political conditions of post-war nationalism.

Certainly there is much to indicate that a leveling process of this nature is going on, fortified by the spirit of nationalism and artificially aided by high protective tariffs and other methods of trade control.

In the first place, there has been the spread of industrial, engineering, and agricultural science to all lands and among all peoples. No longer does a single country and a single people have a monopoly of the technical knowledge required for efficient production. England has sent her engineers and her machines to help establish new industrial plants in Japan and India and wherever there was prospect of profit. America likewise has lent her scientific agriculturists to the Argentines and the Brazilians to help them perfect their farming and pastoral industries and, in these post-war years, has sent her industrial managers to establish, direct and perfect all kinds of industrial enterprises in all parts of the world. Machines, men, patents, managerial skill, capital -- all these have flowed out to the former undeveloped areas. Ideas and methods and inventions are universally exchanged. Even factories have migrated from old to new industrial countries. The old industrial countries have therefore been facing the competition of new countries not only in foreign markets, but in their own domestic markets as well; and often the old markets have been lost. In many cases, as in the former market for American shoes in Brazil, local production has come to supply almost completely the demand.

Furthermore, new technical methods and scientific discoveries have given new opportunities for the spread of industries in other countries and have lessened the dependence of certain regions for supplies that once were secured only by importation. For example, the perfection of new sources of power has given new opportunities for industrialization to countries without coal or with only inferior coal. This is illustrated by the expansion of the use of oil, the perfection of the internal combustion engine, the ability to use low-grade coal, and the improvements in the use of water power. Moreover, such developments as the manufacture of synthetic dyes, the production of artificial nitrates, and the discovery of rayon have given certain countries an opportunity to lessen their dependence on others for essential materials and thus to develop a more balanced domestic production. Obviously, the geographical extension of the areas suited for industrialization has been very great; and doubtless the process will be carried still further by new inventions.

Nevertheless, although these new conditions do operate to bring about the geographic extension of industry and agriculture, there is serious doubt whether this fact diminishes either the necessity or the volume of foreign trade. We shall discuss this subject in a moment.

The spread of industrialization into new areas, already begun before the war, for the reasons just mentioned, was greatly stimulated and hastened by the war. Many countries, shut off from their usual supplies and encouraged by the demand for war materials at exceptionally high prices, could and did develop industries and expand the production of raw materials to meet their own needs and even to export to the belligerents and to their neutral neighbors. Thus the textile mills of Japan and India and China took on a great activity during the war. India and Australia began the manufacture of iron and steel on a large scale. Brazil developed textile and boot and shoe production. Even the industries of older industrial countries like the United States were greatly stimulated by the prevailing conditions.

Furthermore, the war aroused a determination on the part of many countries, both belligerent and neutral, to conserve and strengthen at any cost the advances in diversified production already begun. After the war the determination to secure economic as well as political independence became an obsession of practically all nations, both new and old. Economic self-sufficiency was regarded both as an end in itself and as a means of securing and defending political independence. The chief instruments readily at hand for attempting to gain economic independence were protective tariffs. But the perpetuation of war-created industries by the use of ever-mounting tariff walls did not satisfy the new nationalism. Still other industries, often unnecessary and uneconomic, were created behind tariff barriers to complete the desired national self-sufficiency. Thus began the upward spiraling of tariffs, the establishment of import quotas, and the many other restrictions to foreign trade that multiplied as the post-war decade advanced.

There were also other incentives to set up high tariffs. In a period of widespread financial stress the nations laid hold of tariffs as means of increasing national revenues, to aid in balancing budgets, and to stifle imports in order to stop the outflow of gold. Tariffs were set up also to offset the results of war debt and reparations payments, obligations that could be met ultimately only by the export of merchandise by the debtor countries. But whatever the motive, tariffs as the chief agent of nationalism stimulated the building up of new industrial plants and the opening of new raw material sources in each individual country at the same time that they sought to lessen imports. Each country, acting independently, rushed the development of its productive equipment without planning, without giving thought to its ability to produce effectively, and without consideration of the world's consuming power. Each country sought not only to supply its own markets but to export as well. Produce all, export much, buy nothing -- this appeared to be the slogan. The inevitable result was the expansion of production capacity and of production far beyond the world's ability to consume. There followed, as night the day, declining prices, a consequent lowering of buying power, and finally the general demoralization of trade.

To add to the difficulty, the ordinary effects of protective tariffs on trade (usually less important than generally supposed), were much magnified during the post-war period by the unusual situation resulting from reparations and war-debt obligations. The war debts themselves, as already mentioned, gave further stimulus to the move to bring tariff rates to super-high levels in order to prevent "debt dumping." This made debtor countries less able not only to pay their debts, but, since they could not export, less able also to buy the products of other countries. Foreign markets for the products of newly created industries therefore could not be developed. With imports cut off, exports automatically declined also. The situation was for a time relieved by the huge loans made by the United States to European countries - - loans that so long as they continued kept up the flow of American and other exports. But when the sources of foreign lending dried up in 1929-30 the debtor countries rapidly ceased to import and the creditor countries ceased to export.

Furthermore, the monetary effects of the war debts greatly intensified the harmful results of excessive tariffs. Since the flow of merchandise for debt payments had been curtailed, gold was drained off in excessive amounts from the debtor to the creditor countries -- especially to the outstanding war-debt creditors, the United States and France. The maldistribution of gold that followed resulted in a still further lowering of price levels; and the low price levels in turn added to the actual debt burden of the debtor countries (a 50 percent increase has occurred since 1928) and let loose the whole pack of monetary, exchange and budget troubles that finally in 1931 forced much of the world off the gold standard and demoralized the currencies and exchanges of nearly all countries. Currency depreciation in turn gave added impulse to still higher tariffs aimed against exchange dumping, and to restrictions on the purchase of exchange to help save national finances. Thus the vicious circle was further strengthened, and heavier and still heavier burdens were put on international trade as new and higher tariffs were imposed, as import quotas were set up, and as embargoes and restrictions on foreign exchange were multiplied.

The course of events during the post-war decade may be summarized, then, as follows: There was a tremendous expansion of productive capacity initiated by wartime industrialization; the process was continued after the war by intense nationalism operating behind the shield of high protective tariffs; it was sustained for a time by heavy lending by the United States; but it finally collapsed under the economic and monetary strains and stresses in the over-expanded edifice.

The development of productive capacity throughout the world at first was stimulating to foreign trade, especially to the export trade of the United States. There was an increasing demand abroad for equipment goods, first to rehabilitate the belligerent nations, and then to modernize plants and expand the industries, farms and mines of the neutral nations now bent on economic expansion, and to equip the new nations of central and eastern Europe which had set out to win industrial independence. Equipment goods, usually imported duty free even by the high tariff countries, were the very goods which the United States was particularly well prepared to supply. Industrial, mining and agricultural machinery; road building and construction equipment; store and office equipment; automobiles and trucks; all such merchandise was made in the United States under mass production methods and had been highly perfected by an inventive people. On the score both of quality and cost, the United States has superior advantages in the production of such material.

Furthermore, it was the United States that supplied the capital to finance the rebuilding and equipping of a world bent on increasing production. It did so with such eagerness that American capital flowed abroad in unprecedented amounts. As far as the United States was concerned, then, nationalism in combination with lending abroad very largely nullified for several years the restrictive effects of tariffs, and allowed the exports of the United States to advance from 1922 to 1929 to unprecedented peacetime heights.

Then came the collapse -- first economic and localized, then monetary and world-wide. The world had been overbuilt to produce as a result of artificial stimulation and unplanned expansion; it now found itself caught in its own trade restrictions and unable to sell. Nations obliged to make large payments to foreigners on debts for which no productive enterprises had been created, were shorn of their ability to pay as soon as the United States ceased to loan. With the gold supply centered in two countries, with prices collapsing and with credit restricted, monetary and exchange problems were added to the economic difficulties. It is not strange that under these conditions depression swept across the world and that international trade was disrupted and demoralized. Nor is it strange that the foreign trade of the United States, built so largely upon the export of goods designed to equip the nations of the world with a new or enlarged productive plant, and upon foreign investments that so largely financed the equipment, should have been most severely affected when the crash came.

It would appear from this analysis of foreign trade after the war that the chief factors causing the declines in the movement of international goods were the commercial policies of protection and the trade restrictions imposed almost universally by governments seeking to become economically self-contained. The slump in foreign operating trade is not the result of the working out of economic factors under new conditions and bringing in a new period of national economic isolation; rather is it, in the words of the World Economic Conference of 1927, the result of "the hindrances opposed to the free flow of labor, capital and goods," in the effort to obtain self-sufficiency.[iii]

Let us now stop to examine the economic basis upon which modern foreign trade rests. In the first place it may be said that the principles of foreign trade are fundamentally the same as the principles of domestic trade. Trade is an exchange of commodities between people. If the exchange is across an international boundary it becomes "international trade." But the same reasons, the same motives, even the same methods, are involved whether John Jones of Boston is trading with James Smith also of Boston, or with James Smith in Illinois, or with James Smith in England. This is commonly forgotten in discussions of foreign trade. The fact that trade is international often carries the idea that somehow it is different from domestic trade. There is supposed to be something about it that is mysterious, subtle, even dangerous to national welfare; it is to be tolerated as a necessary evil, not promoted as a means of improving national well-being. This conception lies back of much of our tariff legislation and national commercial policies. But international trade is not between nations, but between individuals residing on opposite sides of a national frontier. This consideration is of the greatest significance in understanding foreign trade.

John Jones trades with James Smith, no matter where located, generally through a middleman or a series of middlemen, for either one or both of two reasons. John Jones is skilled in the making of some product -- say textiles -- and James Smith is most proficient in the making of tools. This simple division of labor makes exchange necessary and profitable to each if both are to obtain the best textiles and the best tools at the lowest cost in labor and money. Or John Jones owns a timber tract and James Smith a potato farm. The difference in the type of resources owned by the two again makes exchange of products between them both necessary and profitable if Jones eats potatoes and Smith uses timber in constructing his home.

What applies to John Jones and James Smith as individuals applies also to groups of peoples and to regions. Certain peoples have certain aptitudes or have acquired certain skills in the producing of specialized goods. The peoples of Asia Minor, for example, have a special skill in making rugs of artistic merit and fine quality; in the Thuringian Forest of Germany special aptitudes exist for making wooden toys; Americans appear to be especially proficient in the invention, production and use of labor-saving machinery. But what the different peoples do in different areas is not only a matter of skill, or aptitude or quality of artistic sense; it is also a matter of physical resources and environment. A certain section of the earth, by virtue of its resources, climate and situation, is well prepared to produce one kind of product;

another section is equipped to produce another and different class or type of product. This is obvious in the case of tin production in Malaya and iron ore in the United States, of bananas in the West Indies and wheat in Argentina; it is less obvious but equally true in the case of industrial areas. Usually the character of one region's products reflects both the character of its resources -- including climate -- and the skills, experience and aptitudes of its people. These two factors -- quality of resources and quality of people -- act and react on each other and result in the "geographical division of industry." Just as the exchange of products between John Jones and James Smith, both in Boston, is to the mutual advantage of each, so the exchange between the citizens of different countries brings advantages to each country and increases its wealth and prosperity. It is obvious that if no such advantages were to be mutually gained there would be no need of trade, either local or international.

But, it may be said, the fact that the United States is so large and has such varied resources, that it is already to such an extent self-sufficient, is evidence that foreign trade need not be regarded as necessary or important to our economic welfare. It is, of course, true that no country, unless it be Russia, could dispense with foreign trade with less hardship than the United States. But a hardship it would be even to the United States. It is conceivable that the United States could be a world to itself; but it would be at the sacrifice of much that it now enjoys.

As a matter of fact, it is impossible to achieve self-sufficiency in the twentieth century world and at the same time maintain existing economic standards. No country is so large or so rich in resources that it can supply all its various industrial needs in this age of science and invention. Certain products occur or can be produced only in certain restricted areas. We cannot alter the geological distribution of minerals or the geographical distribution of rainfall and soils and water power, nor those combinations of advantages that give certain regions, like Central Europe or the northeastern part of the United States, superior advantages for industrial development. Even in regions generally similar in resources, there exist minor differences that give one region certain small but definite advantages over the other, either in cost of production or quality of product or both. And in the modern competitive world these small advantages are important and persistent.

The advantages of the regional division of industry and the consequent international exchange of goods become, not less, but greater with economic development and advancement. Even in the best equipped industrial countries the need of trade in industrial raw materials grows constantly with every scientific discovery and every improvement in technical method. A new development in transportation starts a demand for a new import material -- rubber -- and furnishes a new finished product for export -- the automobile. Technical improvements in methods of steel and tinplate production send ships to the four corners of the world to secure necessary products -- manganese and chrome ore, tungsten, nickel and vanadium, tin and palm kernel oil -- all essential, none of them produced in sufficient quantities in the United States. The perfection of the telephone receiver alone has called to its aid eighteen or twenty import commodities from nearly as many countries.

The woolen industry no longer requires just wool. If cloth is to be produced in the exact quality to meet the demand of the consumer and the competition of manufacturers at home and abroad, many wools from many lands must be blended -- wools from Australia, from the Argentine, from Scotland, from Wyoming. Cotton from the southern states no longer can satisfy the textile manufacturer. To American varieties must be added the special types from Egypt, from Peru, from China, in order to obtain the qualities of finished products desired and the economies demanded by competition. The shoes Americans wear are made from leathers dependent for their particular uses in the shoe on hides from Argentina, on goat skins from Europe, Brazil and Arizona, on calf skins from India, Germany and Chicago. These illustrations indicate how exacting are demands of modern industry. Such conditions of industry can be met only by international trade. There is no such thing as "independence" in modern factory industries. Foreign trade could be eliminated or even greatly curtailed only at the expense of progress and of the individual and collective welfare of American industry and the American people. The success of Gandhi's campaign in India to go back to hand spinning and weaving would not be a more backward step in the industrial world than would be the abandonment by the United States of international trade in favor of an isolated self-sufficiency.

The very fact that industry demands these imports in ever-increasing amounts and varieties itself makes possible and necessary an export trade. Exports must be created to pay for the necessary imports -- and the more is imported, the more is exported. Trade feeds upon itself and grows.

As with raw materials, so with foods and manufactured goods. Industrial populations must be fed; peoples with increasing living standards demand more and better foods. Coffee and sugar and fruits flow in from the tropics; the grassy plains of the continental interiors where are grown the best and cheapest wheat are reclaimed for agriculture and add to the flow of trade. With spreading education and rising living standards, there is an increasing demand also for luxury goods and works of art. Silks and oriental rugs, the art goods peculiar to different peoples --jewelry and embroideries and novelties of all kinds -- swell the total. These are the normal conditions. Tariffs and embargoes may temporarily interfere; patriotic slogans like "Buy British" may have some temporary and slight influence; but they do not alter the basic motives that lie at the bottom of all trade. With their profit and welfare at stake, individuals and industries will not willingly confine their business activities within narrow geographic limits. To abandon or curtail permanently the trade across international boundaries would entail such handicaps upon economic progress that it is inconceivable that an intelligent world would long endure it.

It is a principle of foreign trade that trade grows fastest between the most highly industrialized countries. Industrial Germany before the war was, next to India, the most important market for industrial England; and England in turn was Germany's chief market, taking 14.4 percent of all German exports. Very soon after the war similar relations were reëstablished. And yet these two countries are the most highly industrialized nations of Europe and the most intense rivals.

The highly developed industrial countries of northwestern Europe are by far the most important markets for the United States -- not only for its exports of raw materials and foods, but also for its exports of manufactures. Nearly one-half of all our vast exports to Europe in 1929 were manufactured goods; and Europe for many years has taken more than twice as much of our manufactures as has South America. Japan has been feared as a rival of the industrial countries of the West, and is a growingly important competitor. But despite her growing industrialization Japan has been a rapidly growing importer of the products of the West. Japan's imports per capita increased from $4.41 in 1908 to $17.21 in 1923, a greater per capita increase than in any other country -- and this during a period when the population was growing nearly a million per year. During this period every item of Japan's manufactured imports increased in quantity, with a slight exception in the case of cotton piece goods. Imports increased even more rapidly than exports. As markets these developing countries are more important than as competitors; and this applies to an old and established industrial country like England as well as to a new industrial nation like Japan.

The fact remains, however, that economic considerations have not been controlling in the formation of national commercial policies. Most attempts to moderate the excesses of nationalism and to call a halt to mounting tariff and trade restrictions have proved unavailing. Economic conferences, suggestions for tariff truces, proposals for customs agreements or unions -- all have failed as yet to modify the restrictions that are throttling trade. And yet to bring about revival of trade there seems no alternative to removing existing barriers, the chief of which, of course, are tariffs.

National self-sufficiency is an idle dream. It is simply impossible unless we are prepared to sacrifice much of the advance already made in industry and in economic well-being. To turn back the hands of the clock would be to deceive ourselves; it would aggravate the disease, not cure it. National commercial policy must recognize the economics of the situation and act on it. Although the way out is beset with great difficulties in a world gone tariff mad, two major conditions apparently need to be met if the flow of trade is to be renewed and confidence restored. First, there must be a removal of the excessive trade barriers, principally through the modification of tariffs; secondly, there must be a reduction or cancellation of war debts.

For the United States, no application of sound theory and no experience in the economic history of nations can defend or justify the maintenance of our excessively high tariffs along with our position at the same time as the greatest industrial nation and as the world's greatest creditor. As an industrial nation we must import; and if we import we must export. As a creditor nation we must receive payments, if we receive them at all, in imported goods; and if we revive our lending, we must lend with an export of goods. However we look at it, foreign trade is imperative, unless we choose to abandon our present economic position and curtail our future growth.

The modification of war debts and reparations is not a question of legality or justice, but of expediency and common sense. The requirements of war debt payments are obstacles direct and indirect to the trade of the United States in several particulars. They relate to the United States particularly because payments find ultimate lodgment here and their influence on trade is far out of proportion to their actual size. Their presence is one of the prime factors sustaining the demand for high tariffs both in the United States and in other countries; they are perhaps the most potent basic cause of the maldistribution of gold and the currency afflictions that hold back sound recovery; the payment of them offers artificial competition in world markets to American exports; through their influence on prices, currency and exchange, they help to keep production costs low in Europe relative to those prevailing in the United States; they keep down the living standards of the peoples of the debtor countries; in combination with our own high tariffs and the high tariffs of the debtor countries, they encourage the establishment of American factories in Europe and thus develop American competition against America; they keep open the old sores growing out of the war and are a powerful factor in preventing the return of confidence and sane optimism. Modification or cancellation of them would help restore international credit and start again foreign investments which are now hesitant to embark on new enterprises.

It is impossible to visualize American business interests failing to participate in a large way in the future development of a dynamic world. Private enterprise, with capital, energy, initiative and experience at its command, will refuse to live in narrow isolation. Participation means international trade; and international trade cannot thrive under our present tariff systems nor in a world beset with the problems growing out of the war debts.

[i] Day: "History of Commerce," p. 271.

[ii] "Commerce Year Book" for 1931, vol. 2, p. 679.

[iii] Final Report of the League's World Economic Conference, 1927, p. 12.

G. B. ROORBACH, Professor of Foreign Trade in the Harvard School of Business Administration

A Trade Policy for the 1960s

Raymond Vernon

REUTERS

THE savant who first observed that politics is the art of the possible said much less than seems to meet the eye. The ex ante and the ex post concepts of "the possible" are disconcertingly different. One might better say that politics is the art of enlarging the possible. And one could well add that an indispensable step in the process is to have a view of the goals beyond the possible for which one is reaching.

Our exploration of a trade policy for the 1960s, therefore, will not proceed from the premise that a democratic government is the captive of the parochial interests it represents; on that assumption, we are slated for the dinosaur's fate. Instead, our general frame of reference is this: What trade policy does the decade of the 1960s demand for survival and growth? And what could a determined President hope to achieve, at the outside, if he exploited every possibility in his position of leadership?

In the past decade or two, a deep-seated change has occurred in the traditionally protectionist views of the more highly developed countries of the world. During this period, it has been possible for the twoscore members of the General Agreement on Tariffs and Trade to cut deep into their import barriers. The Organization for European Economic Coöperation managed to implement an unprecedented Code of Trade Liberalization. A European Coal and Steel Community has been achieved and a European Economic Community and European Free Trade Area have followed.

Each of these programs constituted a minor miracle of a sort, patently impossible before it actually occurred. The fact that the miracle none the less occurred can be ascribed to various forces. One of these forces--one which can easily be underemphasized--has been the persistent advocacy by most professional economists in the advanced countries for the reduction of trade barriers and the broadening of markets. The wartime emergencies and post-war problems precipitated economists into posts of key importance, not only in the United States but in many other advanced countries as well. In these posts, influenced by fresh professional analyses, the economists-turned-administrators have supported various programs of trade liberalization.

The basis of the economist's espousal of trade liberalization schemes, it is well to note, has undergone considerable change. Prior to World War II, the United States economist usually based his argument for reduction of trade barriers on some version or other of the comparative-advantage doctrine and, using all the antique illustrations of the virtues of specializing in wheat or cloth, saw the possibility of significant gains for the United States arising out of increased international trade. As the years went on, the economist's views changed somewhat. The underdeveloped areas began to be treated as a different case, demanding their own kind of trade policy. And the rationalization for liberal trade policies in the developed areas of the world grew substantially more complex. Comparative advantage was still regarded as relevant doctrine in many quarters. In addition, however, there is the notion that many efforts of research and production, like those in the field of atomic energy and rocket aircraft, involve such giant fixed costs that development would be impeded unless a huge internal market were available to the developer. Finally, there is the related worry that the control of the industrial structure in some countries and in some products has become so highly concentrated in a few hands that competitive pricing, competitive cost-cutting and competitive product development can be achieved only by merging a number of national markets.

These instincts--they are hardly more than this--have been fortified by various experiences in the postwar world. Extensive reduction of trade barriers by the developed countries through the GATT, the O.E.E.C. and the International Monetary Fund seems to have been a boon to most economies. Even more extensive schemes such as those embodied in the European Economic Community appear to have tripped off a considerable wave of investment and innovation in the countries concerned. And the economic pain associated with the displacement of hitherto protected national interests has not been anywhere near as great as had sometimes been feared.

But the economist's views on trade liberalization would not have been sufficient by themselves to move the mountains which have been shifted during the last decade. Economic rationalizations may have been a necessary condition for progress, but political considerations have provided an essential condition sufficient in itself. In the 1930s, it was a popular political notion that trade bred understanding and interdependence; that as countries expanded their trade, their hostile intentions contracted. This was an article of faith with Cordell Hull and it remains as a thread of conviction in some quarters. But as a galvanizing principle for action, it never had much vitality. Instead, the political justification for the major trade-liberalization projects today relates to the closing of ranks and the mobilization of power against outsiders. So, for instance, the justification to which the United States has been most responsive in opening up its markets to Japan is that the move forestalls Communist China from developing a foothold in the Japanese economy. The main political justification for the European Economic Community is the need to forge a unit so strong that it can bargain effectively with the United States, the Soviet Union or the British Commonwealth. The justification for the EFTA is to present an adequate countervailing force against the strength of the E.E.C.

There is not much doubt that the principal contribution which an appropriate trade policy for the United States has to make in the 1960s is political rather than economic. A critical problem for the United States in the decade ahead is by one means or another to maintain a sense of cohesiveness and common purpose among the advanced countries outside the Soviet sphere. Between 1950 and 1960 there has been a shift from an atmosphere capable of generating a Marshall Plan and a NATO to one in which the Western powers seem unwilling to maintain even their excessively modest commitment to the defense of Europe. British public opinion appears more confused and confusing than at any time since the war's end; some elements seem seized by a mood of pacifism and isolation, while others are so fearful of being isolated from the markets of the European Continent that they are prepared to accept a major reorientation of Britain's external relations. Belgium is licking her Congolese wounds, frustrated and unhappy about the equivocal support of her NATO partners. France is absorbed in the play of her Algerian tragedy, unable to turn to other problems while this one remains unsettled. And the confusion of Europe can easily grow worse before it gets better.

One reason for the confusion and uncertainty of Western Europe--not by any means the only reason--has been the fact that the United States has allowed its own policies to grow blurred and distorted. Our policies in the field of foreign trade and foreign aid illustrate the point in an acute way. An unending series of little concessions to domestic pressures has turned our trade legislation into a group of ambivalent statutes which hamstring the President in any effort to reduce the trade barriers of the United States and which constantly threaten to force him to increase the existing restrictions on imports. Today, his nominal statutory power to reduce tariffs up to 20 percent by negotiation can in practice be applied to a limited range of products. The statutory admonition to the President that he must avoid "serious injury" in the process is couched in such sweeping terms that it takes on a special meaning. It is not enough for him to protect an industry against serious loss or serious unemployment; he must also "protect" its market position in every product it manufactures. It is not enough to guard the industry against an absolute decline in sales volume or employment in each product; the industry must also be ensured that its share of the market will grow along with that of its foreign competitors. And it is not sufficient to authorize the President to restore earlier tariff cuts toward these ends; he is also admonished to raise duties further in some cases or even to lay on import quotas if necessary to achieve the needed level of protection. The same ambivalence has crept into our foreign aid programs, obscuring and confusing their objectives. On the basis of what they see, many countries suspect that our foreign aid programs are principally designed to collect adherents to our side in the cold war, to increase the influence of American business abroad and to get rid of unsaleable surplus products in our economy.

It seems unnecessary to argue the point that the need to maintain a common sense of purpose and of possible success among the Western democracies is more imperative than ever. To contribute to that unity various things will have to be done. First, we need to reestablish unequivocally the fact that there is a clear direction in our long-run policy--a long-run commitment to the continuous reduction of our trade barriers for as long as other developed countries will agree and as rapidly as the problems of internal adjustment permit. The reëstablishment of this image is needed not only for the general reassurance it is likely to give other countries but also for a much more immediate and insistent reason. If the President can cut United States tariffs considerably, it may be possible for a time to ensure that the two rival trading blocs of Europe--the European Economic Community and the European Free Trade Area--will also hold down their external trade barriers. It may be possible to ensure, for instance, that as France and Germany reduce their tariffs on automobiles in favor of each other in accordance with the provisions of the Treaty of Rome, they will also reduce their common automobile tariff as it applies to British and Swedish cars and to American and Japanese cars. And if they do, the economic schism between the European Economic Community and the European Free Trade Area will not grow so swiftly and so deeply as to present a formidable problem for the early future.

To secure the necessary powers to bargain for the reduction of these trade barriers, however, there would have to be great changes in the scope of the President's power to reduce American tariffs and in the way in which he exercised that power in tariff negotiations. If the President had the power to reduce our tariff by 50 percent over a five-year period, without the usual restraints of the present escape clause and peril-point clauses, this might be sufficient to bargain effectively with the European blocs; but any power of much narrower scope would almost surely be insufficient.

At the same time, the President could not sweep under the rug the problems of internal readjustment for the American economy which such tariff reductions might entail. On grounds of both equity and national growth, these problems have to be dealt with. One approach to the problem of adjustment is to give some sectors of the economy more time to make the adjustment if necessary. On that theory, the President could be empowered to restore a tariff rate if a reduction was causing serious difficulty, provided that the reduction would then gradually be put in force again over a specified span of years.

Another approach to the problem is through a trade adjustment program. Displaced labor or capital which needed redeployment could be given an assist by programs of retraining, by providing moving expenses and capital loans, and by technical assistance--operations of a sort well within the experience of the United States Government and of various governments in Europe. The capital and labor which could not be successfully redeployed--the housewives who could not move to another area to find a different job and the capital which was so irretrievably frozen or so highly specialized as to be lost to other pursuits--might require the payment of indemnity; but the United Kingdom, for instance, has handled precisely this problem with remarkable success in shrinking back the size of its cotton textile industry. Programs of this sort do not eradicate the adjustment problem. They can blunt the edge of it sufficiently, however, to ensure that the gains generated from increased trade are not offset by the losses involved in the cost of shifting resources.

Assuming that the problems of trade adjustment can be dealt with, one is entitled to ask whether the current balance-of-payment difficulties of the United States may be a reason for holding back from added steps of trade liberalization. The answer is a fairly unqualified no. On the contrary, it seems quite clear that the United States stands to gain from trade liberalization with Europe in balance-of-payment terms. European firms have had easy access to the United States market for some years. Firms in the United States have just begun to acquire equivalent access to European markets as import licensing systems have begun to be dismantled; and such firms have made only a beginning in the exploitation of these markets. Whether American firms will take full advantage of this recent surge of dismantling depends on their long-run expectations regarding access to these markets. If the present drift of events continues without some new initiatives in liberalizing trade, sellers face more and more discrimination in Europe as the common-market schemes move to completion. If the trend is muffled by measures such as those proposed here, sellers can be counted on to exploit their new opportunities.

Apart from resuming reciprocal reduction of trade barriers, the United States can develop a score of other measures which create a clearer image of its purpose. It would have to amend its disingenuous "national security" provision, which authorizes the President to impose import restrictions whenever imports threaten to impair our national security. Much more to the point as a national security measure would be a statute which granted the President the power to suspend existing import restrictions for some limited period in specified products whenever our national security would be materially strengthened by such a step. Such a power might afford the means for admitting products like Icelandic fish or Egyptian cotton at those critical moments when such a step could ward off the possibility of Soviet penetration into the economies of friendly countries.

Even if we were to make these changes, however, there is a clear risk that two or three years hence we may conclude that we were trying to clean the Aegean stables with a demitasse spoon. What if the crisis of purposelessness in the Atlantic alliance should persist and deepen? What if the European Free Trade Area and the European Economic Community can find no basis for bridging their growing differences? What if France-after-de Gaulle and Germany-after-Adenauer prove so confused in direction and so torn by internal conflict that what is left of the Atlantic alliance seems scarcely worth another ministerial meeting? Then we shall have to offer much larger and more challenging goals to the remnants of the alliance. Taking a leaf from the volumes which Europe has written in the last ten years, we may find that it is our turn to propose a customs union or a free trade area to the other developed countries--one in which the members of the E.E.C., EFTA and possibly Japan, Australia and New Zealand could share.

If this were what political unity demanded, the capacity of the United States to make the decisions essential for its survival would be tested to the utmost. It is hard to envisage a Congress which before the fact would authorize the President to negotiate such an arrangement, or which after the fact would ratify his agreements. We can only hope that, at that stage, our political system would function as effectively as that of France or Germany when they decided to create an economic community.

II

However one envisages the shape of future trade relations among the developed countries, the smell of trouble for the less-developed countries is fairly strong. Europe may be organized around the European Free Trade Area and the European Economic Community or around a new arrangement which embraces both; or the United States may be associated in an even wider arrangement among the developed countries. In either case, unless the implications of these arrangements for trade with the underdeveloped areas are fully considered, these areas may suffer great loss.

There are two segments in the trade of the underdeveloped countries which are especially likely to be sensitive to the creation of economic unions among the developed nations. One of these is trade in manufactured products of a certain type--those based on a comparatively simple, self-contained technology, involving a significant labor cost content and requiring comparatively low transport costs when shipped across international boundaries. Textiles are the classic example of such products. Transistors are a latter-day illustration. It seems inevitable that products which will fill this bill of specifications should be produced in swiftly growing volumes in underdeveloped areas. The costs of transmitting technology across national boundaries are declining rapidly--especially as travel time for key executives is reduced and as better communication makes them constantly accessible to the home office. The costs of transmitting products across national boundaries are also falling swiftly as delivery becomes swifter and more certain; these are critically important factors in the purchase of products for assembly or the purchase of products for consumer merchandising.

The other type of product in which the underdeveloped country has an export potential is, of course, raw materials in either their pristine state or in some form of early fabrication. Advanced countries not uncommonly are also major producers of raw materials; what one of them does not produce, another may. A customs union or other preferential arrangement among them could squeeze underdeveloped areas out of their accustomed markets.

Assuming--as we are doing here--that it is critically important not to impede the development of the laggard areas of the world, we are obliged to tailor the trade agreements among the developed nations to fit our objectives vis-à-vis the underdeveloped countries. The policy of the industrialized West must be that of granting unilateral concessions to these countries in order to keep our markets open to their products.

Once again, we are obliged to ask if we dare pursue this policy in light of our balance-of-payments position. And once again the answer is that the balance-of-payments problem need not represent a deterrent. When underdeveloped countries are offered a chance to sell more goods, their inevitable response is to buy more goods--not to hoard gold or to build up overseas balances. Their import wants are so great that they cannot fail to bring their imports up to exports in a very short order. At the same time, however, the expanded export opportunities offered to these countries are best provided by all the developed nations in concert, not by the United States alone.

Our trade policy toward the underdeveloped countries must do more, however. Through all the haze of embattled statistics, the fact remains that the instability of raw material prices and export earnings constitutes a major obstacle to the sustained development of many of the less advanced countries. A perennial answer to the problem has been commodity agreements of one sort or another. But commodity agreements are notoriously difficult to negotiate. Once negotiated, they typically accomplish less than was hoped for. To a degree and for a time, they may muffle the fluctuations of prices. But when the demand for industrial raw materials falls off or the supply of agricultural products suddenly changes through natural causes, export proceeds inevitably suffer. And when agreements go wrong and seek to impose too high a price on the consumer, as they so commonly do, substitutes swiftly develop or new sources of supply come in. The result is often an irreversible setback for the producers of the product.

We must, of course, continue to study the possibility of reaching agreements to stabilize commodities. But we know enough already to suspect that they will carry us only so far. As a supplement, therefore, we must consider how best to stabilize the supply of foreign currencies of the countries concerned. In theory, the International Monetary Fund can do this; indeed, if pressed, its officials would insist that they do this already. In point of fact, however, no raw-material exporting country can lay its future plans upon the assumption that the I.M.F. will help make up any deficit generated by year-to-year changes in raw material prices or supplies. I.M.F. extensions of credit are commonly hedged about with conditions which countries vulnerable to the rawmaterial problem find it most difficult to meet--the requirement, for instance, that steps to balance budgets and curtail foreign exchange expenditures must be instituted concurrently with the grant of assistance. So countries may be forced to curtail their imports of fertilizer or their expenditures on irrigation as a condition precedent to I.M.F. aid.

Conditions of one sort or another will always be indispensable to a credit-granting institution. But the conditions imposed by the I.M.F., seen through the eyes of the outside observer, have run too much in the tradition of the banker and too little in the tradition of the entrepreneur. They have too easily subordinated the objectives of growth to those of stability. There are times, of course, when stability of some sort is a prerequisite to growth. But there are times, too, when growth is the instrument through which balance is eventually achieved.

Finally, we need to participate more actively and constructively in the development of regional trade arrangements among the underdeveloped nations. The nature of our participation should be shaped by the recognition of two or three hard facts. One is the pervasive role of monopoly or oligopoly in the modern sector of most of these countries, a situation which runs from the granting of credit through to the marketing of products. The other is the insufficiency of individual national markets to support many types of modern industry or to encourage the various specializations so necessary for increased output.

Regional trade arrangements do not automatically solve this sort of problem. On the contrary, they can be used to extend the scope of existing monopolies; they can force some member countries to shift from efficient outside sources for some of their critical products to inefficient inside sources; and they can spread stagnation a little further by creating tight little communities of nations insulated from the effects of outside competition. One can say of these regional trade arrangements, therefore, only that they offer an opportunity for the speed-up of growth, but not an assurance that the speed-up will occur. If in their development they offer wider markets, more opportunities for specialization, more diversified sources of credit and a multiplication in sources of supply, the growth objective will be closer at hand. The influence of the United States should be used to ensure that the arrangements work in that direction.

III

So far we have been looking at the trade relations of the United States with countries outside the Soviet bloc. What is more, we have been assuming--while well aware of the rashness of that assumption--that the countries concerned conduct their foreign trade more or less on a pattern followed by the United States, a pattern in which individual consumers and traders determine the flow of goods across national boundaries. What about our trade relations with the state-trading countries of the world--particularly those which comprise the Soviet bloc?

This is not altogether a new question for the United States, but it presses for a reply today with heightened urgency. Though the United States groped for a solution from time to time in the prewar period, it never really found more than half a solution. Then in the postwar period the problem arose again; but at first it took a form which could easily be handled. In some cases, such as those of Britain and France, state trading was confined to just a few commodities, representing an exception to a general rule. In these cases, the United States sought to apply rules analogous to those which would apply in private trade: the import mark-ups of state-trading entities were thought of as analogous to tariffs, hence negotiable between the selling and the buying countries; the selection of supply sources by the state-trading entities was deemed analogous to the application of rules against discrimination, hence subject to scrutiny and complaint; and so on.

But the problem of dealing with economies fully committed to state direction within and to state trading without posed a very different set of issues. Here, "price," "mark-up" and "discrimination" acquired totally different meanings and all the analogies with private trading began to crumble. Since our political relations with practically all such countries were crumbling as well, there was no real need to face the issue. The United States allowed only a trickle of trade to take place with such countries, over the barriers imposed by our Export Control Act. And under the statutory mandate of the Battle Act we tried to persuade other friendly countries to pursue parallel policies, using the leverage of our foreign aid programs wherever we could.

Today, it is clear that other friendly countries have every intention of expanding their trade with state-directed and state-trading economies such as those of the Soviet bloc, in spite of the feeble United States pressures still being exerted on them. There is reason, therefore, to turn back to this baffling problem of trade between state-directed and free-enterprise economies. Moreover, the desire to find a solution by now seems fairly widespread. Discussions in the Economic Commission for Europe and in the GATT over the past two or three years indicate that many other countries, some of one type, some of the other, would like to find a better means for handling such trade.

The first step for the United States ought to be that of clearing its statutory decks for constructive action. While there is not the space here to debate the point in detail, it seems reasonably clear that the approach pursued in our Export Control Act and in our Battle Act is almost a dead letter. In administering these acts, the United States has assumed that trade with the Soviet bloc in a broadly defined range of products is inevitably harmful, on balance, to our side and that the denial of these products to the Soviet bloc contributes to our security. Two things begin to be distressingly clear, however. In the prevailing mood of the world today, an effective system of denial of industrial goods no longer is possible; there are too many uncontrollable sources from which such goods can come. Besides, there is grave doubt if denial would make much sense even if it could be achieved; the outcome of modern warfare surely is not affected to any extent by holding down the supply of industrial goods to the Soviet bloc. Accordingly, the Export Control Act and the Battle Act should be used only for the control of arms, ammunition and implements of war in trade with the Soviet bloc, not for that broad range of industrial products to which we now attempt to apply it.

Once we have put the security objective in proper perspective, we ought to be clear as to our objectives in attempting to develop a modus vivendi for trade with state-trading economies. Two objectives in particular seem important. First, we want to protect our multilateral system, with its emphasis on nondiscrimination, declining trade barriers and maximum choice, from the corrosive and debilitating effects which are generated when any country in the system tries to accommodate itself to the bilateral, discriminatory patterns of the state trader; that is, we want to check the use of quotas, inconvertible currencies and discriminatory pricing which are the usual stock-in-trade of a state trading entity. Second, we want to be sure that the state trader cannot exploit his monopoly power to such an extent that he walks off with the bulk of the gains from trade.

In order to develop such a system, we need the coöperation of other countries. To get that coöperation, we must make it crystal clear that our objectives are not a part of cold-war military or political strategy--at least not in the usual sense. The amendment of the Battle Act should go some distance in that direction. But to make the point clearer still and to give the President the necessary powers to develop a modus vivendi, it would also be useful to amend the Trade Agreements Act so that the President was authorized in his discretion to suspend the provisions requiring trade discrimination against the Soviet bloc.

With these powers in hand, the President could aggressively try to develop reasonable trade relations with the bloc. In all likelihood, he would have to move on two fronts. He would need to learn what ground rules our friends are prepared to accept as a basis for such trade; and he would have to try to learn the enigmatic intentions and desires of the Soviet bloc in the trade field. As far as our friends were concerned, those with convertible currencies and open trading systems might be expected to agree that they would avoid the use of discriminatory trade measures favoring the Soviet bloc, including the use of clearing accounts, import licensing systems which reserved some share of the domestic market to Soviet products, and so on; that they would consult on problems of serious market disruption generated by Soviet pricing practices; and that they would try to develop joint counter-moves with us in cases in which the Soviet bloc was using the threat to cut off its trade or the promise to expand it as a means of political penetration of some friendly country.

What the Soviet bloc might agree to as appropriate rules of the game in the trade field is much less clear. In contacts with Soviet representatives on trade matters thus far, one gets the disconcerting sense that an enormously wide gulf exists in the communication of basic points of view on the subject. Any system in which governments guarantee neither markets nor sources of supply is one which the Soviet side seems to have genuine difficulties in comprehending. Whether they understand the system or not, Soviet trade representatives seem to find it hard to believe that governments cannot really reassert a directive role over their trade if they choose; the question, as the Soviet side sees it, is whether they choose. The chances of developing an early modus vivendi with the Soviet bloc, therefore, does not seem high. But it may not be too early to launch the long process of communication which must precede an agreement.

A common thread runs through all these proposals, coloring our suggestions regarding trade with Western Europe, trade with the underdeveloped nations and trade with the Soviet bloc. As a nation, we have been of two minds. We have had no real doubts where our destiny was pushing us--toward greater and greater economic and political involvement with the rest of the world. Yet, from time to time, we have cast a wistful look back to the times when economic and political isolation were available as a real alternative. We have punctuated our bold moves of engagement with incongruous counter-moves of disengagement; we have reduced our tariffs while imposing import quotas on products like lead, zinc and oil; we have increased our aid while enlarging the conditions on its use which would protect our agriculture and our textile industry. As a result, we appear the reluctant dragon--powerful yet afraid. What we have to shed is fear--fear of the loss of foreign exchange, fear of the ability of our domestic industry to respond to its opportunities and its problems, fear of the tactics of the Soviet trader. If economic engagement is a battle, then the battle is inevitable. And we had best be getting on with it.

RAYMOND VERNON, Professor of International Trade and Investment, Harvard Business School; senior staff member of the Joint Congressional-Presidential Commission on Foreign Economic Policy, 1954; formerly Acting Director, Office of Economic Defense and Trade Policy, Department of State; author of "Trade Policy in Crisis"

Trade, Investment and Deindustrialization: Myth and Reality

Sol C. Chaikin

REUTERS

The American labor movement has basically concentrated on domestic issues-with the notable exception of its vigorous efforts to further the cause of human rights, free trade unionism and political democracy throughout the world. This focus on the United States has been the result of both the sheer size of the American economy and work force and the specific circumstances which gave rise to the rapid growth of the labor movement in the 1930s.

The renaissance of organized labor in this country during the depression years was based mainly in the manufacturing sector. In those days, international trade accounted for a minute part of the nation's total output of goods and services. It was, therefore, manifest that the problems of the national economy that culminated in the Great Depression resulted from deficiencies in domestic policy. Gradual economic revitalization in the New Deal years reinforced the views of labor leaders that the viability of the American economy was inextricably and almost exclusively linked with the domestic scene.

In the early 1960s, workers in a number of labor-intensive industries, particularly the apparel industry, began to experience economic distress. For some, the problem was outright loss of jobs; for the majority, earnings failed to keep pace with average manufacturing wages. That this could occur during what was to become the longest period of sustained economic growth in American history was cause for consternation. What was happening compelled those affected to look beyond our borders.

It rapidly became obvious that the dilemma was due to market dislocations in the wake of a growing tide of imports. Unions might have been expected to respond by calling for a cessation of all labor-intensive imports. The International Ladies' Garment Workers' Union, however, did not follow that path. Unlike most unions in the United States, the ILGWU was founded by immigrants who arrived in this country with a firm commitment to the international solidarity of working people. The ILGWU leadership needed no lessons in the importance of international economic cooperation to maintain world peace. It rejected and continues to oppose a philosophy of extreme protectionism.

The threat to American jobs and living standards that had been limited to a few industries has now multiplied to the point where it affects workers-and many employers-in almost every industry. The issue is no longer the viability of entrepreneurial manufacturing. The specter of deindustrialization is not only apparent, but has continued to grow at a geometric pace.

In the course of more than 40 years as an officer of the ILGWU, I have been closely connected with the industrial scene. Especially since becoming the union's president in 1975, I have often discussed the loss of American manufacturing with my corporate counterparts. I have heard the concern of other union leaders in the highest councils of the labor movement and that of workers on the shop floor, along with the thinking of my opposite numbers in the developed and developing nations. Insights have also been gained in exchanges with government leaders in the United States and abroad and through participation in negotiations affecting both bilateral and multilateral trade.

The experiences of the apparel industry in particular and of the nation's manufacturing base in general have compelled me to think through more thoroughly the current implications of postwar national economic policy. I would like to share these explorations and some of the resulting conclusions.

II

By the end of the Second World War, U.S. trade policy had shifted radically from the autarky of the 1930s to an ideology of "free trade." International cooperation created by the wartime alliance and the emergence of the United States as the dominant Western power were catalysts in this change. In the immediate postwar years, the output of the United States represented an unprecedented share of global industrial production. By 1948, three years after the end of the war, American output still represented more than half of the world's industrial product. America's newfound love affair with free trade was, consequently, solidly based upon a pragmatic assessment of domestic potential.

Prosecution of the war had brought important changes in the American economy. Fabrication of war material and the growth of the armed forces had reduced depression-related unemployment to a point where the dream of a full employment economy seemed possible. Capital outlays, encouraged by military needs, and research and development, both of which were underwritten by the government, had helped to modernize industry, yielding impressive gains in output and productivity.

Military expenditures declined sharply with the end of the war and millions of discharged servicemen reentered the domestic work force. The likelihood of a postwar slump was advanced by most economists, who foresaw a severe downturn once pent-up demand for consumer goods, created during the war years, was satisfied. The most effective way to avoid that prospect was to ensure new outlets for American industrial capacity.

If only in purely economic terms, the postwar U.S. commitment to a greater degree of unrestricted trade made a great deal of sense. Given the destruction of industrial plant in much of Europe and Japan and the time period they needed to rebuild, extraordinary advantages of the United States in capacity, technology and productivity permitted the economy to prosper. While Europe and Japan were rebuilding their industrial bases, American manufacturers enjoyed an unchallenged share of world markets which helped to facilitate rapid conversion of the economy to peacetime production and avert an economic downturn.

Postwar trade policy also enhanced opportunities to attain strategic political goals. The United States sought through the Marshall Plan to assist in the reconstruction of devastated European economies as an integral part of an effort to create and strengthen stable democracies. The Marshall Plan contributed significantly to Europe's recovery as did investment by American corporations, encouraged by government policy.

While the U.S. economy initially benefited from this policy, there were mid-and long-term costs associated with these efforts. In time, financial assistance, investment, shared industrial know-how and the rebirth of war-devastated economies began to diminish the advantage American manufacturing enjoyed in the period immediately following World War II.

As American investment in Europe continued to grow, the relative availability of capital for domestic investment declined. Earnings of European subsidiaries of U. S. corporations were not fully repatriated, further increasing the gap between potential and actual domestic capital formation. While overseas investments by U. S. corporations enhanced the profitability and competitiveness of these corporations, they restricted growth possibilities in the domestic economy.

The implicit restriction of domestic growth and the conscious sharing of the global market had aims which could not be calculated in purely economic terms. They were linked with efforts to avoid social unrest in Western Europe and to the establishment of a strong Western Alliance. The absence during the past 37 years of global military conflict, and especially of regional warfare in Europe, has been one outcome of U.S. policy. Its value is incalculable.

American policy toward postwar Japan had similar ramifications. Emergence of a stable, friendly and economically viable order in Japan was, as in Western Europe, a vital American concern. Japan, and Asia as a whole, however, did not readily offer as significant a market in the immediate postwar years as did Europe. Nonetheless, for similar strategic reasons the United States provided aid and shared technology. The Korean War contributed to the rebirth and growth of basic Japanese industry as Japan became an important supply base for American and U.N. forces. Further substantial gains to the Japanese economy took place later, during the Vietnam War. The United States also provided an additional critical inducement to Japanese industries by establishing and helping to maintain until 1971 a foreign exchange rate favorable to the Japanese, even as that country pursued a highly protectionist trade policy.

America's postwar export predominance could not continue indefinitely, especially after Germany, France and Japan recreated and further developed their industries with the most advanced available technology. Throughout the 1950s and into the early 1960s, aided by the absence of large-scale military expenditures, both Japan and the principal countries of Western Europe enlarged plant and equipment and increased consumer output, thereby creating near full-employment economies and raising living standards. As their industrial plants grew, these nations devoted greater attention to increasing exports. American multinationals captured a share of the domestic and export markets in Western Europe and, to a far lesser extent, in Japan. Initially, the domestic economy in the United States was not as severely affected as had been anticipated earlier. The unbroken domestic growth of the 1960s made the markets of Western Europe and Japan relatively less important.

III

As a result of U. S. government policies and private encouragement, as well as the need to pay for raw material imports used in its growing industrial machine, Japan increasingly pursued a model of export-oriented development in a number of key industries. In this, of course, Japan was not alone. If Japan were an isolated case, perhaps trade policy would not bear so heavily on our current economic problems. But Japan is not an isolated case. Rather than acknowledging that there are limits to the American economy's ability to absorb imported goods, U. S. policy has been one of encouraging developed and developing nations to increase their exports to this country.

Continuation of a policy of relatively unrestricted trade without incurring disastrous internal results must be viewed both in the context of the domestic economic circumstance and, because the actions of the United States have international implications, in terms of foreign policy goals.

The consequences of this policy for domestic manufacturing have changed and intensified in the course of the last two decades. Yet, despite the growing importance of the problem, discussion of import-penetrated industries was, as recently as ten years ago, extremely narrow in scope and short in duration. The sectors concerned-primarily labor-intensive industries-were few, and, to most observers, imports did not appear to be a general threat to U.S. manufactures. Industries experiencing difficulty competing with foreign goods were viewed merely as isolated cases.

In the 1970s the nation came to learn that excessive import penetration was not peculiar to such labor-intensive industries as apparel, textiles or home electronics. The experience in these sectors was merely a preview of similar dislocations which have now affected almost every facet of American manufacturing.

Many nostrums have been suggested over the last 20 years. When the members of the ILGWU were first confronted with the rising tide of apparel imports from developing countries, we were advised that the solution in our labor-intensive industry was simple. Domestic industry, it was said, should become more competitive by improving worker productivity.

Even in the less-developed countries, however, apparel is manufactured with essentially the same state-of-the-art technology employed in the advanced nations. Frequently, manufacture abroad has been implanted by American corporations. Designs and production techniques created in the United States and supported by American merchandising skills are used in the developing countries. Capital, technology and managerial know-how have been internationalized, leaving no opportunity for domestic apparel manufacturers to obtain a meaningful edge in productivity. Consequently, wages represent the only area in which the domestic industry can compete in an open market with imports from the developing world.

By the standards of other manufacturing in the United States, wages in the domestic apparel industry are not high. Across the country, a sewing machine operator earns an average of $5.00 to $5.50 per hour. With benefits, this comes to total compensation of roughly $6.75 per hour. But workers in the major exporting countries earn a small fraction of this amount-less than $1.00 per hour in Hong Kong, less than 40 cents per hour in Taiwan, Korea or Singapore, about 20 cents per hour in India and even less in Sri Lanka and the People's Republic of China. For garment workers in the United States to compete with such wage levels, even taking into account shipping costs and applicable tariffs, would mean that they would have to accept total compensation of hardly more than $1.00 per hour.

When we brought this to the attention of the policymakers, they responded that additional constraints on apparel imports were still unwarranted. If the domestic apparel industry could not compete on a global basis, so be it. The displaced workers, they contended, would find other work in such industries as shoe production, novelties or plastics, where the skills were highly compatible. Yet these labor-intensive industries were afflicted with the same malady-they too were losing jobs in the wake of growing imports from low-wage areas.

Policymakers and corporate spokesmen then suggested that the loss of labor-intensive manufacturing jobs should not be cause for alarm. People displaced by imports, they maintained, could be retrained for better jobs in capital-intensive industries-autos, steel or, better yet, the technology-intensive growth industries. Such a stratagem, however, had first to cope with limitations on upward or even horizontal job mobility.

IV

Even under the best of economic circumstances, occupational adaptability is far from perfect. As the shortcomings of the War on Poverty of the late 1960s clearly demonstrated, the American labor force has a broad spectrum of skills. High levels of employment and minimal unemployment, therefore, require a full spectrum of job opportunities-from the least skilled to the most advanced. Fitting people into job slots is a complex and frequently disheartening exercise, especially when an industry or a substantial fraction of it is phased out of existence. Limitations on occupational adaptability, which some economists slough off as "structural unemployment" (as though there are no human bodies behind that bland concept), are compounded by constraints on mobility created by family ties, inadequate financial resources, educational limitations, lack of access to information regarding available jobs, or de facto sex or racial discrimination.

In periods of economic stagnation or retrogression, it is difficult, if not impossible, to upgrade workers whose skills have become technologically or economically obsolete. Particular attention must, therefore, be paid to the availability of jobs in industries where skills are roughly compatible. Otherwise, massive sectoral unemployment results. Trends in several key industries thus have a critical bearing upon trade policies and, more broadly, upon industrial development and growth.

Between 1965 and 1981, the import share of developed countries in the domestic U.S. auto market grew from six percent to over 27 percent. Foreign-made trucks accounted in 1973 for only five percent of domestic purchases; in 1981, the figure had risen to 20 percent. The pattern in steel, the nation's backbone, parallels the auto industry's experience. From barely five percent in 1962, the import share of the developed countries in the domestic steel market increased nearly fivefold to almost 25 percent in 1981.

It is currently being said that the decline in the market share of domestic auto and steel output, as in many labor-intensive manufacturing industries, may well be an affordable price to pay for a productive restructuring of the American economy. This argument suggests that basic manufacturing is a drain on the resources available to technology-intensive industries. The latter, it is contended, should be the mainstay of an economically advanced nation. The proponents of this view concede that it will result in some permanent unemployment, but, they argue, the long-run result will be a more competitive economy. The problem presented by occupational adaptability is acknowledged, but subordinated to the conclusion that promotion of high-technology industries will ultimately produce the most effective means to secure real economic growth. Such growth, it is said, would in time provide for considerably lower levels of unemployment.

Even if the enormous problem of occupational adaptability is ignored, dependence upon technology-intensive industries as the primary source of manufacturing employment is conceptually flawed. It fails to take account of the small labor component in technology-intensive production, compared with either labor-intensive or even most capital-intensive manufacturing.

Thus, under the most ideal of circumstances, reliance on technology-intensive production could not support present levels of manufacturing employment, let alone reduce current high unemployment. The practical deficiencies of this development concept are underscored, moreover, by evidence that the market shares for domestically produced technology-intensive goods are themselves declining.

A case in point is the American electronics industry, a field that truly grew out of American ingenuity. The basic new discoveries in the industry were made in this country over past decades, with defense and space programs providing enormous resources for research and development and guaranteeing a market for innovation. America's infrastructure has been second to none, and our ability to provide industry with the best trained minds has been unparalleled. As recently as 15 years ago, the global preeminence of the United States in electronics surpassed achievements in any other industry. Yet what should have been an enormous advantage has now dissolved.

The erosion began in consumer electronics. From negligible import penetration 20 years ago, we have moved to the opposite extreme. By 1978, the import share for videotape players and household radios was 100 percent. There was no domestic production in these products. In the same year, imports accounted for 90 percent of all domestic purchases of citizens band radios, 85 percent of all black and white television sets, 68 percent of all electronic watches and 64 percent of all stereo components. Even such sophisticated consumer electronics as color television sets and microwave ovens had large import shares. The figures (respectively 18 percent and 25 percent for 1978), however, do not tell the entire story; they understate the actual significance of import penetration because products assembled domestically and counted as American production include substantial overseas value-added in the form of foreign-produced components, sub-assemblies, circuit boards and complete chassis.

If the evaporation of American manufacturing leadership were limited solely to consumer electronics, perhaps we could console ourselves with the preeminence we have maintained in the most sophisticated areas of research. Even here, however, the outlook is increasingly distressing. Semiconductors, for example, represent literally the most home-grown U.S. industry, and epitomize the cutting edge of America's technological strength. Yet from a starting point of zero import penetration in 1975, Japanese firms alone have captured 40 percent of the U.S. semiconductor market and are rapidly moving into the international arena. Nor are the Japanese content merely to produce what has been created in this country. In less than a decade, they have made impressive progress in areas of high-technology research that were once the exclusive domain of American enterprise. The United States no longer holds the lead in such exotic processes as electron-beam lithography or memory circuit design. Rather, this country must now struggle to maintain parity in these and many other areas of high technology.

Even the computer, that great American technological achievement, is not safe from the mounting pressure of foreign competition. U.S. Industrial Competitiveness, a July 1981 publication of the Federal Office of Technology Assessment, concluded that, ". . . the Japanese have managed great strides since 1970. . . . Japanese hardware now seems largely competitive with American. . . . While . . . Japanese computer firms have yet to establish any real presence in the U.S. market, they clearly intend to try."

V

The demonstrated ability of foreign competitors to rapidly displace key American manufacturers in both the domestic and international markets suggests a fundamental weakening of the American economy. Lagging productivity is often cited as a cause. Yet, while the rate of productivity growth in the United States has been relatively low throughout the 1970s, the absolute level of American manufacturing productivity remains the highest in the world and the differential is substantial compared with that of our major trading partners. In absolute terms, Japanese and West German productivity levels in 1980 were respectively 66.3 percent and 88.3 percent of the American figure.1

Lagging productivity growth-from 1973 to 1980 it rose at an annual rate of only 1.7 percent-is itself symptomatic of a more profound malaise. Like any symptom, it raises a number of ancillary questions. Why has the American economy (not unlike that of Great Britain) increasingly failed to replace many of its worn-out, antiquated, uncompetitive factories? Why has plant capacity utilization been so low during most of the 1970s that it currently rests at one of the lowest levels since the Great Depression? Why have major American corporations been drawn increasingly toward acquisition of other large companies and toward continued high levels of foreign investment?

Broadly speaking, this country has been following policies which can only lead to intensified deindustrialization. Unrestricted import penetration (during more than a decade of economic stagnation and retrogression) and insufficient new investments have played a vital contributing role in this process.

To the extent that imports have captured significant shares of the American market, demand for domestically manufactured goods has declined and there has been a substantial drop in domestic output. The resulting excess of capacity requires fixed overhead to be amortized on the basis of fewer units of production. The consequently high capital consumption costs per unit represent an inflationary pressure which results in higher prices and lower profit margins. The former diminish the competitiveness of U.S.-based industry, and the latter decrease the attractiveness of new productive investment.

Another inflationary pressure which accompanies unused capacity is reduced labor productivity. Managerial and professional staff cannot always be reduced in proportion to cuts in output. The same is often true of technical, maintenance or clerical staff who must perform essential functions irrespective of the level of output. Increased unitized labor costs which accompany excess capacity place an added burden on import-penetrated industries. Additionally, layoffs of key managerial and professional personnel, now taking place at an increasing rate, lead to sizable losses in investment, both in skills and in special knowledge of the firm and industry.

The negative effects of high levels of unused capacity in key industries have become even more self-perpetuating for two reasons. First, in relatively short order, supplier industries are affected as demand for industrial commodities decreases substantially. The high and persistent unemployment caused by diminished output has a snowball effect, reducing consumption and restricting growth in nearly every economic sector. Second, excess capacity affects management investment decisions. In competitive, entrepreneurial industries such as, for example, apparel and consumer electronics, the general response to imports has been to shift further from manufacture to importation and distribution. Although the strategies vary among specific corporations, the major corporations in this country have dealt with unused capacity by increasing overseas investments, by mergers and acquisitions, or by speculation in currency, commodities and various financial instruments.

Finally, there is a propensity on the part of consumers who have altered their purchasing patterns in favor of imports to maintain that pattern. Irrespective of any future efforts by American producers to regain the market, a sizable residual level of demand for imports will remain.

VI

From 1950 to 1980, direct foreign investment by American companies expanded from \$11.8 billion to \$213 billion, an average annual growth rate in excess of ten percent. The comparable average for domestic investment in the same years was less than seven percent. This latter figure, however, is deceptively high, since in recent years massive amounts of money counted as productive investment have actually been used to finance corporate mergers and acquisitions.

Direct foreign investments divert assets which could stimulate domestic growth, improve productivity and increase American competitiveness in world markets. Tens of billions of dollars have been used to substitute foreign jobs for jobs in the United States. Mergers and acquisitions, which have dominated domestic corporate finance in recent years, have neither spurred growth nor created jobs. Resultant concentration of ownership, however, has contributed to the furtherance of oligopoly and with it increased levels of inflation.

The rationale behind U.S. Steel's acquisition of Marathon Oil is a case in point. At a time when the American share of both domestic and world steel output is shrinking and when mass layoffs have crippled entire communities, expending $6.4 billion to purchase a thriving energy company would not appear to be the best way to serve the interests of the nation. The motivating logic was, perhaps, best expressed by Thomas Graham, Chairman of Jones & Laughlin Steel Corporation, who, in a November 23, 1981 interview with The New York Times, stated: "There's too much capacity in the free world. We in the U.S. have been victimized by imports for 20 years. It would be an imprudent businessman who would expand until those problems are solved."

What he describes is part of a vicious cycle. Low levels of real domestic investment in past decades and excessive import penetration deprive American manufacturers of the incentive to expand. Plants become obsolete, further eroding competitiveness. Firms that lack resources die or are swallowed up. Those that have resources produce an increasing share of their output overseas, adding directly to domestic unemployment, diverting capital from domestic investment and making the United States even less competitive. Others engage in acquisitions which neither increase output nor cut costs. Those with adequate resources have engaged in speculation in the dollar, earning huge profits at the expense of price levels. Investment in financial instruments in lieu of productive outlays is yet another variation of the domestic deindustrialization process.

On January 29, 1982, The Wall Street Journal reported that, rather than expand its high-technology base, Bendix Corporation "may be content to keep its $500-million pool of cash in short-term investments." Citing a rate of return for its investment portfolio more than double that of its manufacturing equity, Bendix Chairman William M. Agee concluded: "We may be an investor of money for an extended period of time."

These alternative processes have renewed and intensified the cycle of deindustralization; they are largely responsible for the loss of more than half of all the jobs in consumer electronics and large segments of steel, auto, home appliances, shoe production, tire and rubber output and apparel. There is no reason to believe that the trend will not continue to develop in every aspect of manufacture, simply because neither business nor government appears willing to do anything about it.

Since Japan has become the highly touted model of what to do, it is of interest that the Japanese have avoided this circular dilemma. As reported in The Journal of Commerce of November 6, 1981, Dr. Edwards Deming, often referred to as the prime architect of Japan's postwar boom, has observed:

Management has failed in this country. The emphasis is on the quarterly dividend and the quick bucks, while the emphasis in Japan is to plan decades ahead. The next quarterly dividend is not as important as the existence of the company 5, 10 or 20 years from now. One requirement for innovation is faith that there will be a future.

Dr. Deming's last point should be emphasized in view of the apparent conclusion in some quarters that American manufacturing is expendable. Some of our economic pundits even suggest that industrialized countries, particularly the United States, abandon manufacturing and concentrate on service industries.

VII

The notion of an economy based entirely on services raises several distinct problems. Elimination of manufacturing jobs removes the usefulness of skills for which there is no analogue in the service sector, and creates insurmountable problems with respect to occupational adaptability. Loss of investment in the training of literally millions of industrial workers represents an additional massive cost to the economy. Because there are relatively few well-paying jobs in the service sector, an economy devoid of manufacturing would also necessarily experience a general decline in living standards.

Aside from the direct economic effects, a pure service economy in the United States would diminish and ultimately eliminate the nation's capacity to provide the technological edge upon which American defense strategy rests. The viability of defense industry is inextricably linked with the highly diversified nature of American manufacturing. Equally essential is the ability to produce components to maintain and operate the defense apparatus. Forfeiture of America's industrial base would, in time, reduce the United States to the status of a client nation with respect to the purchase of arms.

Additionally, an economy which forfeits its right to produce for its own needs would also be unable to encourage general technological skill or innovation. Forfeiture of this country's goods-producing sector would compel the best technological minds to migrate.

Unrestricted trade and the investment practices of the multinationals, as I have contended throughout this article, can only lead to an America ultimately devoid of manufacturing. Nevertheless, present trade and investment policies must also be viewed in a broader context than just the domestic economy. The United States has responsibilities and strategic interests that must also be considered. They relate as well to nations seeking economic development.

VIII

Developing countries have been encouraged to adopt a rapid industrial development model, one that is heavily dependent upon export-oriented manufacture. However, the proposition that rapid industrialization of developing countries via exports contributes to the establishment of stable democracies is highly questionable. American trade policy toward Japan, for example, was only one component in a comprehensive plan that included genuine fostering of human rights and the establishment of institutions necessary to the existence of a participative democracy, including the creation of a national labor movement. The absence of similar efforts in the developing nations has severely limited the liberalizing role of trade. This is particularly clear with respect to those nations' chief resource-cheap labor.

In a world in which capital, technology, managerial skills and transportation techniques are largely internationalized, labor costs take on a special importance. Often labor represents the only meaningful variable in production costs. Consequently, rising wages make national economies that are dependent upon export income vulnerable to competition from other developing nations. This vulnerability is exacerbated by the difficulties associated with transition from export-oriented rapid development to an integrated industrial economy.

In those nations that have been characterized as new industrial countries, the policy has been to maintain artificially low wage rates and to permit unconscionable employment practices. These practices have resulted in economic polarization and repression of workers' rights-outcomes which perpetuate autocratic rule.

In short, unrestricted trade and investment do not benefit the majority of American workers or employers who depend upon the domestic market, nor do they benefit the majority of people in the developing nations. They serve neither American strategic nor political interests. Who, then, benefits from present policy?

The multinational corporations have the best of both worlds in developing nations. Their massive resources place them in an enviable position to negotiate with a prospective host country, enabling them to exact favorable conditions. Tax abatements, donations of land, site preparation, and waiver of requirements that they comply with government regulations are among the standard concessions made to global firms.

Less publicized is the de facto subsidization of profits which occurs when the host country takes measures to keep wages artificially low. The incentive for repressive measures in developing countries comes, additionally, from the certain knowledge that there are other developing nations eager to host multinationals, nations where living standards are even lower.

How then should the United States deal equitably with assistance to developing nations, and, at the same time, maintain existing jobs, create additional employment, arrest the declining role of American industry and rebuild its industrial base?

IX

There are a number of specific measures that would facilitate reindustrialization in the United States and lead to positive development for both the United States and its trading partners. Implementation of a rational system of fair trade should certainly be a priority. Central to such a trade policy would be import quotas negotiated on a global basis in those sectors where import penetration has significantly diminished domestic employment and threatens to continue this process.

Increments in imports should be linked to the ability of the American economy to absorb them. Massive disruptions in domestic markets, the result of large increases in import levels from exporting countries, should be avoided. Negotiated import quotas would permit exporting nations to know in advance the potential size of the market in the United States and their share in it, and permit them to plan accordingly. Moreover, allocation on a global basis would prevent the rapid shift of market shares to nations where living standards are even lower than in the traditional exporting nations. A rational policy of fair trade can protect job opportunities in exporting as well as importing nations.

Let me emphasize that I am in no way advocating a revival of autarky. A return to the protectionism that characterized American trade policy in the 1920s and 1930s would be disastrous. I am just as convinced, however, that if we continue our present policy, mounting political pressure will make total protectionism unavoidable. Little time is available to begin corrective measures. The evident trend toward autarky is not likely to abate in the wake of anticipated levels of unemployment in excess of ten percent and the fear of continued high levels of unemployment, even with economic recovery.

Profit-seeking, regardless of its costs to our nation and people, has been central to the process of deindustrialization. The rate of return on U.S. direct investments abroad is, as I have observed, significantly higher than profits on domestic investments. Many of the largest corporations and banks make 50 percent or more of their profits abroad, providing an irresistible incentive to those with enough resources to operate on a global basis. The allure also holds for diversification, via mergers and acquisitions.

This is not an indictment of the business community. I am saying, however, that in the interest of short-term profits America may be losing sight of its priorities. Most critical among such priorities is an acceptance of the principle that full employment, a viable goods-producing sector and decent living standards are essential to the national interest and to the interests of those nations that depend upon the strength of our economy.

A rational policy of fair trade is only a starting point. A common ground among labor, industry and government in pursuit of full employment must be found. To those who counsel that such a goal would be excessively costly, I say simply that the costs are miniscule compared with the price of high unemployment. Economic chaos caused by the Reagan Administration's shortsighted policies now threatens to result in the highest federal deficits in American peacetime history. This cost is a mere shadow of the penalty that unemployment places on the national economy, in terms of foregone income and missed improvements in the quality of American life.

To compete in both the domestic and world markets, this nation must increase productivity, not lower the American living standard. A meaningful commitment to full employment will increase demand, allow idle plant to be more fully utilized and result in new productive investment and important increments in productivity. In such an environment, fears of technological or import-related displacement would be largely mitigated and technological innovation permitted to proceed at an unprecedented rate, to the benefit of Americans as well as the people of other countries.

1 These estimates are those of the Bureau of Labor Statistics. The BLS data were cited before a congressional subcommittee by Under Secretary of Labor Malcolm R. Lovell, Jr., who noted that: "International comparisons of productivity are very difficult to make. The best available data [by the BLS] show that the United States has a higher output per employed person than other major developed countries, but that the gap is being narrowed." Statement of Mr. Lovell before the Subcommittee on Trade of the House Committee on Ways and Means, October 21, 1981, xeroxed statement, p. 10. The relevant BLS table is unpublished but available on request under the title, "Real Gross Domestic Product . . . per Capita and . . . per Employed Person, 1950-1980." The figures presented by Mr. Lovell have since been slightly revised, to those given above.

Sol C. Chaikin has been President of the International Ladies' Garment Workers' Union since 1975. He is a Vice President of the AFL-CIO, and a member of its Executive Council and of its Trade and International Affairs Committees. He is also deputy member of the Executive Committee of the International Confederation of Free Trade Unions, and was a member of the U.S. delegation to the Belgrade and Madrid sessions of the Conference on Security and Cooperation in Europe.

Beyond Free Trade

Robert B. Reich

REUTERS

The United States is now engaged in a divisive debate over international trade. On one side are disciples of the principle of free trade-the touchstone of American trade policy in the postwar era. Free traders argue that the interests of the United States, and of the world, continue to lie in reducing barriers, subsidies and other government interventions which distort the natural pattern of specialization and trade among countries. On the other side are those calling for policies to protect American industry from foreign competition. Protectionists argue that imports are causing massive unemployment and eroding the nation's industrial base.

The two camps have recently found common ground in the view that the United States must "get tough" with trading partners which protect or subsidize their own industries. By threatening to close American markets or subsidize American traders if other nations fail to abandon their own interventions, free traders and protectionists can both serve their concerns. More than 30 bills were introduced in the 97th Congress urging government action to enforce reciprocity by retaliating against foreign trade barriers and subsidies. Last December the Senate adopted a resolution sought by a Florida-based machine-tool manufacturer; the measure endorsed the manufacturer's request for President Reagan to deny investment tax credits to U.S. companies that purchase Japanese computerized machine tools, on the grounds that Japanese industrial policies give Japan's machine-tool manufacturers an unfair competitive advantage. The Reagan Administration is now warning the Japanese that the United States will commence formal countervailing duty proceedings unless the

Japanese cease their practice of favoring certain industries with low-interest loans and special immunities from antitrust constraints.

The Administration also has asked Congress for a $2.66-billion standby fund to match export financing by foreign governments. Already the Administration is providing generous subsidies on the sale of $150-million worth of wheat flour to Egypt, in retaliation against state-assisted flour exports by France. Even the Council of Economic Advisors-long a bastion of free trade purism-has embraced the strategy of retaliation. In its 1983 report to Congress the Council asserted that "even though costly to the U.S. economy in the short run, [retaliation] may . . . be justified if it serves the strategic purpose of increasing the cost of [trade interventions] by foreign governments."1

It is an ideal political solution. By framing the issue as the proper American reaction to foreign transgressions we need not directly face the painful choice between free trade and protection. We can avoid articulating the national goals underlying our trade policy. Protection can be the sword of the free traders in their assault upon foreign trade practices while it simultaneously serves as a shield for those anxious to preserve American jobs. Everyone seems to win.

But no one wins. Import barriers that merely preserve established businesses impose heavy costs on American consumers who must now pay more for the goods they purchase. Barriers and domestic subsidies reduce producers' incentives to innovate and to invest in new products and processes by relieving the pressure of foreign competition. They reduce workers' incentives to seek retraining and to relocate for new jobs. At the same time, interventions aimed at preservation retard the development of other nations' economies; in particular, they block the less-developed nations from "inheriting" the industries for which they are becoming better suited by virtue of their cheaper labor or favored access to markets and raw materials. Finally, they tempt other nations to retaliate in kind, and risk triggering a trade war of import barriers and export subsidies spiraling devastatingly higher, as they did in the 1930s. There is nothing new about any of these arguments. They have been used for years by the free traders themselves. They are no less valid against free traders who now endorse tactical protectionism as a bargaining chip against our trading partners.

The problem is that the classic principle of free trade no longer offers any practical or politically compelling alternative to protectionism. The recent collapse of free-trade ideology into retaliatory protectionism attests to the bankruptcy of that ideal in the present international economy. The sources of this breakdown lie deeper than the current worldwide recession and an over-valued dollar, both of which obviously imperil political assent to an open trading system. The free-trade ideal has been eroding-both within the United States and among America's trading partners-for over a decade. The erosion originates in the profound structural changes that have been reshaping the world's economy.

Since the late 1960s the economies of the United States and every other industrialized nation have been rocked by the emergence of Japan as a powerful exporter of steel, automobiles, and advanced consumer electronics products; by the emergence of South Korea, Taiwan, Hong Kong, the Philippines, Mexico, and Brazil as efficient producers of synthetic textiles, footwear, automobile components, and simpler consumer products, and the rapid movement of some of these nations into steel production and shipbuilding; by improvements in the technology of transportation, communications, and international financial and engineering services, all of which have permitted manufacturing processes to be fragmented and parcelled out across the globe to wherever specific tasks can be performed most efficiently; by the progressive saturation of the American and some West European markets with standard consumer products like automobiles and appliances, and the sudden growth of Asian and Latin American markets for these goods; and by the emergence of certain new technologies (optic fibers, semiconductors, lasers, recombinant DNA) whose commercialization-although critical to the continued competitiveness of a wide range of businesses-entails large investments and greater risks than most firms are accustomed to accepting.

These changes have put governments in industrialized nations under pressure to maintain employment in steel, autos, textiles, consumer electronics, and shipbuilding; to help upgrade plants and equipment in these and other industries; to encourage scrapping of excess capacity; to organize marketing or purchasing cartels; to provide retraining and relocation assistance for workers laid off in distressed industries; to sponsor new industries in hard-hit regions; to underwrite energy costs; to help convert capital equipment to lower-cost energy sources; to sponsor research and development; to nurture new technologies and underwrite the costs and risks of bringing them to market.

Policies inspired by new foreign competition operate either by raising the barriers to entry or by altering the cost structures of selected industries. Entry barriers have been raised through changes in antitrust laws, rules governing patents, trademarks and licensing, health and safety regulations, and government procurement restrictions, and by orderly marketing agreements and voluntary export restraints, as well as by straightforward tariffs and quotas. Costs have been reduced through government-subsidized loans, loan guarantees, tax credits, accelerated depreciation allowances, employment and training subsidies, research grants, and favorable credit or tax treatment for purchasers. Most of these interventions have been targeted selectively-on specific industries rather than across the board-because the sharp disruptions of the last 15 years have imposed disparate burdens and created different opportunities across industries.

Reviewing the widely varying forms and effects of intervention reveals that current American trade policy harbors an inherent contradiction: Our government must not intervene, since intervention by assumption distorts production and saps our competitive strength. At the same time, we must not permit other governments to intervene, since intervention gives our industrialized rivals unfair competitive advantage. Recognizing the contradiction illuminates the reality that free-trade ideology obscures.

Some interventions, rooted in incoherent economic goals or political pressure to spare powerful minorities the pain of adjustment, impose net costs on a country. Some interventions shift adjustment costs onto other countries, benefitting the nation undertaking them but burdening the rest of the world. And some interventions are strictly positive-sum, accelerating economic progress and adding to the world's wealth. To dismiss all these interventions as lamentable "distortions" is neither economically illuminating nor politically compelling. Refusing to discriminate among the different types of interventions prevents us from rejecting the first, resisting the second, and encouraging the third.

Many interventions respond to important side effects of market decisions-the large social costs and social benefits that surge through national economies under stress. To fail to intervene-even if inaction were politically possible-would be to allow severe dislocations to occur by default. We may take issue with specific interventions, specifically those which do not accommodate changes in the global economy, but merely prop up the status quo. But to object to all interventions on the ground that barriers and subsidies are at odds with the ideal of free trade sets principle above ultimate purpose. Free trade is not an end in itself, but a means to a higher living standard for the world's people. Government interventions that make economic transitions smoother, more equitable, and more efficient can serve precisely this purpose.

What is the proper end of U.S. trade policy? The issue no longer can be weighed on the familiar scales of free trade versus protection. Our failure to craft a national strategy for responding to the structural changes occurring in the world's economy confines us to a confused and contradictory trade policy. Our trading partners do not know what we want because we have failed to articulate it, or even to acknowledge the choices we face. By default, we are adopting a trade policy that preserves our old industrial base, and freezes structural change and progress in the United States and around the globe.

II

The postwar American ideal of free trade assumed a steady expansion of capital-intensive, standardized production within all industrialized nations. Comparative advantage among them was perceived to depend upon differences in the relative abundance of capital and labor, which in turn depended on national differences both in citizens' willingness to defer consumption and accumulate capital, and in the historic inheritance of capital stock. Comparative advantage was assumed to change over time; even the "backward" nations would eventually progress sufficiently to support capital-intensive industries. But development would be evolutionary, and shifts would be slow, regular, and predictable. It stood to reason that the best policy for ensuring both steady expansion and steady change would be a gradual reduction in trade barriers. That way, each nation could exploit large economies of scale in the type of production in which it currently enjoyed a comparative advantage, while incremental changes in investment and capital accumulation slowly altered the terms of trade.

Neoclassical trade theory was built upon a much older intellectual foundation. Adam Smith and David Ricardo had based their potent arguments for free trade principally on geographic differences in natural endowments, implying a quite static distribution of advantages. A nation had no choice but to realistically accept the economic station its land and climate had assigned it. As machine-based industry developed and spread, later theorists refined the model to accommodate the importance of physical capital. This "factor-proportions" model turned on the observation that some peoples were better than others at making and using machines, for reasons that had little to do with natural resources. Comparative advantage became less a matter of given endowments, more a matter of chosen investments.

Yet because it grew out of an era when technologies changed gradually, and when colonialism and devastating world wars stifled or distorted international economic adjustment, neoclassical trade theory never fully acknowledged the profound difference between comparative advantage as a fact of natural endowments and comparative advantage as an ever-changing product of social organization and choice. Until very recently, observing that the United States was rich in capital while Korea was rich in unskilled labor seemed as comfortably solid a comparison as observing that Portugal was sunny and suited for grapes while Ireland was verdant and suited for sheep. This was the theoretical basis of the free-trade principle that informs American trade policy today.

Just as the Ricardian model had viewed world trade largely in terms of the textile industry which Britain then dominated, so was the U.S. postwar trade policy shaped by attention to America's dominant industries: steel, chemicals, automobiles, rubber, and electrical machinery. Stability and predictability, to ensure that fixed costs could be recovered, were the only principles of public policy necessary to encourage investment. Potential efficiencies in world-scale production promised to preserve American dominance in these industries.

The postwar free-trade ideal was appropriate to its time, an era of unprecedented mass consumption of standardized goods. A new, relatively homogeneous generation of consumers was exercising pent-up demands for homes, cars, and all sorts of steel and plastic gadgets. Throughout the 1950s and 1960s the American economy grew less by innovating than by expanding the scale of its basic production processes and thus reducing unit costs. Western Europe followed that lead. There were relatively few breakthroughs in new products or processes, and very little real competition. But demand seemed insatiable and prosperity reigned. Free trade both enabled the rest of the world to share in this expansion and permitted the United States to preserve its preeminence.

The ideal was codified in the General Agreement on Tariffs and Trade (GATT), signed in 1947, and articulated in more detail in the subsequent Dillon (1960-1961) and Kennedy (1963-1967) rounds of tariff negotiations. It was expressed in the principles of non-discrimination, reduced government intervention and the formal negotiation of trade disputes. The GATT structure succeeded reasonably well because all parties (except the less-developed nations) had a stake in making the system work so they could share in American-led prosperity; and because the United States possessed sufficient economic and political power to enforce its vision. The volume of world trade increased dramatically, exceeding annual growth in world production. Between 1913 and 1948, world trade had risen two and a half percent per year on average; world production, only two percent; between 1948 and 1973, trade increased by seven percent per year, and world production by five percent.

The principal departures from the ideal were agricultural commodities and textiles, the two areas where potential foreign competition threatened American producers from the start. U.S. representatives to GATT insisted on an exception for primary commodities. The United States already had restricted imports of dairy products, wheat, and peanuts. Sugar quotas went into effect in 1948. Later came "voluntary" agreements with Taiwan on mushrooms, with Australia and New Zealand on beef, and with Mexico on strawberries and tomatoes. Farm subsidies were similarly exempt: in 1955, when the contracting parties to GATT adopted provisions limiting the use of export subsidies, they effectively excluded primary commodities from coverage. By 1982, the United States was spending over $18 billion a year on purchasing and storing wheat, dairy products, and corn, and on providing low-interest loans to farmers; the government spent over $2 billion merely to raise milk prices (a sum that just about equalled the year's net new lending by the Export-Import Bank to promote overseas sales by American manufacturers).

Policies to preserve the textile industry followed a related logic of escalating preservationism. In 1957 Japan agreed to limit its textile exports to the United States. This was followed five years later by a multilateral agreement (the Long Term Arrangement) designed to protect North America and Europe against cotton textiles from Japan and other developing nations; it was extended in 1967 and again in 1970. In 1971 the United States initiated agreements with Hong Kong, Taiwan, and Japan, restricting their exports of wool and man-made fibers. Then in 1974 came the first Multi-Fiber Agreement, which restricted synthetic textiles as well. The latest Multi-Fiber Agreement allows importing nations to negotiate bilateral quotas with exporters. About 80 percent of U.S. textile imports are now covered by individual country restrictions. The United States recently has imposed new restrictions on textile exports from Hong Kong, South Korea, and Taiwan, limiting them to an annual increase of just 1.5 percent per year. In mid-January 1983, the Reagan Administration reduced quotas on some textiles and clothing from China (not a signatory of the Multi-Fiber Agreement) and froze other Chinese textile and clothing exports at or near existing levels.

These two exceptions to the postwar ideal of free trade contained the seeds of its disintegration. Agriculture and textiles were the only significant sectors where free trade would impose major adjustment costs on American producers. The world market for farm goods was limited. Competitors in Canada and Australia had not been crippled by war. And American agricultural interests expected that once the worst of the devastation was repaired, West European nations would soon become largely self-sufficient in food, and even exporters. Thus American farmers saw little to gain and much to lose from free trade, and simply rejected the principle. (In fact the potential world market and the American competitive edge have both proved greater than expected, and for decades the United States has tried to recant its own exception and bring agriculture under the banner of free trade.)

In textiles the causes were different but the effect was the same: some American interests foresaw sizable immediate losses from free trade, and U.S. negotiators obtained exemptions from the rules. The world market for textiles, unlike the market for food, was expected to grow, but early in the postwar era it was clear that low-wage countries were better suited for much textile manufacturing.

In nearly every other industry, free trade promised nothing but expanding American exports. Accepting the principle was painless, and its limits unexamined. But in both cases where free trade would have called for substantial immediate adjustment on the part of significant economic groups in the United States, the principle was unceremoniously abandoned. There were no public policies to guide adjustments of this magnitude.

The free-trade principle-and the codes and institutions that were growing up around it-made no reference to the problem of structural adjustment. These early departures from the ideal foreshadowed its widespread breakdown today.

Even when the adjustment problems of the United States and Western Europe loomed larger in the 1970s, America continued to view the issues narrowly in terms of the free-trade ideal. During the Tokyo Round of negotiations, the United States continued to seek international agreements to limit government interventions that "distort" international trade. Several of the codes that emerged-governing public procurement practices and non-tariff barriers-were informed by the free-trade ideal. But the subsidies code reflected no consensus on what sorts of subsidies were out of bounds; the code did little more than establish processes to ensure that retaliation was not disproportionate to the offense.

III

During the 1970s trade accords became progressively less coherent or conclusive because the premises on which the postwar free-trade ideal had been founded were no longer applicable to large segments of industrialized economies. Comparative advantage was no longer an almost static phenomenon based on slowly evolving capital endowments. The hourly output of workers in certain less developed nations like South Korea and Taiwan was quickly catching up to the output of workers in the United States and other industrialized nations because they were starting to use many of the same machines, purchased from international engineering and capital-equipment firms with money borrowed from international banks.

The pace of structural change was dramatic. In the mid-1960s, Taiwan, Hong Kong, Korea, Brazil, and Spain specialized in simple products that required large amounts of unskilled labor but little capital investment or technology-clothing, footwear, toys, basic electronic assemblies. Japan's response was to shift out of these products and into processing industries like steel and synthetic fibers, which called for substantial capital and raw materials, but still used mostly unskilled and semi-skilled labor and incorporated relatively mature technologies not subject to major innovations. Ten years later, the newly industrialized countries had followed Japan into basic capital-intensive processing industries. Japan, meanwhile, had become an exporter of steel technology instead of basic steels, and moved its industrial base into products like automobiles, color televisions, small appliances, consumer electronics, and ships-businesses requiring technological sophistication as well as considerable investment in plant and equipment.

By 1980, Taiwan and the other rapid industrializers had themselves become major producers of complex products like automobiles, color televisions, tape recorders, CB transceivers, microwave ovens, small computers, and ships. Korea already has the world's largest single shipyard; the Pohang steel mill is one of the most modern plants in operation. Almost all the world's production of small appliances is now centered in Hong Kong, Korea, and Singapore. Meanwhile, poorer countries like Malaysia, Thailand, the Philippines, Sri Lanka, and India are inheriting the production of clothing, footwear, toys, and simple electronic assemblies.

Far from halting this migration of high-volume, standardized production, automation actually has accelerated it. Sophisticated machines are readily transported to low-wage countries. Robots and computerized machines are substituting for semi-skilled workers. Automated inspection machines are reducing the costs of screening out poor-quality components, thereby encouraging firms in industrialized nations to farm out production of standardized parts to developing nations.

In the face of this rapid movement into high-volume, standardized production, Japan-and to a lesser extent West Germany and France-have sought to shift their industrial bases to products and processes that require skilled workers-precision castings, specialty steel, special chemicals, and sensor devices, as well as the design and manufacture of fiber-optic cable, fine ceramics, lasers, large-scale integrated circuits, and advanced aircraft engines. Skilled labor has become the only dimension of production where advanced industrialized nations can create and retain an advantage. Technological innovations can be bought or imitated by anyone. Production facilities can be established anywhere. Financial capital now flows around the globe at the speed of an electronic impulse. But production processes that depend on skilled labor must stay where the skilled labor is.

Some skill-intensive products or processes require precision engineering, complex testing, and sophisticated maintenance. Others are tailored to the special needs of customers. The remainder involve technologies that are changing rapidly. All three categories are relatively secure against low-wage competition. All depend largely on experience and know-how-often developed within teams of employees who blend traditionally separate business functions of design, engineering, purchasing, manufacturing, distribution, marketing, and sales. Just as the main source of comparative advantage changed over a century ago from static natural endowments to slowly accumulated capital stocks, so now the new importance of skill-intensive production makes comparative advantage a matter of developing and deploying human capital. This second change is more dramatic than the first. In a very real and immediate way, a nation chooses its comparative advantage. The flexibility of its institutions and the adaptability of its work force govern the scope of choice. Decisions on human-capital development define a nation's competitive strategy.

Most discussions of Japan's competitive success focus, either admiringly or accusingly, on its tactics, while neglecting the fact that these tactics are effective largely because they are rooted in a coherent strategy for progressively adopting higher-skilled, higher-valued economic activities.

As Japan has reduced its commitment to basic steel, basic petrochemicals, small appliances, ships, and simple fibers, it has dramatically expanded its capacity in the higher-valued, more specialized segments of these industries. Japan's production of high quality polyester-filament fabrics, requiring complex technologies and skilled labor, now accounts for 40 percent of its textile exports. Japan's steel production has shifted to custom-cast steels with new additives and different levels of purification: high tensile-strength steel, light enough to be used in fuel-efficient cars; steel mixed with silicon, designed to improve the efficiency of power transmissions and electric motors; corrosion-resistant steel. While it upgrades its steel production processes, Japan is moving rapidly into wholly new industries. Already Japan has more than half of the world market in 64K memory chips. It has led in the introduction of the next generation-256K chips. It is on the verge of outpacing the United States in super computers. It is gaining significant shares of the world market in industrial ceramics and composite materials. It is substantially ahead in photovoltaics and the application of robotics.

West Germany and France are having more difficulty adapting their economies, but each country is making progress. Although the recent recession has slowed industrial adjustment in both nations, West Germany continues to shift into specialty steel, precision machinery, specialty chemicals, and biotechnologies; France, into aircraft, nuclear-powered generators, satellite technology, and electronic switching equipment.

These nations' governments are working with their businesses and labor unions to accomplish the shift. They are ensuring that managers obtain long-term capital and that workers obtain retraining. They are selectively raising entry barriers and reducing costs in an effort to alter the pattern of national investment, and thereby to accelerate structural change in their economies. They have undeniably made mistakes. On occasion they also bow to the demands of older industries to maintain the status quo. Often, they find it difficult to achieve consensus about the best strategy for adjustment. They are having problems coping with the current recession while trying to maintain flexibility. But these nations understand the inevitability and urgency of structural change, and the central importance of easing and accelerating the transition.

As the free-trade ideal has become hopelessly inadequate to guide these shifts, international economic agencies and formal trade processes sponsored by the United States have been gradually bypassed and enfeebled. Only the easiest of disputes are settled within the GATT system; most major issues of global economic change are dealt with outside it. Bilateral, voluntary export agreements are the rule. Japan now voluntarily limits its exports to Western Europe of automobiles, machine tools, television tubes, and video tape recorders; and its exports to the United States of automobiles, semiconductors, and many other items. The European Community limits its sales of steel to the United States.

Quotas, tariffs, and other barriers are being imposed on a wide range of products. The European Community maintains a tariff of 17 percent on integrated circuits. Australia, South Africa, Spain, Mexico, and 26 other nations require fixed percentages of domestic content in automobiles assembled within their borders. France is restricting imports of video tape recorders by subjecting them to detailed inspections and deliberate delays.

Some government subsidies are being devoted to older industries. Over the last five years the European Community has invested more than $30 billion in steel. Other subsidies are being directed at emerging businesses. In 1982, Japan unveiled two programs that together devote $750 million to pursuing world leadership in developing and producing the next generation of computers. Japan's $200-million project to develop very-large-scale integrated circuits already has enabled that nation to take the lead in that field. France is spending $20 billion on electronics over the next five years; Germany and France together are investing heavily in satellite technology.

The GATT, which condones or condemns trade practices exclusively by reference to market standards, has little to say about the growing fraction of trade conducted largely outside market channels, such as transfers of raw materials and intermediate goods within multinational firms and issues concerning wholly or partly public enterprises. Several governments are increasing their ownership interests in industry. West European governments already have equity holdings in petrochemicals, steel, railways, coal, gas, oil, shipbuilding, telecommunications, airlines, aerospace, and automobiles. Of Western Europe's 50 largest industrial companies, governments have an ownership stake in 19. In France alone, public corporations now account for almost 30 percent of French sales, 22 percent of the nation's workforce, and almost 52 percent of all industrial investment. These state-owned companies typically subsidize other companies by selling certain goods and services at prices below cost. France has long subsidized the sale of state-supplied coal. State-owned or state-managed banks in many West European nations and in Japan provide special supports to exporting companies. State-owned companies also typically purchase what they need from domestic suppliers. Most national railways, telecommunications, and power-generating entities are excluded from the GATT procurement code.

The free-trade ideal has also been crumbling within the United States. In many respects its erosion here has been more dramatic than elsewhere, and has set a precedent for other nations. Since the late 1960s, the pattern has become well established: American industries suddenly faced with foreign competition have threatened to file complaints with the government alleging foreign "dumping" in the United States of goods priced lower than production costs, or foreign subsidies which render the imports unfairly cheap. Anxious to avoid protracted litigation and the trade and diplomatic frictions accompanying it, the United States often has responded by negotiating a voluntary agreement with the exporting nation, setting a limit to the volume of exports shipped to the United States. As structural changes continue and the exporter adapts by becoming more efficient, the drama repeats itself, with the resulting restrictions becoming even tighter than before.

In 1969, U.S. steel producers pressured the government to obtain voluntary limits on the tonnage of steel that could be exported to the United States from Western Europe and Japan. When these failed to stem the tide, the industry filed anti-dumping petitions. In 1978, the Carter Administration agreed to impose a "trigger-price" mechanism, which effectively barred imported steel from entering the country at any price below the computed cost of production by Japan's most efficient producer plus transport charges, overhead, and a stipulated profit margin. After the steel industry filed new anti-dumping petitions in 1980, the trigger price was increased by 12 percent. After the steel industry again filed countervailing duty cases in 1982, alleging that steel exporting nations were unfairly subsidizing their industries, the Reagan Administration negotiated a formal quota on steel exports from Western Europe, limiting sales to 5.44 percent of the U.S. market. Other steel exporting nations now are seeking similar quota shares of the U.S. market.

In 1977, the U.S. government negotiated a marketing agreement with Japan, limiting Japanese exports of assembled color televisions to just under 1.6 million units annually. Similar agreements subsequently were negotiated with Taiwan and South Korea. In 1978, the government substantially increased tariffs on CB radio transceivers. In 1981, the Reagan Administration forced Japan to limit its automobile exports to the United States to 1.68 million vehicles; this has predictably encouraged other importing nations to demand similar assurances from the Japanese. At about the same time the Administration allowed duties to be reimposed on $3.8-billion worth of imports from Hong Kong, South Korea, Taiwan, Brazil, and Mexico, substantially increasing the protection accorded American manufacturers of car parts, electrical goods, fertilizers, and chemicals. Meanwhile, officials pressured Japanese electronic equipment manufacturers to limit their exports to the United States and to provide assurances about minimum prices. Congress has also been busy devising new barriers: there is now a 25-percent tariff on trucks manufactured abroad, and 80 percent of the parts of federally funded mass-transit vehicles must be fabricated in the United States.

All told, by 1982 the U.S. product sectors protected overtly by non-tariff barriers-when weighted by each sector's share of total consumption in manufacturing-covered 34 percent of the market for American manufacturers. In Japan the comparable figure was 7 percent; in Canada, 10 percent; in West Germany, 20 percent; in France, 32 percent.2

American industries threatened by foreign competition also have been propped up by a wide assortment of government subsidies, special tax provisions, and subsidized loans and loan guarantees. These forms of assistance have mushroomed since the late 1960s, as global competitive pressures have increased. In 1981, for example, the overall rate of U.S. tax subsidies to business as a percent of manufacturing fixed investment (the difference between the actual tax reduction resulting from the purchase of plant or machinery and what that tax reduction would have been under a neutral formula based on estimates of the asset's useful life) was 12.8 percent. In France, the rate was 4.4 percent; in Japan and West Germany the rate was actually negative.3 By 1982, tax expenditures benefiting American business-in the form of targeted tax credits, special depreciation allowances, and accelerated depreciation-totalled $222 billion. That same year U.S. government-subsidized loans to business totalled over $7 billion in direct outlays; an additional $8.7 billion was allocated in the form of new commitments for loan guarantees. None of the tax expenditures, and only a portion of the loans, appeared as direct outlays in the federal budget.

Finally, the United States continues to grant substantial subsidies and impose severe trade barriers under the pretext of national security. Approximately 55 percent of all research and development in the United States is funded by the government (a much higher percentage than in any other industrialized nation), and the bulk of this support is linked to national defense: government outlays for defense research and development have increased by about $9 billion since 1981, while non-defense research and development has increased by only $600 million. Some of these expenditures, more or less by chance, yield spin-offs of new commercial products. Most are narrowly designed for military hardware.

Some connections to national defense are even more attenuated. Merchant shipping is assumed to be a "strategic" industry; as a result, foreign merchant ships are barred from U.S. coastal trade, while the American government spends approximately $500 million per year subsidizing the shipbuilding industry. The United States is now quietly negotiating bilateral cargo-shipping deals with the Philippines,

Indonesia, and South Korea-in effect cartelizing several Pacific shipping lines. Crude oil from Alaska's North Slope may not be shipped to Japan, for fear that such trade will compromise America's hoped-for energy independence. Recently, the U.S. government pressured American Telephone and Telegraph (AT&T) to award a large fiber-optics contract to a U.S. company rather than to Fujitsu, the lowest bidder, out of fear that the United States might otherwise grow too dependent on Japan for this strategically important product. (Protection of the U.S. watch industry was once defended on the ground that only watchmakers had the skills necessary for designing bomb sights, and recent demands for barriers against Chinese textiles warn of the danger of inadequate domestic capacity for making military uniforms.)

Demands for relief of U.S. industries in competitive trouble are growing louder. This is understandable. In 1980-before the current recession got underway-58 percent of the U.S. labor force was employed in an industry which had experienced an overall decline in employment since 1973. In addition, four of the industries with slow employment growth (tobacco, automobiles, primary metals, textiles) were among the five industries with the largest average plant size.4 Adjustments are particularly difficult for these groups. Private risk capital is generally unavailable for restructuring these industries toward higher value-added and more competitive production. Workers have no ready alternative employment in the geographic area; and they are reluctant to leave for fear of losing seniority rights and pension credits at work, selling their homes at depressed prices and buying new homes in regions where homes cost much more, and sacrificing whatever employment security their spouse might have in a local job.

The free-trade ideal is not necessarily incompatible with these mounting worldwide demands for import barriers and subsidies. The United States could continue to view all these measures-both abroad and at home-as exceptions and stopgaps, and seek to contain them. Or we could continue to ignore their variety, ubiquity, and magnitude, and concentrate instead on the shrinking arena in which the ideal of free trade still applies. Or we could redefine "free trade" in such a way that many of these measures fall within a margin of permissible departures from the ideal. Or we could simply match other nations' barriers and subsidies (and expect them to match our own) in an attempt to create a "level playing field" for free trade.

The United States could embark upon any one of these strategies, or all of them. But any such attempt would be futile, because the traditional choice between free trade and protection has become almost irrelevant to the dynamic of structural change in the world economy. Free trade is almost a sideshow. The central issues of international trade policy now concern the relative speed at which national economies are evolving to higher value-added production.

IV

The practical policy choices facing the United States and every other industrialized nation are whether (and to what extent) to preserve existing jobs and industries, and whether (and how) to help move capital and labor to higher value-added and more competitive production. Both choices imply an active role for government. But the first is politically and administratively easier to accomplish than the second, at least in the short run. Most people are afraid of change, particularly when they suspect that its burdens and benefits will fall randomly and disproportionately. By the same token, many policies to preserve the status quo-like barriers against foreign competition and special tax benefits propping up deteriorating balance sheets-do not entail active and visible government intervention. No bureaucrats intrude on corporate discretion. Congress votes no budgets. The costs do not appear on any national accounts, and those who bear them are seldom aware of the source or extent of the burdens.

On the other hand, policies designed to ease and accelerate an economy's transition to higher value-added and more competitive production often require that governments work closely with business and labor to ensure that the sharp changes required do not impose disproportionate costs on some or windfalls for others; that workers have adequate income security and opportunities for retraining; that emerging industries have sufficient capital to cope with the high costs and risks of starting up when these costs and risks are beyond what private investors are willing to endure; and that industries in difficulty have sufficient resources to reduce capacity in their least competitive parts and restructure their most competitive. All of these activities entail an active and explicit government role.

The most attractive option is obvious. Preservationism, here or abroad, imperils our future prosperity and that of the rest of the world. The international economy can be compared to a mill wheel driving the process of structural change in each national economy, pushing each into higher-valued production, and generating, ultimately, an ever-richer world. The current that propels the wheel is the flow of goods and services from country to country. Any attempt to dam up the current-say, to maintain jobs in the U.S. steel industry by blocking exports of Brazilian steel-reduces the current's force and slows down the wheel. Brazil has smaller earnings with which to repay its international loans and its growth is stalled. It thus imports fewer U.S. products, and America's growth is slowed. Once the mill wheel begins to decelerate, it is difficult to restore the momentum short of unblocking all the dams and letting the current surge. But the sort of convulsive economic adjustments required to get the world economy moving again under these circumstances are far more difficult to arrange. In the present period of slow growth and high unemployment, a progressively larger proportion of firms and workers become hostage to protectionist policies.

The alternative to preservationism-rapid movement to higher value-added production-is not without its own strains and disruptions. For 15 years American and West European industry has been buffeted by Japan's speedy shift into steel, automobiles, and consumer electronics; the movement of South Korea, Taiwan, and Brazil into these same product areas is now causing further strains. Meanwhile, Japan's forays into advanced microelectronics and composite materials seriously threaten

America's future industrial base-as does West Germany's shift into biotechnologies and France's rapid development of telecommunications technology. In addition, competition among nations for leadership in the same emerging businesses creates what might appear to be its own zero-sum game.

But these sorts of tensions and disruptions are the necessary price of a dynamic world economy. Transformations to higher value-added production enlarge the world's wealth. They speed the current under the mill wheel. They generate cheaper and higher-quality products for consumers worldwide. Japan's automobile successes have hurt the American automobile industry, but the fact is that Americans now have access to better automobiles at lower costs; so, too, with steel from Brazil and new drugs from West Germany.

The apparent zero-sum standoff in international competition for leadership in the same emerging businesses is illusory. Competition to develop new products and serve new markets fuels innovation and change. Emerging products and processes can take an infinite variety of forms, incorporating different features and serving different product "niches." Moreover, the race to improve on products and processes already in the market-leapfrogging over competitors' current offerings-makes the current flow even faster. Such shifts are a positive-sum game.

The American interest lies in promoting the rapid transformation of all nations' industrial bases toward higher-value production, while discouraging zero-sum efforts to preserve the status quo. But this strategy requires that the United States abandon its condemnation of all government interventions as illegitimate departures from the free trade ideal.

U.S. trade policies have had just the opposite effect, discouraging positive adjustments at home and abroad. Part of the problem is that America's failure to discriminate between desirable government interventions and undesirable ones-treating them all as somehow illegitimate and thereby forcing them outside the channels of international scrutiny and negotiation-has ceded much of the initiative to political coalitions bent on preserving the status quo. Informal voluntary export agreements of the sort now covering substantial portions of the world market for steel, automobiles, textiles, and consumer electronics are almost certain to be undertaken as last-ditch efforts to save jobs.

America's formal trade policies also have signaled to our trading partners that we deny the legitimacy of active adjustment. For example, when the U.S. Commerce Department determined last June that Britain was unfairly subsidizing British Steel-but failed to consider that the subsidies were being used by British Steel to reduce capacity and retrain redundant workers-the United States appeared to reject this adjustment strategy outright. Yet capacity reductions and retraining programs organized by affected industries with government help are among the most effective ways of easing the shift of capital and labor out of declining sectors. Indeed, the U.S. steel industry stands to gain substantially from such reductions in world steel-making capacity. This is not to suggest that all subsidies to distressed industries are positive. Subsidies distort the world economy, and injure the United States, when they serve simply to maintain existing production facilities and jobs at the expense of other nations.

Similarly, when the U.S. Commerce Department preliminarily determined earlier this year that Matsushita was "dumping" radio pagers in the United States at a price that did not permit Matsushita to recover its costs-but failed to consider that Matsushita actually was pricing in anticipation of significant gains in experience and scale efficiencies as it expanded-the United States appeared to deny legitimacy to the aggressive marketing necessary to rapidly commercialize new technologies. Anticipatory pricing to gain high market share in an emerging industry is one of the most effective investments that growing businesses can make-with or without the aid of their governments. Consumers of radio pagers the world over stand to gain from the rapid emergence of such a low-cost product. But we should not turn a blind eye to all instances of foreign pricing below production costs. Such pricing policies in declining businesses merely serve to retard structural change, and may export unemployment during down-turns in a business cycle.

Or consider our formal stand on high technology trade. When the United States argued at last November's GATT Ministerial Meeting that developing nations should remove all import barriers against products incorporating advanced technologies, and industrialized nations should stop subsidizing the commercialization of these technologies, the United States merely seemed bent on maintaining its own lead. Yet the right kinds of government interventions can validly help these nations gain the know-how and production scale that will let them become highly efficient producers in some of these new areas. Other import barriers and domestic subsidies can also of course simply shield obsolete domestic technologies from superior foreign ones and retard global economic progress.

Perhaps the saddest irony is that our formal machinery for responding to the allegedly unfair practices of our trading partners has tended perversely to block industrial change at home. In recent years, America's primary interventions in trade policy have arisen from anti-dumping and countervailing duty cases, the results of which can only shield domestic producers from foreign rivals. As international competition has intensified, many U.S. firms have used these mechanisms to shield their domestic market and avoid the pressure to adapt.

The United States has had a countervailing duty law since 1897. Yet duties were only imposed 41 times in the law's first six decades. None were imposed between 1959 and 1967. But as foreign competition heated up between 1967 and 1974, the government imposed duties 17 times. In 1976, the United States entered 15 countervailing duty orders; in 1978, 12. In recent years duties have been used less to offset subsidies on exports from our industrialized trading partners, and more to block incursions by developing countries using aggressive pricing to break into new markets. Of the 38 cases since 1979 where the government found that foreign export promotion measures warranted duties, 22 concerned imports from seven newly industrialized nations.5

Prior to 1973, the United States had never countervailed against a domestic subsidy (as opposed to direct export subsidies); since then it has done so more and more often. Once the Commerce Department finds dumping or subsidization, and the International Trade Commission determines that U.S. companies have been injured (even if the foreign practice was not the major cause of the injury), customs officials have no choice but to levy duties on the imports. Even a preliminary finding of "reasonable indication" of unfair practice and domestic injury triggers a requirement that the importer post bond for the estimated duty. Together, these provisions give domestic industries enormous leverage in their battles to ward off foreign competitors.

The current spate of bills in Congress calling for "reciprocity" against foreign trade barriers and subsidies-and the Reagan Administration's new "get tough" policies threatening retaliation against these practices-suffer from the same perversity. Even if a foreign trade barrier or subsidy is patently a zero-sum attempt to preserve the status quo, it makes no sense for the United States to express its opposition in a way that retards industrial adjustment in this country as well.

In short, the United States has no coherent trade strategy. It has no principles for determining which practices of foreign nations and firms should be opposed, and which practices should be encouraged or even emulated. Posing the issue as free trade versus protection is no longer valid in a world economy undergoing rapid structural change where all governments are active participants, either orchestrating or retarding adjustment. That outmoded choice offers no guidance to political leaders in all industrialized nations who must respond to the needs of thousands of workers displaced by imports. Because the United States has no realistic policy, and because the old choice offers no practical alternative, the real choice-between preservation and adjustment-is being made implicitly by the United States in favor of preservation.

V

What sorts of principles might guide a new trade policy to encourage positive adjustment at home and among our trading partners? I can only suggest a rudimentary framework-no more than a set of guidelines for further debate and discussion. The details would need careful examination and elaboration by policymakers and negotiators.

First, however, two notes of caution: the United States still accounts for over one-fifth of global production and nearly one-fourth of the total national product of all non-communist nations; in dollar value, our exports of goods comprise almost 50 percent of the world's total. The dollar remains a medium of exchange for 80 percent of non-communist trade, and constitutes 75 percent of central bank reserves. Thus the size and influence of the American economy places limits on what actions the

United States can take toward our trading partners without shifting the dynamics of the world economy. We cannot merely imitate the successful strategies of another nation, like Japan, which has learned to play well a particular kind of game; our actions inevitably alter the rules of the game itself.

The second point to bear in mind is that "industries" are, strictly speaking, just convenient fictions. They are in fact shifting groups of competitors, clustered around particular products and processes. Rarely are two firms engaged in precisely the same effort. The clustering is thicker for some products and processes than for others, and the pattern is always changing. At any given time some clusters will be doing quite well; others, poorly. Thus it is misleading to speak about the decline of "steel" or "textiles" as a whole, or the emergence of "semiconductors." Some businesses associated with steel-certain specialty steels or steel minimills, for example-remain highly competitive within advanced nations; some textile businesses will continue to perform successfully. On the other hand, some activities entailed in making semiconductors (like stuffing circuit boards), and the manufacture of some lines of standardized semiconductors (like 16K RAMS) probably can be undertaken more efficiently in a developing nation. Thus in seeking to accelerate adjustment we should not aim to abandon broad categories of activities like steel, nor to embrace broad categories like semiconductors. Instead, we should aim to shift all of these clusters of businesses to higher value-added segments and more competitive outputs.

A new trade policy that assumes and accommodates structural change in the world economy would distinguish among three distinct categories of trade friction, each linked to a different type of business: (1) low-skilled, standardized businesses; (2) cyclical businesses; and (3) high-skilled, emerging businesses. A strategic trade policy would be designed to facilitate adjustment within each category.

Low-skilled, standardized businesses can be found in basic steel, cotton and simple synthetic textiles, metal-working, most shipbuilding, and basic chemicals. These businesses are characterized by long runs (or large batches) of fairly simple commodities, technologies that are evolving slowly, a relatively low level of skills demanded in the production process, and often intensive use of energy. Notwithstanding that capital costs may be high in some of these businesses, it is relatively easy for newly industrialized nations like South Korea, Taiwan, Hong Kong, Singapore, Brazil, and Mexico to pursue them and become strong competitors. Their labor costs are low, they often have access to cheap raw materials, and their markets for such standardized products often are growing rapidly.

The task for the United States and other advanced industrial nations is to ease the adjustment of their firms and workers out of these businesses as quickly as possible. The least competitive firms should be induced to close, thereby giving the more competitive time in which to consolidate operations and shift to higher value-added production. Underutilized plant and equipment should be scrapped or put to other uses. Workers should be retrained. New businesses should be encouraged to move into affected communities. All this typically requires an infusion of external resources, since distressed businesses and their communities are unlikely to possess the wherewithal to do it themselves.

Thus government subsidies linked directly to these adjustments should be encouraged, both within the United States and in other advanced industrial nations. A similar case can be made for some protection from lower-cost imports for a limited time during the transition, if it is specifically linked to a plan for capacity reductions and retraining. Domestic consumers will pay higher prices for these goods in the interim, but the higher prices may be viewed as a justifiable tax to help finance the transition. In fact, one import relief law (the so-called "escape clause") explicitly provides for protection in order to facilitate "orderly adjustment," although this proviso is generally ignored in practice. An escape clause with enforceable adjustment requirements might serve as a vehicle for useful negotiations between industry and government on the pace and direction of adjustment.

For example, Japan's recent efforts at redeploying people and capital out of low-skilled, standardized businesses have been relatively successful. Since 1978 the government has helped businesses organize adjustment cartels to scrap excess capacity and find alternative employment for their workers. Between 1979 and 1981, public and private agreements concerning 14 businesses led to an average capacity cut of 23 percent, accompanied by a rise in capacity utilization from 69 percent to 79 percent and an increase in the ratio of imports to domestic production from 15 percent to 24 percent. Shipbuilders have cut back production by 37 percent; aluminum smelting, by 62 percent; urea production, 42 percent; ammonium, 26 percent; nylon and polyester fiber, 12 percent; wet phosphoric acid, 18 percent. Of course not all such efforts have met with success. Electric-furnace steel manufacturers have used the cartel's protection to increase capacity by 14 percent. And other Japanese steel-makers, faced with competition from cheap South Korean steel, are pressing the government to impose anti-dumping levies. But the officially sanctioned machinery for scrapping and retraining has in general eased adjustment.

Other advanced nations are installing such adjustment mechanisms with varying degrees of success. If the United States is to have any workable alternative to protection, it must create similar instruments for easing the transition. At a minimum, the United States should refrain from countervailing against foreign subsidies, or retaliating against foreign trade barriers, when these practices are directly tied to capacity reductions and retraining programs.

On the other hand, the United States can legitimately object to certain of our trading partners' practices-like subsidizing exports and setting prices below production costs-which merely retard the shift of capital and labor out of these businesses. Such preservationist policies complicate adjustment and concentrate its costs. They can make it harder to design and implement national transition strategies. Even more objectionable, in terms of the ultimate goal of worldwide economic advance, these policies often end up slowing growth within developing nations (which otherwise would shift into these low-skilled, standardized businesses), and thus constrain the expansion of export markets for more complex goods produced in advanced nations.

But is makes no sense for the United States to retaliate against these zero-sum policies by imposing countervailing duties or anti-dumping levies on imported products that have benefitted from them, or by providing American manufacturers in the same businesses with export subsidies of their own. These steps merely retard economic change in the United States while at the same time imposing even greater hardships on developing nations. Instead-for a whole range of low-skilled, standardized businesses-the United States should seek international agreements with other advanced industrial nations, establishing targets and timetables for capacity reductions, the scrapping or conversion of existing plant and equipment, and retraining of workers. The United States might seize the initiative by proposing an international adjustment fund to help finance these transitions. Payments into the fund would be proportional to a nation's current employment in designated low-skilled, standardized businesses; drawing rights would be proportional to a nation's reductions in capacity and employment.

The European Community already has undertaken a few tentative steps in this direction, but these initiatives have been hampered in part by contrary U.S. policies. In December 1979, for example, member governments agreed to a Commission proposal to extend aid to the European textile industry for capacity reductions and conversion of plant and equipment. But it was particularly difficult for the Community to implement this policy due to the continuous flow into Western Europe of cheap U.S. synthetic fibers whose manufacturers had access to petroleum feedstocks at regulated prices below world market levels. During the past five years the Commission also has recommended targets for capacity reductions in steel, and has provided funds for conversions. But these steps too have been only partially successful. Although the Commission has the power to require that member states' steel subsidies be used for capacity reductions and retraining, certain nations-like Italy-actually have increased capacity during the interim. Moreover, the recent flow of tax benefits and government-subsidized loans from the United States to its own steel industry, coupled with mounting efforts to protect American steel from foreign competition, has emboldened some European steel-makers to demand similar preservationist policies there.

Agreements among advanced industrial nations concerning targets and timetables for phasing out low-skilled, standardized businesses would need to be complemented by trade policies accommodating developing nations' adoption of these same businesses. For example, while no legitimate function is served in advanced nations by granting these businesses export subsidies or in pricing these products below production costs, trade practices like these can in some cases help developing nations achieve the production scale necessary to become profitable. For developing nations shifting into standardized businesses, export subsidies and below-cost pricing policies are often best viewed as investments to gain economies of scale. At the least, therefore, a trade policy geared to adjustment would not indiscriminately counter developing nations' export promotion measures with countervailing duties or anti-dumping levies.

Cyclical businesses typically entail high fixed costs in plant, equipment, and labor. They also are quite sensitive to even small declines in aggregate demand, since prospective buyers often will delay purchases until markets recover. Taken together, these two features-high fixed costs and business-cycle sensitivity-guarantee trouble for these businesses during recessions. Large numbers of employees are laid off; investments in new equipment are postponed. When the economy picks up again, it is often difficult for firms in these businesses to regain their competitive footing, particularly if firms in other nations have been cushioned during the trough. In the meantime, the social costs of unemployment often are substantial.

In all advanced industrial nations there is an understandable temptation to grant these cyclical businesses special treatment during recessions-to subsidize them, to help them price below production costs, and to block imports-thereby maintaining employment and capacity rather than bearing the social costs of unemployment and the high unit costs of reduced capacity. But this strategy quickly can turn into a zero-sum game. With every advanced nation seeking in effect to export its unemployment and excess capacity problems, no costs are avoided; they are merely shifted to the least nimble international player.

For the United States in particular this is a losing game. Some other nations may be small enough and their trade sufficiently inconspicuous to impose temporary costs on other nations without running the risk of retaliation. For obvious reasons, the United States is not in this enviable position. We cannot keep our cyclical businesses afloat at the expense of the rest of the world because other nations facing similar problems surely will respond in kind.

Our trade position is made doubly difficult because GATT mechanisms can seldom effectively counter such foreign practices. The formal machinery of anti-dumping, countervailing duties, and escape-clause proceedings is generally too cumbersome; informal negotiations leading to voluntary export agreements are too slow. By the time imports have claimed a noticeable market share, it is often too late for U.S. businesses to recoup. They will have already laid off workers and delayed investments.

Nevertheless, we should view these foreign trade practices in perspective. Periods of worldwide unemployment and underutilized capacity are caused by declining demand, not by predatory trade practices. Zero-sum trade practices can reallocate and concentrate these costs, but they do not create them. The long-term competitiveness of America's cyclical businesses has been jeopardized more by their short-sighted investment and employment practices than by unfair foreign trade measures.

For example, not until 1975 did the Japanese begin to make substantial headway in semiconductors. And they could do so in large part because American chip-makers were standing still. As the U.S. economy was staggering under the impact of the oil-price rise, commercial purchasers of semiconductors in the United States reduced their demand sharply. The government's defense and aerospace budgets were contracting at the same time. As a result, U.S. chip-makers cut their capital equipment purchases by half and laid off thousands of skilled workers. By contrast, the Japanese chip-makers-with their tax privileges, government loans and subsidies still in place-could afford to maintain capacity and improve their technology in anticipation of the next economic upturn. When the market began to rebound, American chip-makers had difficulty attracting back skilled workers and regaining technological momentum. Still smarting from the recession, American executives were reluctant to add new capacity. When the market took off again in 1978, they were caught short. Just to keep its own customers supplied, Intel was forced to buy chips from Hitachi at the rate of 200,000 a month; International Business Machines (IBM) had to purchase 10 million Japanese chips for its small computers. By the end of 1978 the Japanese chip-makers had captured 40 percent of the world market for 16K RAMS. History has been replayed for both semiconductors and machine tools in the current recession.

Thus a "tough" U.S. trade policy for cyclical businesses is less relevant to their competitive strength than industrial and macroeconomic policies designed to reduce their vulnerability to recessions. In many of these businesses we have failed to maintain competitiveness because our capital markets do not provide adequate long-term financing, because our workers lack durable ties to their firms, and because we have chosen to control inflation by periodically cooling the U.S. economy to a near freeze. Other advanced industrial nations have adopted quite different policies. For example, our trade conflicts with Japan over cyclical businesses have been most intense during periods when the yen was undervalued (1970-71, 1976-77, and 1981-82). In the most recent period, that disparity has been directly related to America's tight money and loose fiscal policies, and Japan's loose monetary and tight fiscal policies.

Thus, the U.S. trade strategy for cyclical businesses should be twofold: first, we should continue to discourage foreign export subsidies and below-cost pricing. But more important, we should seek to coordinate our macroeconomic policies with those of our trading partners, so that currency values do not fall too far out of line with underlying trade demand. And we should create counter-cyclical industrial policies which would help maintain employment and capacity in our key cyclical businesses during troughs in the business cycle. These policies might take the form of development banks to provide long-term financing, and government-subsidized retraining vouchers to allow employees to use recessions as occasions to upgrade their skills.

Emerging businesses in advanced industrial nations are characterized by rapid technological change. All depend largely on skilled labor. Examples include the design and fabrication of optical-fiber cable, large-scale integrated circuits, advanced aircraft engines, complex polymer materials, and products derived from recombinant DNA. Many of these businesses are found in the higher-valued, more specialized segments of older industries-for example, automobile transaxles, aramid (high-strength synthetic) fibers, and corrosive-resistant steel. And in many of these businesses, such as office communications and computer-aided manufacturing, the traditional line between goods and services is becoming blurred.

Every industrialized nation is racing to gain scale and experience in these businesses; national strategy, not natural endowment, is the key to competitive advantage. Every nation-including the United States, through the back door of the National Aeronautics and Space Administration (NASA) and the Department of Defense-is subsidizing research, development, and commercialization. Some nations also are erecting import barriers on the theory that these businesses represent "infant industries" which must be temporarily sheltered. Finally, in anticipation of burgeoning markets, some firms are setting prices substantially below current production costs. Which of these practices should the United States oppose? Which should it emulate?

Subsidies to accelerate development should be welcomed. New, higher-valued products and new processes for generating them add to the world's wealth. Even if every nation aims for leadership in the same field, this will not become a zero-sum game, since an infinite range of variations and improvements can be achieved, and intense competition will spur even greater progress.

For emerging businesses featuring rapid technical change and continuously evolving products, even below-cost pricing should be welcomed as a positive-sum strategy. Such a pricing strategy signals the anticipation of a substantial drop in costs and prices as producers gain greater scale and experience. The producer gambles that there will be sufficient demand to generate a healthy return if and when the firm gains a substantial market position; the gamble is made more risky by the possibility that a competitor will bring out a new product generation in the meantime. Because this form of competition keeps prices low, all consumers benefit. Moreover, given the dynamic nature of the market, below-cost pricing under these circumstances is not predatory-any competitor can leapfrog to a new and better product. Below-cost pricing is just one means of investing in (and betting on) a particular production generation.

The United States has two handicaps in this race. The first is the share of resources devoted to defense-related research and development, which leads only occasionally and by accident to commercially competitive products or processes. This problem is best addressed by boosting support for non-defense research and development, and by creating a new mechanism (perhaps a White House Industrial Development Board) capable of assessing the effects of major defense projects on U.S. commercial competitiveness and identifying alternative plans for achieving defense objectives in ways that offer richer benefits for the rest of the economy.

The second handicap takes the form of antitrust policies which discourage joint research ventures among domestic firms in international competition. This can be remedied by altering the antitrust laws explicitly to permit such joint ventures when the world market share of the relevant U.S. firms is under, say, 25 percent.

But there is no reason why the United States should erect trade barriers against foreign emerging businesses which enjoy targeted subsidies or set prices below production costs. Barriers only reduce domestic competition. They allow American producers to opt out of the international race for the next cheaper or better generation. So long as markets are growing and changing rapidly, the financial health of domestic firms in these businesses depends not on heavy investment in existing production capacity or on a stable pool of customers, but on rapid adaptation and quick exploitation of new opportunities-a set of organizational skills that can be honed best in a highly competitive global market.

Nor does the "infant industry" argument provide a sound rationale for protecting emerging businesses. Such protection rarely will help a domestic firm catch up to a foreign competitor enjoying a head start in scale and experience. Since technologies are changing rapidly, a better strategy is to encourage domestic firms in their efforts to leapfrog to the next product generation and establish a leading position there. Domestic producers intent on making such a leap may benefit from government subsidies (particularly in cases where the prospect of delayed and contingent returns makes venture capital markets balk), but not from protection against imports of the product they aim to surpass.

Import barriers may also jeopardize the international competitive positions of domestic industrial purchasers who would have to pay more for their supplies, or settle for components of poorer quality. U.S. pressure on Japan to reduce exports of 64K RAMS surely places American computer manufacturers at a competitive disadvantage relative to Japanese computer manufacturers who have ready access to better and cheaper chips. Similarly, were the President to disallow investment tax credits for the purchase of numerically controlled machine tools manufactured in Japan, as some machine-tool makers have urged, American producers of automobiles and construction equipment would no longer have access to superior Japanese machine tools at a low cost.

The United States should oppose foreign trade barriers which block U.S. exports of high-technology products. But because such tactics are apt to hurt these other nations at least as much as they do U.S. producers, the United States has an opportunity through international negotiations to convince its trading partners that the route to competitive success in emerging businesses lies more in the right kind of subsidies than in import barriers.

A final facet of the American strategy for emerging businesses concerns the investments in the education, training, and group learning which now define advanced nations' comparative advantage and determine their capacity to adopt new high-value businesses. Financial capital formation is becoming a less important determinant of a nation's well-being than human capital formation. Financial capital is highly mobile; international savings are flowing around the globe to wherever they can be put to use. Nor is basic invention any longer the key to competitive leadership. Technological innovations can be bought or imitated by anyone: Britain has continued to lead the world in major technological breakthroughs while its economy declines. But a nation's store of human capital-the skills and knowledge embedded within the work force-is relatively immobile internationally, and directly determines the speed and efficiency with which new products can be developed and brought to market.

The quality of public education will continue to be critically important. But since many of the most relevant skills can best be learned on the job, it is becoming increasingly important to develop and attract emerging businesses that will invest aggressively in the training and development of their employees.

Some 70 percent of the value added in American manufacturing currently derives from firms that have branches, subsidiaries, or joint ventures outside the United States; a similar percentage of manufacturing income in Japan, West Germany, Sweden, and Britain is earned by multinational enterprises. Thus the internal decisions of these firms help shape the pattern of international employment. But the important issue is not how these multinationals allocate jobs. It is how they allocate their investment in people.

Japanese multinationals, for example, are now actively engaged in worldwide investment programs. But their underlying strategies are geared to increasing the real wages of Japanese workers over the long term. Japanese companies are establishing facilities in America and Western Europe for assembling automobiles, trucks, and appliances. Because these assembly facilities require relatively low-skilled labor, they do not threaten the interests of progressively more skilled Japanese workers. So long as the highest-value portion of the production process remains behind in Japan, foreign-based assembly facilities contribute to the standard of living of Japan's citizens by increasing the demand for the sophisticated components they produce.

Meanwhile, Japanese companies are entering joint ventures with American companies in the emerging fields of biotechnology, "fifth generation" computers, fiber optics, and advanced integrated circuits. By the terms of these agreements, most advanced research and engineering are to be done in Japan. The U.S. firms thereby gain access to the Japanese market, but Japan reaps the more durable benefit of investments in its human capital. Japanese firms also are producing aircraft under licensing agreements with McDonnell Douglas and Lockheed, rather than buying the aircraft outright; this arrangement enables Japanese workers to learn about up-to-date aircraft manufacturing systems and technologies. In the short run these joint ventures and licensing agreements are more expensive than direct purchases would be, but in the long run they will increase the store of skills and knowledge embedded in the Japanese work force and thereby permit Japan to be more competitive in these industries in the future. The extra cost simply represents sound investments in human capital.

At the same time many Japanese producers are supplying American manufacturers with high value-added products and components. Xerox already is producing many of its small copiers in Japan. Motorola operates an integrated-circuit design center and a test center there. AT&T soon will be selling in the United States cellular mobile-telephone equipment produced in Japan. Of the 16 U.S. firms that built manufacturing facilities in Japan during the first half of 1982, ten were in the business of making advanced semiconductors, and four in biotechnology and fine chemicals. Beginning in 1984, both General Motors and Ford will be importing subcompacts, diesel engines, and transaxles from Japan. All these arrangements also serve to develop Japanese know-how, rather than the long-term skills of the American work force.

Governments in many other nations are beginning to distinguish between direct investments in their nations which merely create new jobs and those which also increase the quality of their labor force. They therefore are bargaining with multinationals for more human capital investment: Italtel, Italy's state-owned telecommunications equipment manufacturer, recently entered into an agreement with General Telephone and Electronics (GTE) to develop an electronic telephone-switching system for the Italian market on condition that the manufacturing facilities be in Italy. GTE gets an inside track on future business in Italy, but Italtel gets the know-how. France has invited Motorola to establish a semiconductor division there and has offered investment incentives on condition that Motorola set up a research and development department in France to help train French engineers. Various governments' conditional offers of market access have led IBM to establish nine research laboratories in Europe and Asia. Ireland is offering incentives for multinationals to establish full-scale manufacturing, research and development, and European-wide administrative facilities in that country.

The United States must understand that government expenditures in the form of subsidies, loan guarantees, and tax benefits designed to keep or lure high value-added emerging businesses within the United States, are no less legitimate investments in the education of America's labor force than are investments in the public schools. Properly conceived, these are not zero-sum efforts to increase employment at home at the expense of employment elsewhere; they are positive-sum policies to enhance the skills and know-how of American workers while increasing the wealth-creating potential of the world. In the long run they may constitute our most important strategy for emerging businesses.

VI

These guidelines for active trade strategies that distinguish among declining, cyclical, and emerging businesses are no panacea for trade conflicts. Frictions will remain. Indeed, policies based on the principles outlined here would surely inspire heated debates about which businesses fit within each category, and whether trade practices in fact are being used to shift to higher value-added production or merely to preserve the present industrial base.

The point is not so much to reduce or eliminate frictions, but to change the nature of the debate and the focus of attention. Rather than preoccupy ourselves (and our trading partners) with endless and empty disputes over whether a particular practice constitutes an unwarranted subsidy, a particular firm is engaged in dumping, a certain domestic industry has suffered an injury, or certain non-tariff barriers are disruptive to free trade, these new trade strategies would focus the debate squarely on the central question of whether the practices in question serve to accelerate adjustment or maintain the status quo.

The international economy is changing too rapidly to expect that we can discover any immutable principles to guide it automatically on its way. Structural changes are painful, and the vagaries of politics inevitably will play a larger role in setting trade policy in the United States and in every other nation in the years ahead. Thus we need a set of strategic concepts which are consistently applied and which clearly alert our trading partners to what we conceive to be our interest. For the same reason, a formal, court-like apparatus for fact-finding and disposition of trade disputes will prove to be less useful than an ongoing process of political debate and negotiation, in which all sides are permanently engaged.

The choice is clear. The forces of preservation will continue to gain ground without U.S. leadership in the opposite direction. Already steel, autos, textiles, and video tape recorders have succumbed to fixed world quotas on their way to becoming cartel arrangements. The United States should approach our trading partners with a lively awareness that adjustment is inherently difficult, that active government intervention is inevitable and sometimes desirable, and that-through explicit strategies and an ongoing process of negotiation and compromise-we can change zero-sum international conflict into a positive-sum enterprise for world growth.

1 Economic Report of the President, February 1983, Washington: GPO, 1983, p. 61.

2 Estimate from William Cline, "Exports of Manufactures from Developing Countries: Performance and Prospects for Market Access," Washington: Brookings Institution, 1982. This estimate does not reflect the severity of the protection accorded the products in question.

3 See Bulletin for International Fiscal Documentation, Organization for Economic Cooperation and Development, July 1981.

4 See R. Lawrence, "Deindustrialization and U.S. Competitiveness: Domestic and International Forces in U.S. Industrial Performance 1970-1980," Washington: Brookings Institution, October 19, 1982.

5 Mexico, Uruguay, Argentina, Spain, Brazil, Republic of Korea and Taiwan. Trade Action Monitoring System, Office of the U.S. Trade Representative.

??

??

Robert B. Reich teaches business and public policy at the John F. Kennedy School of Government, Harvard University. He is co-author with Ira Magaziner of the recently published book, Minding America's Business, and is author of the forthcoming book, The Next American Frontier.

Competitiveness: A Dangerous Obsession

Paul Krugman

REUTERS

THE HYPOTHESIS IS WRONG

In June 1993, Jacques Delors made a special presentation to the leaders of the nations of the European Community, meeting in Copenhagen, on the growing problem of European unemployment. Economists who study the European situation were curious to see what Delors, president of the EC Commission, would say. Most of them share more or less the same diagnosis of the European problem: the taxes and regulations imposed by Europe's elaborate welfare states have made employers reluctant to create new jobs, while the relatively generous level of unemployment benefits has made workers unwilling to accept the kinds of low-wage jobs that help keep unemployment comparatively low in the United States. The monetary difficulties associated with preserving the European Monetary System in the face of the costs of German reunification have reinforced this structural problem.

It is a persuasive diagnosis, but a politically explosive one, and everyone wanted to see how Delors would handle it. Would he dare tell European leaders that their efforts to pursue economic justice have produced unemployment as an unintended by-product? Would he admit that the EMS could be sustained only at the cost of a recession and face the implications of that admission for European monetary union?

Guess what? Delors didn't confront the problems of either the welfare state or the EMS. He explained that the root cause of European unemployment was a lack of competitiveness with the United States and Japan and that the solution was a program of investment in infrastructure and high technology.

It was a disappointing evasion, but not a surprising one. After all, the rhetoric of competitiveness, the view that, in the words of President Clinton, each nation is "like a big corporation competing in the global marketplace", has become pervasive among opinion leaders throughout the world. People who believe themselves to be sophisticated about the subject take it for granted that the economic problem facing any modern nation is essentially one of competing on world markets, that the United States and Japan are competitors in the same sense that Coca-Cola competes with Pepsi, and are unaware that anyone might seriously question that proposition. Every few months a new best-seller warns the American public of the dire consequences of losing the "race" for the 21st century.1 A whole industry of councils on competitiveness, "geoeconomists" and managed trade theorists has sprung up in Washington. Many of these people, having diagnosed America's economic problems in much the same terms as Delors did Europe's, are now in the highest reaches of the Clinton administration formulating economic and trade policy for the United States. So Delors was using a language that was not only convenient but comfortable for him and a wide audience on both sides of the Atlantic.

Unfortunately, his diagnosis was deeply misleading as a guide to what ails Europe, and similar diagnoses in the United States are equally misleading. The idea that a country's economic fortunes are largely determined by its success on world markets is a hypothesis, not a necessary truth; and as a practical, empirical matter, that hypothesis is flatly wrong. That is, it is simply not the case that the world's leading nations are to any important degree in economic competition with each other, or that any of their major economic problems can be attributed to failures to compete on world markets. The growing obsession in most advanced nations with international competitiveness should be seen, not as a well-founded concern, but as a view held in the face of overwhelming contrary evidence. And yet it is clearly a view that people very much want to hold, a desire to believe that is reflected in a remarkable tendency of those who preach the doctrine of competitiveness to support their case with careless, flawed arithmetic.

This article makes three points. First, it argues that concerns about competitiveness are, as an empirical matter, almost completely unfounded. Second, it tries to explain why defining the economic problem as one of international competition is nonetheless so attractive to so many people. Finally, it argues that the obsession with competitiveness is not only wrong but dangerous, skewing domestic policies and threatening the international economic system. This last issue is, of course, the most consequential from the standpoint of public policy. Thinking in terms of competitiveness leads, directly and indirectly, to bad economic policies on a wide range of issues, domestic and foreign, whether it be in health care or trade.

MINDLESS COMPETITION

Most people who use the term "competitiveness" do so without a second thought. It seems obvious to them that the analogy between a country and a corporation is reasonable and that to ask whether the United States is competitive in the world market is no different in principle from asking whether General Motors is competitive in the North American minivan market.

In fact, however, trying to define the competitiveness of a nation is much more problematic than defining that of a corporation. The bottom line for a corporation is literally its bottom line: if a corporation cannot afford to pay its workers, suppliers, and bondholders, it will go out of business. So when we say that a corporation is uncompetitive, we mean that its market position is unsustainable, that unless it improves its performance, it will cease to exist. Countries, on the other hand, do not go out of business. They may be happy or unhappy with their economic performance, but they have no well-defined bottom line. As a result, the concept of national competitiveness is elusive.

One might suppose, naively, that the bottom line of a national economy is simply its trade balance, that competitiveness can be measured by the ability of a country to sell more abroad than it buys. But in both theory and practice a trade surplus may be a sign of national weakness, a deficit a sign of strength. For example, Mexico was forced to run huge trade surpluses in the 1980s in order to pay the interest on its foreign debt since international investors refused to lend it any more money; it began to run large trade deficits after 1990 as foreign investors recovered confidence and began to pour in new funds. Would anyone want to describe Mexico as a highly competitive nation during the debt crisis era or describe what has happened since 1990 as a loss in competitiveness?

Most writers who worry about the issue at all have therefore tried to define competitiveness as the combination of favorable trade performance and something else. In particular, the most popular definition of competitiveness nowadays runs along the lines of the one given in Council of Economic Advisors Chairman Laura D'Andrea Tyson's "Who's Bashing Whom?": competitiveness is "our ability to produce goods and services that meet the test of international competition while our citizens enjoy a standard of living that is both rising and sustainable." This sounds reasonable. If you think about it, however, and test your thoughts against the facts, you will find out that there is much less to this definition than meets the eye.

Consider, for a moment, what the definition would mean for an economy that conducted very little international trade, like the United States in the 1950s. For such an economy, the ability to balance its trade is mostly a matter of getting the exchange rate right. But because trade is such a small factor in the economy, the level of the exchange rate is a minor influence on the standard of living. So in an economy with very little international trade, the growth in living standards, and thus "competitiveness" according to Tyson's definition, would be determined almost entirely by domestic factors, primarily the rate of productivity growth. That's domestic productivity growth, period, not productivity growth relative to other countries. In other words, for an economy with very little international trade, "competitiveness" would turn out to be a funny way of saying "productivity" and would have nothing to do with international competition.

But surely this changes when trade becomes more important, as indeed it has for all major economies? It certainly could change. Suppose that a country finds that although its productivity is steadily rising, it can succeed in exporting only if it repeatedly devalues its currency, selling its exports ever more cheaply on world markets. Then its standard of living, which depends on its purchasing power over imports as well as domestically produced goods, might actually decline. In the jargon of economists, domestic growth might be outweighed by deteriorating terms of trade.2 So "competitiveness" could turn out really to be about international competition after all.

There is no reason, however, to leave this as a pure speculation; it can easily be checked against the data. Have deteriorating terms of trade in fact been a major drag on the U.S. standard of living? Or has the rate of growth of U.S. real income continued essentially to equal the rate of domestic productivity growth, even though trade is a larger share of income than it used to be?

To answer this question, one need only look at the national income accounts data the Commerce Department publishes regularly in the Survey of Current Business. The standard measure of economic growth in the United States is, of course, real GNP, a measure that divides the value of goods and services produced in the United States by appropriate price indexes to come up with an estimate of real national output. The Commerce Department also, however, publishes something called "command GNP." This is similar to real GNP except that it divides U.S. exports not by the export price index, but by the price index for U.S. imports. That is, exports are valued by what Americans can buy with the money exports bring. Command GNP therefore measures the volume of goods and services the U.S. economy can "command", the nation's purchasing power, rather than the volume it produces.3 And as we have just seen, "competitiveness" means something different from "productivity" if and only if purchasing power grows significantly more slowly than output.

Well, here are the numbers. Over the period 1959-73, a period of vigorous growth in U.S. living standards and few concerns about international competition, real GNP per worker-hour grew 1.85 percent annually, while command GNP per hour grew a bit faster, 1.87 percent. From 1973 to 1990, a period of stagnating living standards, command GNP growth per hour slowed to 0.65 percent. Almost all (91 percent) of that slowdown, however, was explained by a decline in domestic productivity growth: real GNP per hour grew only 0.73 percent.

Similar calculations for the European Community and Japan yield similar results. In each case, the growth rate of living standards essentially equals the growth rate of domestic productivity, not productivity relative to competitors, but simply domestic productivity. Even though world trade is larger than ever before, national living standards are overwhelmingly determined by domestic factors rather than by some competition for world markets.

How can this be in our interdependent world? Part of the answer is that the world is not as interdependent as you might think: countries are nothing at all like corporations. Even today, U.S. exports are only 10 percent of the value-added in the economy (which is equal to GNP). That is, the United States is still almost 90 percent an economy that produces goods and services for its own use. By contrast, even the largest corporation sells hardly any of its output to its own workers; the "exports" of General Motors, its sales to people who do not work there, are virtually all of its sales, which are more than 2.5 times the corporation's value-added.

Moreover, countries do not compete with each other the way corporations do. Coke and Pepsi are almost purely rivals: only a negligible fraction of Coca-Cola's sales go to Pepsi workers, only a negligible fraction of the goods Coca-Cola workers buy are Pepsi products. So if Pepsi is successful, it tends to be at Coke's expense. But the major industrial countries, while they sell products that compete with each other, are also each other's main export markets and each other's main suppliers of useful imports. If the European economy does well, it need not be at U.S. expense; indeed, if anything a successful European economy is likely to help the U.S. economy by providing it with larger markets and selling it goods of superior quality at lower prices.

International trade, then, is not a zero-sum game. When productivity rises in Japan, the main result is a rise in Japanese real wages; American or European wages are in principle at least as likely to rise as to fall, and in practice seem to be virtually unaffected.

It would be possible to belabor the point, but the moral is clear: while competitive problems could arise in principle, as a practical, empirical matter the major nations of the world are not to any significant degree in economic competition with each other. Of course, there is always a rivalry for status and power, countries that grow faster will see their political rank rise. So it is always interesting to compare countries. But asserting that Japanese growth diminishes U.S. status is very different from saying that it reduces the U.S. standard of living, and it is the latter that the rhetoric of competitiveness asserts.

One can, of course, take the position that words mean what we want them to mean, that all are free, if they wish, to use the term "competitiveness" as a poetic way of saying productivity, without actually implying that international competition has anything to do with it. But few writers on competitiveness would accept this view. They believe that the facts tell a very different story, that we live, as Lester Thurow put it in his best-selling book, Head to Head, in a world of "win-lose" competition between the leading economies. How is this belief possible?

CARELESS ARITHMETIC

One of the remarkable, startling features of the vast literature on competitiveness is the repeated tendency of highly intelligent authors to engage in what may perhaps most tactfully be described as "careless arithmetic." Assertions are made that sound like quantifiable pronouncements about measurable magnitudes, but the writers do not actually present any data on these magnitudes and thus fail to notice that the actual numbers contradict their assertions. Or data are presented that are supposed to support an assertion, but the writer fails to notice that his own numbers imply that what he is saying cannot be true. Over and over again one finds books and articles on competitiveness that seem to the unwary reader to be full of convincing evidence but that strike anyone familiar with the data as strangely, almost eerily inept in their handling of the numbers. Some examples can best illustrate this point. Here are three cases of careless arithmetic, each of some interest in its own right.

Trade Deficits and the Loss of Good Jobs. In a recent article published in Japan, Lester Thurow explained to his audience the importance of reducing the Japanese trade surplus with the United States. U.S. real wages, he pointed out, had fallen six percent during the Reagan and Bush years, and the reason was that trade deficits in manufactured goods had forced workers out of high-paying manufacturing jobs into much lower-paying service jobs.

This is not an original view; it is very widely held. But Thurow was more concrete than most people, giving actual numbers for the job and wage loss. A million manufacturing jobs have been lost because of the deficit, he asserted, and manufacturing jobs pay 30 percent more than service jobs.

Both numbers are dubious. The million-job number is too high, and the 30 percent wage differential between manufacturing and services is primarily due to a difference in the length of the workweek, not a difference in the hourly wage rate. But let's grant Thurow his numbers. Do they tell the story he suggests?

The key point is that total U.S. employment is well over 100 million workers. Suppose that a million workers were forced from manufacturing into services and as a result lost the 30 percent manufacturing wage premium. Since these workers are less than 1 percent of the U.S. labor force, this would reduce the average U.S. wage rate by less than 1/100 of 30 percent, that is, by less than 0.3 percent.

This is too small to explain the 6 percent real wage decline by a factor of 20. Or to look at it another way, the annual wage loss from deficit-induced deindustrialization, which Thurow clearly implies is at the heart of U.S. economic difficulties, is on the basis of his own numbers roughly equal to what the U.S. spends on health care every week.

Something puzzling is going on here. How could someone as intelligent as Thurow, in writing an article that purports to offer hard quantitative evidence of the importance of international competition to the U.S. economy, fail to realize that the evidence he offers clearly shows that the channel of harm that he identifies was not the culprit?

High Value-added Sectors. Ira Magaziner and Robert Reich, both now influential figures in the Clinton Administration, first reached a broad audience with their 1982 book, Minding America's Business. The book advocated a U.S. industrial policy, and in the introduction the authors offered a seemingly concrete quantitative basis for such a policy: "Our standard of living can only rise if (i) capital and labor increasingly flow to industries with high value-added per worker and (ii) we maintain a position in those industries that is superior to that of our competitors."

Economists were skeptical of this idea on principle. If targeting the right industries was simply a matter of moving into sectors with high value-added, why weren't private markets already doing the job?4 But one might dismiss this as simply the usual boundless faith of economists in the market; didn't Magaziner and Reich back their case with a great deal of real-world evidence?

Well, Minding America's Business contains a lot of facts. One thing it never does, however, is actually justify the criteria set out in the introduction. The choice of industries to cover clearly implied a belief among the authors that high value-added is more or less synonymous with high technology, but nowhere in the book do any numbers compare actual value-added per worker in different industries.

Such numbers are not hard to find. Indeed, every public library in America has a copy of the Statistical Abstract of the United States, which each year contains a table presenting value-added and employment by industry in U.S. manufacturing. All one needs to do, then, is spend a few minutes in the library with a calculator to come up with a table that ranks U.S. industries by value-added per worker.

The table on this page shows selected entries from pages 740-744 of the 1991 Statistical Abstract. It turns out that the U.S. industries with really high value-added per worker are in sectors with very high ratios of capital to labor, like cigarettes and petroleum refining. (This was predictable: because capital-intensive industries must earn a normal return on large investments, they must charge prices that are a larger markup over labor costs than labor-intensive industries, which means that they have high value-added per worker). Among large industries, value-added per worker tends to be high in traditional heavy manufacturing sectors like steel and autos. High-technology sectors like aerospace and electronics turn out to be only roughly average.

This result does not surprise conventional economists. High value-added per worker occurs in sectors that are highly capital-intensive, that is, sectors in which an additional dollar of capital buys little extra value-added. In other words, there is no free lunch.

But let's leave on one side what the table says about the way the economy works, and simply note the strangeness of the lapse by Magaziner and Reich. Surely they were not calling for an industrial policy that would funnel capital and labor into the steel and auto industries in preference to high-tech. How, then, could they write a whole book dedicated to the proposition that we should target high value-added industries without ever checking to see which industries they meant?

Labor Costs. In his own presentation at the Copenhagen summit, British Prime Minister John Major showed a chart indicating that European unit labor costs have risen more rapidly than those in the United States and Japan. Thus he argued that European workers have been pricing themselves out of world markets.

But a few weeks later Sam Brittan of the Financial Times pointed out a strange thing about Major's calculations: the labor costs were not adjusted for exchange rates. In international competition, of course, what matters for a U.S. firm are the costs of its overseas rivals measured in dollars, not marks or yen. So international comparisons of labor costs, like the tables the Bank of England routinely publishes, always convert them into a common currency. The numbers presented by Major, however, did not make this standard adjustment. And it was a good thing for his presentation that they didn't. As Brittan pointed out, European labor costs have not risen in relative terms when the exchange rate adjustment is made.

If anything, this lapse is even odder than those of Thurow or Magaziner and Reich. How could John Major, with the sophisticated statistical resources of the U.K. Treasury behind him, present an analysis that failed to make the most standard of adjustments?

These examples of strangely careless arithmetic, chosen from among dozens of similar cases, by people who surely had both the cleverness and the resources to get it right, cry out for an explanation. The best working hypothesis is that in each case the author or speaker wanted to believe in the competitive hypothesis so much that he felt no urge to question it; if data were used at all, it was only to lend credibility to a predetermined belief, not to test it. But why are people apparently so anxious to define economic problems as issues of international competition?

THE THRILL OF COMPETITION

The competitive metaphor, the image of countries competing with each other in world markets in the same way that corporations do, derives much of its attractiveness from its seeming comprehensibility. Tell a group of businessmen that a country is like a corporation writ large, and you give them the comfort of feeling that they already understand the basics. Try to tell them about economic concepts like comparative advantage, and you are asking them to learn something new. It should not be surprising if many prefer a doctrine that offers the gain of apparent sophistication without the pain of hard thinking. The rhetoric of competitiveness has become so widespread, however, for three deeper reasons.

First, competitive images are exciting, and thrills sell tickets. The subtitle of Lester Thurow's huge best-seller, Head to Head, Is "The Coming Economic Battle among

Japan, Europe, and America"; the jacket proclaims that "the decisive war of the century has begun . . . and America may already have decided to lose." Suppose that the subtitle had described the real situation: "The coming struggle in which each big economy will succeed or fail based on its own efforts, pretty much independently of how well the others do." Would Thurow have sold a tenth as many books?

Second, the idea that U.S. economic difficulties hinge crucially on our failures in international competition somewhat paradoxically makes those difficulties seem easier to solve. The productivity of the average American worker is determined by a complex array of factors, most of them unreachable by any likely government policy. So if you accept the reality that our "competitive" problem is really a domestic productivity problem pure and simple, you are unlikely to be optimistic about any dramatic turnaround. But if you can convince yourself that the problem is really one of failures in international competition, that imports are pushing workers out of high-wage jobs, or subsidized foreign competition is driving the United States out of the high value-added sectors, then the answers to economic malaise may seem to you to involve simple things like subsidizing high technology and being tough on Japan.

Finally, many of the world's leaders have found the competitive metaphor extremely useful as a political device. The rhetoric of competitiveness turns out to provide a good way either to justify hard choices or to avoid them. The example of Delors in Copenhagen shows the usefulness of competitive metaphors as an evasion. Delors had to say something at the EC summit; yet to say anything that addressed the real roots of European unemployment would have involved huge political risks. By turning the discussion to essentially irrelevant but plausible-sounding questions of competitiveness, he bought himself some time to come up with a better answer (which to some extent he provided in December's white paper on the European economy, a paper that still, however, retained "competitiveness" in its title).

By contrast, the well-received presentation of Bill Clinton's initial economic program in February 1993 showed the usefulness of competitive rhetoric as a motivation for tough policies. Clinton proposed a set of painful spending cuts and tax increases to reduce the Federal deficit. Why? The real reasons for cutting the deficit are disappointingly undramatic: the deficit siphons off funds that might otherwise have been productively invested, and thereby exerts a steady if small drag on U.S. economic growth. But Clinton was able instead to offer a stirring patriotic appeal, calling on the nation to act now in order to make the economy competitive in the global market, with the implication that dire economic consequences would follow if the United States does not.

Many people who know that "competitiveness" is a largely meaningless concept have been willing to indulge competitive rhetoric precisely because they believe they can harness it in the service of good policies. An overblown fear of the Soviet Union was used in the 1950s to justify the building of the interstate highway system and the expansion of math and science education. Cannot the unjustified fears about foreign competition similarly be turned to good, used to justify serious efforts to reduce the budget deficit, rebuild infrastructure, and so on?

A few years ago this was a reasonable hope. At this point, however, the obsession with competitiveness has reached the point where it has already begun dangerously to distort economic policies.

THE DANGERS OF OBSESSION

Thinking and speaking in terms of competitiveness poses three real dangers. First, it could result in the wasteful spending of government money supposedly to enhance U.S. competitiveness. Second, it could lead to protectionism and trade wars. Finally, and most important, it could result in bad public policy on a spectrum of important issues.

During the 1950s, fear of the Soviet Union induced the U.S. government to spend money on useful things like highways and science education. It also, however, led to considerable spending on more doubtful items like bomb shelters. The most obvious if least worrisome danger of the growing obsession with competitiveness is that it might lead to a similar misallocation of resources. To take an example, recent guidelines for government research funding have stressed the importance of supporting research that can improve U.S. international competitiveness. This exerts at least some bias toward inventions that can help manufacturing firms, which generally compete on international markets, rather than service producers, which generally do not. Yet most of our employment and value-added is now in services, and lagging productivity in services rather than manufactures has been the single most important factor in the stagnation of U.S. living standards.

A much more serious risk is that the obsession with competitiveness will lead to trade conflict, perhaps even to a world trade war. Most of those who have preached the doctrine of competitiveness have not been old-fashioned protectionists. They want their countries to win the global trade game, not drop out. But what if, despite its best efforts, a country does not seem to be winning, or lacks confidence that it can? Then the competitive diagnosis inevitably suggests that to close the borders is better than to risk having foreigners take away high-wage jobs and high-value sectors. At the very least, the focus on the supposedly competitive nature of international economic relations greases the rails for those who want confrontational if not frankly protectionist policies.

We can already see this process at work, in both the United States and Europe. In the United States, it was remarkable how quickly the sophisticated interventionist arguments advanced by Laura Tyson in her published work gave way to the simple-minded claim by U.S. Trade Representative Mickey Kantor that Japan's bilateral trade surplus was costing the United States millions of jobs. And the trade rhetoric of President Clinton, who stresses the supposed creation of high-wage jobs rather than the gains from specialization, left his administration in a weak position when it tried to argue with the claims of NAFTA foes that competition from cheap Mexican labor will destroy the U.S. manufacturing base.

Perhaps the most serious risk from the obsession with competitiveness, however, is its subtle indirect effect on the quality of economic discussion and policymaking. If top government officials are strongly committed to a particular economic doctrine, their commitment inevitably sets the tone for policy-making on all issues, even those which may seem to have nothing to do with that doctrine. And if an economic doctrine is flatly, completely and demonstrably wrong, the insistence that discussion adhere to that doctrine inevitably blurs the focus and diminishes the quality of policy discussion across a broad range of issues, including some that are very far from trade policy per se.

Consider, for example, the issue of health care reform, undoubtedly the most important economic initiative of the Clinton administration, almost surely an order of magnitude more important to U.S. living standards than anything that might be done about trade policy (unless the United States provokes a full-blown trade war). Since health care is an issue with few direct international linkages, one might have expected it to be largely insulated from any distortions of policy resulting from misguided concerns about competitiveness.

But the administration placed the development of the health care plan in the hands of Ira Magaziner, the same Magaziner who so conspicuously failed to do his homework in arguing for government promotion of high value-added industries. Magaziner's prior writings and consulting on economic policy focused almost entirely on the issue of international competition, his views on which may be summarized by the title of his 1990 book, The Silent War. His appointment reflected many factors, of course, not least his long personal friendship with the first couple. Still, it was not irrelevant that in an administration committed to the ideology of competitiveness Magaziner, who has consistently recommended that national industrial policies be based on the corporate strategy concepts he learned during his years at the Boston Consulting Group, was regarded as an economic policy expert.

We might also note the unusual process by which the health care reform was developed. In spite of the huge size of the task force, recognized experts in the health care field were almost completely absent, notably though not exclusively economists specializing in health care, including economists with impeccable liberal credentials like Henry Aaron of the Brookings Institution. Again, this may have reflected a number of factors, but it is probably not irrelevant that anyone who, like Magaziner, is strongly committed to the ideology of competitiveness is bound to have found professional economists notably unsympathetic in the past, and to be unwilling to deal with them on any other issue.

To make a harsh but not entirely unjustified analogy, a government wedded to the ideology of competitiveness is as unlikely to make good economic policy as a government committed to creationism is to make good science policy, even in areas that have no direct relationship to the theory of evolution.

ADVISERS WITH NO CLOTHES

If the obsession with competitiveness is as misguided and damaging as this article claims, why aren't more voices saying so? The answer is, a mixture of hope and fear.

On the side of hope, many sensible people have imagined that they can appropriate the rhetoric of competitiveness on behalf of desirable economic policies. Suppose that you believe that the United States needs to raise its savings rate and improve its educational system in order to raise its productivity. Even if you know that the benefits of higher productivity have nothing to do with international competition, why not describe this as a policy to enhance competitiveness if you think that it can widen your audience? It's tempting to pander to popular prejudices on behalf of a good cause, and I have myself succumbed to that temptation.

As for fear, it takes either a very courageous or very reckless economist to say publicly that a doctrine that many, perhaps most, of the world's opinion leaders have embraced is flatly wrong. The insult is all the greater when many of those men and women think that by using the rhetoric of competitiveness they are demonstrating their sophistication about economics. This article may influence people, but it will not make many friends.

Unfortunately, those economists who have hoped to appropriate the rhetoric of competitiveness for good economic policies have instead had their own credibility appropriated on behalf of bad ideas. And somebody has to point out when the emperor's intellectual wardrobe isn't all he thinks it is.

So let's start telling the truth: competitiveness is a meaningless word when applied to national economies. And the obsession with competitiveness is both wrong and dangerous.

FOOTNOTES:

1 See, for just a few examples, Laura D'Andrea Tyson, Who's Bashing Whom: Trade Conflict in High-Technology Industries, Washington: Institute for International Economics, 1992; Lester C. Thurow, Head to Head: The Coming Economic Battle among Japan, Europe, and America, New York: Morrow, 1992; Ira C. Magaziner and Robert B. Reich, Minding America's Business: The Decline and Rise of the American Economy, New York: Vintage Books, 1983; Ira C. Magaziner and Mark Patinkin, The

Silent War: Inside the Global Business Battles Shaping America's Future, New York: Vintage Books, 1990; Edward N. Luttwak, The Endangered American Dream: How to Stop the United States from Becoming a Third World Country and How to Win the Geo-economic Struggle for Industrial Supremacy, New York: Simon and Schuster, 1993; Kevin P. Phillips, Staying on Top: The Business Case for a National Industrial Strategy, New York: Random House, 1984; Clyde V. Prestowitz, Jr., Trading Places: How We Allowed Japan to Take the Lead, New York: Basic Books, 1988; William S. Dietrich, In the Shadow of the Rising Sun: The Political Roots of American Economic Decline, University Park: Pennsylvania State University Press, 1991; Jeffrey E. Garten, A Cold Peace: America, Japan, Germany, and the Struggle for Supremacy, New York: Times Books, 1992; and Wayne Sandholtz et al., The Highest Stakes: The Economic Foundations of the Next Security System, Berkeley Roundtable on the International Economy (brie), Oxford University Press, 1992.

2 An example may be helpful here. Suppose that a country spends 20 percent of its income on imports, and that the prices of its imports are set not in domestic but in foreign currency. Then if the country is forced to devalue its currency, reduce its value in foreign currency, by 10 percent, this will raise the price of 20 percent of the country's spending basket by 10 percent, thus raising the overall price index by 2 percent. Even if domestic output has not changed, the country's real income will therefore have fallen by 2 percent. If the country must repeatedly devalue in the face of competitive pressure, growth in real income will persistently lag behind growth in real output.

It's important to notice, however, that the size of this lag depends not only on the amount of devaluation but on the share of imports in spending. A 10 percent devaluation of the dollar against the yen does not reduce U.S. real income by 10 percent, in fact, it reduces U.S. real income by only about 0.2 percent because only about 2 percent of U.S. income is spent on goods produced in Japan.

3 In the example in the previous footnote, the devaluation would have no effect on real GNP, but command GNP would have fallen by two percent. The finding that in practice command GNP has grown almost as fast as real GNP therefore amounts to saying that events like the hypothetical case in footnote one are unimportant in practice.

4 "Value-added" has a precise, standard meaning in national income accounting: the value added of a firm is the dollar value of its sales, minus the dollar value of the inputs it purchases from other firms, and as such it is easily measured. Some people who use the term, however, may be unaware of this definition and simply use "high value-added" as a synonym for "desirable."

> Value Added Per Worker, 1988 (in thousands of dollars)

cigarettes 488

petroleum refining 283

autos 99

steel 97

aircraft 68

electronics 64

all manufacturing 66

Paul Krugman is Professor of Economics at the Massachusetts Institute of Technology. His most recent book is Peddling Prosperity: Economic Sense and Nonsense in the Age of Diminished Expectations (W. W. Norton).

Workers and the World Economy: Breaking the Postwar Bargain

Ethan B. Kapstein

Roosevelt signs the G.I. Bill into law on June 22, 1944 in the Oval Office.

The global economy is leaving millions of disaffected workers in its train. Inequality, unemployment, and endemic poverty have become its handmaidens. Rapid technological change and heightening international competition are fraying the job markets of the major industrialized countries. At the same time systemic pressures are curtailing every government's ability to respond with new spending. Just when working people most need the nation-state as a buffer from the world economy, it is abandoning them.

This is not how things were supposed to work. The failure of today's advanced global capitalism to keep spreading the wealth poses a challenge not just to policymakers but to modern economic 'science' as well. For generations, students were taught that increasing trade and investment, coupled with technological change, would drive national productivity and create wealth. Yet over the past decade, despite a continuing boom in international trade and finance, productivity has faltered, and inequality in the United States and unemployment in Europe have worsened.

President Bill Clinton may have been right to proclaim that 'the era of big government is over,' and perhaps the American people will ultimately decide that those who need assistance should look elsewhere for help. But if the post-World War II social contract with workers--of full employment and comprehensive social welfare--is to be broken, political support for the burgeoning global economy could easily collapse. For international economic integration is not some uncontrollable fact of life, but has deepened because of a series of policy decisions taken by the major industrial powers over the last 45 years. It is time to recognize that those decisions, while benefiting the world economy as a whole, have begun to have widespread negative consequences. The forces acting on today's workers in here in the structure of today's global economy, with its open and increasingly fierce competition on the one hand and fiscally conservative units-states--on the other. Countermeasures, therefore, must also be deep, sustained, and widespread. Easing pressures on the 'losers' of the new open economy must now be the focus of economic policy if the process of globalization is to be sustained.

It is hardly sensationalist to claim that in the absence of broad-based policies and programs designed to help working people, the political debate in the United States and many other countries will soon turn sour. Populists and demagogues of various stripes will find 'solutions' to contemporary economic problems in protectionism and xenophobia. Indeed, in every industrialized nation, such figures are on the campaign trail. Growing income inequality, job insecurity, and unemployment are widely seen as the flip side of globalization. That perception must be changed if Western leaders wish to maintain the international system their predecessors created. After all, the fate of the global economy ultimately rests on domestic politics in its constituent states.

The spread of the dogma of restrictive fiscal policy is undermining the bargain struck with workers in every industrial country. States are basically telling their workers that they can no longer afford the postwar deal and must minimize their obligations. The current obsession with balanced budgets in the United States and the Maastricht criteria in Europe must be replaced by an equally vigilant focus on growth and equity. National responses to this global problem are likely to fail, as any state that deviates from 'responsible' economic policies will be punished by currency markets and bondholders. States must now reorient their economic policies toward growth, but it should be done as part of a coordinated international effort. Calling for such economic policy coordination might seem utopian in the current political environment, but it has been done before.

The world may be moving inexorably toward one of those tragic moments that will lead future historians to ask, why was nothing done in time? Were the economic and policy elites unaware of the profound disruption that economic and technological change were causing working men and women? What prevented them from taking the steps necessary to prevent a global social crisis?

THE GREAT TRANSFORMATION

The current predicament is hardly unprecedented. Writing in Progress and Poverty in 1879, the reformer Henry George observed that 'at the beginning of this marvelous era it was natural to expect, and it was expected, that laborsaving inventions would lighten the toil and improve the condition of the laborer; that the enormous increase in the power of producing wealth would make real poverty a thing of the past.' George chronicled the many technologies, such as the steam engine and telegraph, that had been introduced in his lifetime, and the great explosion in commerce and trade that followed.

But far from heralding an era of prosperity, 'disappointment has followed disappointment. From all parts of the civilized world come complaints of industrial depression . . . of want and suffering and anxiety among the working classes.' George observed that the massive investment in technology had only resulted in increasing returns to capital and falling wages for working people. Thus 'the mere laborer has no more interest in the general advance of productive power than the Cuban slave has . . . in the price of sugar.'

During the nineteenth century, the world enjoyed a secular increase in trade and investment under the aegis of a liberal Great Britain, while the adoption of the international gold standard created the illusion of domestic financial stability. But profound social dislocation accompanied this process of globalization and would eventually contribute to its undoing.

Britain's decision in 1846 to lift the Corn Laws, which had long protected domestic agriculture, is the classic example of a policy consciously designed to globalize the economy in favor of specific interests. With industrialization, the Manchester factory owners needed more labor. The simple solution was to get farm hands off the land and pay them low wages. The most efficient way to achieve this goal was to introduce foreign competition in agricultural products, forcing down prices and ensuring that farmers and tenants could no longer earn their livelihood. Labor flooded into the cities, and these workers were paid relatively low wages because the price of food--their major expenditure--was falling.

Throughout the Industrial Revolution various regulations that had long governed economic life--many dating back to the Middle Ages--were dismantled, and rural laborers found their traditional ways of life torn asunder. Workers became commodities like grain and coal, with demand for and supply of their services a function of market requirements. Such a laissez-faire approach to labor markets was inherently unstable, as the philosopher Karl Polanyi later explained in The Great Transformation. He described the process by which landless working people throughout Europe entered a world of urban poverty, creating a political cauldron. During periods of prolonged depression these laborers became easy prey for extremist political forces. Polanyi argued that it was the complete unraveling of economic and labor market regulations and traditions in the nineteenth century that caused such tremendous social and political upheaval in the early twentieth, culminating in the collapse of the world economy and the outbreak of the First and Second World Wars.

The Great Transformation was published in 1944, the year that the Bretton Woods conference to restructure the international economy was held. And it was Polanyi's version of history that the postwar policymakers brought with them. As Treasury Secretary Henry Morgenthau said, 'All of us have seen the great economic tragedy of our time. We saw the worldwide depression of the 1930s. We saw currency disorders develop and spread from land to land, destroying the basis for international trade and international investment and even international faith. In their wake, we saw unemployment and wretchedness. . . . We saw their victims fall prey . . . to demagogues and dictators. We saw bewilderment and bitterness become the breeders of fascism, and finally, of war.' The post-World War II global economy resulted from a series of conscious policy decisions, reached in the belief that increased economic exchange could be a force for world peace and prosperity.

The postwar leaders were committed to rebuilding the world economy, but this time with a significant difference. In globalization's previous incarnation, governments had done little to protect working people from its malign effects, and their mistake exacted a price in revolutions and war. Having learned from that experience, statesmen now designed a liberal world economy that maintained an active domestic role for the state in order to ensure that equity and growth went hand in hand.

Thus the new global economy would include both domestic and international components. Of greatest significance, the state would supervise most aspects of economic life. In the United States, for example, the Truman administration passed the Employment Act, which set as its objective full employment, and the G.I. Bill, which provided veterans with education and housing benefits. Across Europe, ambitious social welfare policies were enacted. In every industrial country, labor was not to be treated as a commodity, subject to the free market's destructive whims, and the organization of workers into labor unions was actively encouraged. The implicit agreement struck between states and their societies-what John G. Ruggie has termed the bargain of 'embedded liberalism'--ensured that the gains from economic globalization would be used to compensate the losers in the interests of political stability.ffi

Western leaders constructed international regimes for money and trade that by charter were to be responsive to domestic political and economic concerns. When they launched the General Agreement on Tariffs and Trade (GATT) to liberalize and expand commerce among the member states, they also established safeguards to protect workers from unfair trade practices and to assist those who were displaced. When they created an international monetary system to avoid ceaseless rounds of competitive currency devaluation, they also established the International Monetary Fund (IMF) as a lender of last resort for balance-of-payments emergencies. When they formed a European Common Market to promote regional trade and investment, they also permitted states to retain considerable autonomy in social policy.

But the Bretton Woods order would prove unsustainable. It was very generous to workers and capitalists, but it required high levels of economic growth. The oil crises of 1973-74 and 1978-79 hammered the industrial countries, prompting stagflation, that insidious mixture of stagnation and inflation. Furthermore, increasing foreign trade meant greater competition for national firms, while financial deregulation permitted capital to become more footloose. These developments, in turn, led to widespread corporate restructuring and a glut of unskilled labor, which translated into higher unemployment, less tax revenue, and greater pressure on state resources. The crisis of the welfare state had begun.

Faced with the exploding costs of cradle-to-grave support for increasingly idle populations, Western states in the 1980s began to adopt stringent monetary and fiscal policies. Workers, of course, have had little say in this process. Indeed, what governments are really trying to do is break their postwar deal with workers while maintaining their commitment to an open economy. They cannot have it both ways, and instead the policy focus should be on negotiating a package that helps workers adjust to ongoing economic changes.

WORKERS OF THE WORLD

Nobody disputes that the past two decades have been cruel to unskilled workers in the industrial countries. Growing income inequality has given rise to millions of working poor in the United States, and this sorry condition is now becoming apparent in Western Europe. Between 1973 and 1993 the real hourly wage of Americans without a high school diploma fell from $11.85 an hour to $8.64 an hour. In the early 1970s households in the top 5 percent of the income bracket earned 10 times more than those in the bottom 5 percent; today they make almost 15 times more. Similar trends are evident in Britain and even that most egalitarian country, Sweden.

Workers have been further squeezed by the decline in manufacturing employment. Manufacturing employment in the United States fell by 1.4 million between 1978 and 1990. Those who lost their jobs were, in general, the unskilled, and when they found new work it was usually at lower pay. The experience has now become familiar to middle managers as well, as evidenced by the recent spate of major corporate layoffs. The failure of the industrial sector to generate new jobs has been a major cause of labor's economic problems, and perhaps some of America's social problems more generally. Fully two percent of all working-age American men are behind bars.

In Western Europe, the unemployment figures are frightening. In France, average unemployment between 1969 and 1973 was 2.6 percent; today it is over 11 percent. In Germany the rate was below 1 percent; today it is approaching 10 percent. In Belgium, the unemployment rate has quadrupled over the past 20 years. The Europeans have created a lost generation of workers and are now suffering for it in terms of increased crime, drug abuse, violence against immigrants, and the increasing popularity of extremist political groups. In this context, it is sobering to realize that Germany's current level of four million unemployed is the highest it has been since the early 1930s.

At the same time, there has been a dramatic decline in unionized labor in both the United States and Europe. The unionized portion of the U.S. labor force has dropped by more than one-third--from 25 to 16 percent--since the 1970s, and organized labor is also declining in Austria, France, Germany, Italy, the Netherlands, Switzerland, and the United Kingdom.Û Labor is losing its political voice, and the consequences of its demise--lower wages and benefits for unskilled workers, greater job insecurity, and less political interest in the economic losers--should not be dismissed.

Further, it should be recalled that organized labor in the north has been a prime mover behind unionization and the promotion of human rights in the developing countries of the south. International activism by unions has been a help to workers in Latin America and other countries struggling to win the right to collective bargaining, as well as better health and safety standards. Now that all industrial workers-unionized or not--could benefit from this type of activism in such countries as China and India, and other non- or anti-union regions of the world, organized labor is no longer vigorous enough to play this role. To be sure, unions are hardly perfect; they too form entrenched interests that hinder labor market flexibility and job creation. But their historical role in economic development and social equity has been forgotten.

THE BATTLE OF THE CAUSES

Solutions to these bleak trends need not await some consensus among economists about their causes. Policymakers debating these issues are like firefighters idly wondering what started the blaze while the house burns to the ground. The two traditional culprits that have once again emerged from the economics literature are trade and technology. A third, cited by few economists but by some journalists and politicians, is immigration.

Economists who focus on the effects of trade, such as Adrian Wood, have argued that the contemporary problems of unskilled workers in the north are linked to a strong increase in trade between north and south and a change in its composition.Ü Historically, the developing countries provided the industrial world with agricultural goods and raw materials in exchange for manufactured goods. The gains from such trade have been analyzed and extolled by economists since David Ricardo, sustaining the free trade movement.

Such trade is rightly celebrated, since it makes nations wealthier than they would otherwise be. More recently, however, the south has moved into the business of manufacturing, from clothing to consumer electronics. Today such goods account for over 50 percent of the south's exports and surpass its commodity exports in value. As is well known, workers in these developing countries are generally paid peanuts for their labor--less than a dollar an hour in such countries as China, India, and Pakistan--and in many countries, including China, they are prevented by law from forming unions or otherwise bargaining collectively.

According to a theory proposed by Paul A. Samuelson and Wolfgang Stolper in 1941, two countries that practice free trade and have the same technology should eventually see their wages equalize. In effect, wages in the First World are forced down by competition from developing countries in similar industries. Ironically, even though falling wages would seem to confirm Stolper-Samuelson, some economists are now claiming that its assumptions are wrong.Ý

In Western Europe wages are less skewed than in the United States, but the continent has paid for relative equality with higher unemployment. Economic theory also helps to explain why this is so. If Germany begins importing Polish goods produced with unskilled labor, and regulations and other rigidities prevent wages from falling to Polish levels, unemployment among unskilled German workers will rise in the absence of new job creation.

Many American economists, such as Paul Krugman and Robert Z. Lawrence, contest these explanations. They point out that foreign trade remains too small a share of economic activity in most industrial nations to be responsible for such large and pervasive phenomena as unemployment and income inequality, and they assert that technology must be responsible for these changes. According to this school of thought, the introduction of new technology--say, computers-creates a surplus of unskilled labor. At the same time, the new technology increases the demand for the skilled workers who know how to run it, raising their wages. As a result, income inequality widens because of the good old-fashioned law of supply and demand. The evidence for this line of reasoning is the heavy investment in new technology by manufacturing during the 1980s, when growing wage inequality became apparent in the United States.

But economists are wrong to treat trade and technology as competing explanations. A significant share of new technology, for example, has been induced by foreign competition. Indeed, when one looks at those industries that have suffered great job losses on the one hand and enjoyed significant investment in new technology on the other, they are concentrated in sectors, like steel and automobiles, that have faced tremendous pressure from imports. Still, the widespread introduction of technology across many sectors suggests that domestic competition spurred much of this investment.

As a general explanation, technology is unsatisfactory. It is never clearly distinguished from other kinds of capital, and there is no reason that its introduction must in principle reduce the wages of the unskilled. Technology is for economists the residual that accounts for everything their theories cannot.

Yet a final explanation for labor's lament is immigration. During the 1980s the United States had the largest immigration boom in its postwar history. Between 1980 and 1989 more than six million legal immigrants alone came to its shores. In 1994 more than three million arrived illegally. The net effect of legal migration has been positive. The new arrivals bring needed skills, create businesses and jobs, and raise output. At the same time, the pool of unskilled labor has also increased, forcing down their wages. As with other facets of globalization, increased migration benefits countries overall, but it hurts some groups. The failure to address their dislocation will allow nativists to seize the debate, creating a more permissive environment not only for protectionism but for hate crimes, as is already evident in Western Europe.

RETRAINING REDUX

Whichever explanation is most important, the fact remains that technological change, free trade, migration, and other forces such as defense cuts create losers as well as winners. The rationale for open economies is that, in principle, the gains will outweigh the losses for the country as a whole; thus, the winners can afford to compensate the losers. Under GATT and Bretton Woods, this compensation took the form of such short-term measures as trade adjustment programs, which provide unemployment insurance, retraining, and even support for moving to new communities. When a robust economy was creating lots of good jobs, everyone was made better off. But that is no longer the case. Today, a worker who loses his job is likely to find a new one only at lower pay. Indeed, as The New York Times reported earlier this year, 65 percent of workers who ultimately find jobs after a layoff do so only at lower levels of pay, and Morris Kleiner of the University of Minnesota has found that most such workers are still earning much less even five years later.

According to an analysis of dislocated defense workers in New England, defense workers should have an easy time finding new jobs, given their skills and experience with computers, precision tools, and quality control--even if these attributes have not been tested in the context of more highly competitive enterprises. But even among these workers, one in five of those who found new jobs had wage rates that 'represented a pay cut of 40 percent or more.' Indeed, over 60 percent of all dislocated workers 'had noticeably lower hourly earnings.'fi Their experience with retraining should also counsel caution. Some could not afford the costs associated with these programs, while others had difficulty matching training opportunities to projected new job requirements. For still others, the lack of growth prospects in even distantly related industries raised questions about whether retraining was really a good investment. Overall, as the World Bank's 1995 World Development Report concluded, results are mixed regarding the value of training in helping unemployed workers find new jobs.

But even if training is a good investment, the cost of providing it to all unemployed workers is prohibitive. There are now some 34 million unemployed persons in the member countries of the Organization for Economic Cooperation and Development (OECD). If the average cost of retraining for each worker is $7,000, the total bill would be $238 billion. For the United States, with its 7 million unemployed, the total would be $49 billion. Today, the U.S. government spends about $10 billion on work-related education and training. In the current fiscal environment, it is difficult to imagine that number rising by the required amount.

On the contrary, these programs are being cut back. Since 1992, funds for labor market training and other active measures have fallen in such countries as Canada, Germany, Sweden, and the United States, the last especially ironic since Secretary of

Labor Robert Reich is one of training's greatest devotees (though in fairness, he does have to contend with a Republican Congress). Incredibly, public spending for higher education has also fallen. In the United States, such expenditures were cut 10 percent in the early 1990s, and in Britain only marginally less. At the same time, in countries with federal structures, where the constituent states were expected to assume increased public burdens, local crises and fiscal stringency prevented them from taking up the slack. This is the very problem facing many Russian regions and American states.

It is odd that training has become the mom and apple pie of economists and public officials across the political spectrum when it could at best provide only a partial answer to the problems of dislocated workers, at least given the knowledge base about what works at current spending levels. Indeed, one learns in economics that policymakers should choose the most direct and efficient means for solving problems. This lesson suggests that if the concern is income inequality, policies should be adopted to close the income gap. If the concern is unemployment, more jobs should be created. Training should not be abandoned, of course, but it is not by itself a solution.

KEEPING GROWTH DOWN

In developing positive solutions, however, it is important to recognize that declining rates of economic growth, caused largely by a drop-off in productivity, are hurting all workers. Curiously, analysts have paid less attention to these indexes than to unemployment and inequality. But had the industrial countries continued to grow in the 1990s at their earlier postwar rates, many current headline issues would hardly attract attention. If growth had remained at the 1960s average of 3.5 percent instead of current levels of just over 2 percent, more jobs of all kinds would have been created, rectifying unemployment in Europe and obviating inequality in the United States.

In truth, this productivity slowdown remains a puzzle. Why is it happening if the industrial countries have invested heavily in technology and opened their economies to foreign competition? These things should have spurred productivity growth. At present there is no good answer, though hypotheses focus on such diverse factors as the widespread shift from manufacturing to services in the north, and the decline in educational attainment, especially in science and math, among workers in many of the industrial countries.

Between 1971 and 1978, according to the OECD, the members of the Group of Seven (G-7) enjoyed an average economic growth rate of 3.5 percent per year, and this during a period of severe oil shocks, with the consequent rise in energy prices and inflation. Since 1989, by contrast, growth has averaged 2.1 percent. For Japan, the drop has been even steeper. Its average growth between 1971 and 1978 was 4.5 percent, a number that has fallen in the 1990s to 2.4 percent. Meanwhile, between 1979 and 1994, unemployment in the OECD rose from 17.7 million and a rate of 5.1 percent to 34 million and a rate of 8 percent.

Unfortunately, this slowdown in the 1990s followed on the heels of a period of inflation, deficit spending, and increasing government debt levels around the industrial world. In the G-7 the interest payments on government debt rose from 1.6 percent of GDP in 1980 to 2.5 percent in 1990. Today the figure stands at 2.8 percent. In order to stabilize their financial affairs, states adopted stringent monetary and, more recently, fiscal policies--in short, policies deemed sustainable or credible by financial markets. These policies privileged financial stability over employment. They were the welfare state's equivalent of a grapefruit diet. The problem is that, as with all diets, they can become obsessive and cause more harm than good.

Over time, special interest groups have become entrenched around particular sets of policies, creating bureaucratic sclerosis. Restrictive economic policies--reduced deficits, reduced spending, reduced taxes, and the most exalted deity, low inflation--have favored financial interests at the expense of workers and have created an international rentier class. For anyone with money to invest, the last 20 years have been bountiful. Fiscally restrictive policies have become an ideology of this class for all practical purposes, defended in the pages of the leading newspapers and economic journals and most of the Beltway think tanks. Public officials who adopt restrictive measures are labeled 'responsible' by editorialists, and the markets reward their behavior, sustaining the ideology.

The politics of financial credibility has played out somewhat differently across the industrial world. In the United States they have centered around the balanced budget debate between President Clinton and Congress. Indeed, they led to Clinton's Hoover-like statement about big government in his recent State of the Union address. Policies have targeted inflation and fiscal expansion in recent years, but the benefits of this approach have yet to be widely shared. At the same time, polling data and other evidence, such as the results of the Republican presidential primaries, suggest that the American people are becoming increasingly worried about their economic security and want the government to do something about it. And this concern is not solely a local phenomenon. What in America was once called the battle between Wall Street and Main Street has now become global.

The budget debate is a case of ideology overriding economics. In fact, there is no reason a balanced budget must always be favored over Keynesian deficit spending. As economist Robert Eisner wrote in How Real Is the Federal Deficit? in 1986, 'Deficits can be too small as well as too large.' He reminds us that when 'there is slack in the economy, deficit-induced demand stimulates output and employment.' It may well be the case that Clinton has gone too far in agreeing with congressional Republicans about the need to balance the budget over the next seven years.

But there is no direct correlation between deficit spending and inflation, as Japan demonstrates. During most of the postwar era Japan has had far higher deficits than the United States as a percentage of GNP, but lower inflation. The reason is Japan's credibility when it comes to maintaining monetary stability. Given Japan's high savings rate, the markets have confidence in its ability to finance long-term debt obligations. Today Japan is the only industrial country that is taking a Keynesian approach to its economic problems, and its latest growth figures suggest that fiscal expansion has been beneficial. There is, in short, no reason that moderate fiscal relaxation must generate high inflation. Moreover, to the extent that Japanese levels of inflation become somewhat higher than those in the United States, they would contribute to easing tensions over the yen-dollar exchange rate.

In contrast, leaders in Europe, where deficits are also higher than in the United States, have demanded a rapid reduction in government spending in order to meet the criteria of the Maastricht treaty on monetary union. With Germany setting the economic rules of the game according to its domestic preferences, European states that wish to participate in the planned union must reduce their budget deficits to 3 percent of GDP by 1999. In France, where deficits are now running at 5 percent of GDP, the rules mean applying the ax to the state budget. These policies reflect an obsessive fear of Europe's traditional bouts of inflation, but the major central banks have done a credible job of maintaining monetary stability. What has been the point of adopting these anti-inflationary policies if they do not permit governments some fiscal room to maneuver?

Even in Russia one can see restrictive fiscal policies dismantling earlier contracts between the state and society. Thus, under stringent IMF discipline, Russia too must reduce its budget deficit. Those hardest hit have been pensioners, the unemployed, and the poor--again, the people most in need of state services. The collapse of the social safety net in Russia explains why the Communist Party received the largest share of the vote in the December 1995 Duma elections and why its leader, Gennadi Zyuganov, may be elected the country's president in June 1996.

LOOSENING UP

To meet the growing problems of working people, governments must develop a coherent package of economic policies and programs supported by international policy coordination that generates renewed growth. Such a strategy, which will require some fiscal relaxation, has some costs, but the consequences of doing nothing will be worse, since disastrous measures like protectionism and nativism are again being mentioned, even in economically literate circles.

The starting point for any policy effort of this kind is the normative assertion that the appropriate goal of economic policy is to improve the lives of the citizenry. Monetary and fiscal policies should be structured in such a way as to ensure the fundamental promise that working people can earn a living wage. This means that in every industrial country policies must be directed toward helping people cope with the consequences of economic change. Of course, the appropriate policy mix will vary. In the United States, job insecurity, income inequality, and the plight of the working poor are now chief concerns. In Europe, job creation is key. Thus the policy for Europe would permit greater fiscal relaxation and that for the United States more income redistribution.

The argument that present-day fiscal restrictions must be maintained in order to balance budgets and stabilize national economies is without merit. The critical issue on the fiscal side is how governments spend the money. Just as with corporate investment, there is a difference between investments that are likely to yield long-term benefits and those that throw money down rat holes. To take an extreme case, no American during World War II said that the investment in armaments was a bad one, and it was gladly financed through bond issues and payroll taxes. Contemporary critics who would say that spending money on labor policies is unfair to the nation's children forget that the best thing that can be bequeathed to the next generation is social peace.

An expansionary strategy must include both microeconomic and macroeconomic elements, coupled with international policy coordination. Microeconomic policies, like the expansion of education and training, are needed to provide workers with the skills that will enable them to rejoin the labor market or find better career prospects. But these policies and programs are of little value if the economy is not producing good jobs. Macroeconomic policies, like fiscal relaxation and changes in taxation, are therefore required to provide a stimulus to spur economic growth. Taken together, these micro- and macroeconomic policies should translate into a better-educated and more productive work force. Finally, international policy coordination is necessary so that countries can develop expansionary policies within a collective framework, avoiding competitive currency depreciations that in the long run hurt everyone.

Governments that wish to assist unskilled workers have four choices: protectionism, education and training, public works programs and employment subsidies, and tax policy and income transfers. All of them entail costs, which must be paid for in one way or another.

Protectionism has received both renewed attention and scrutiny since candidate Patrick Buchanan's victory in the New Hampshire presidential primary. Buchanan, an avowed 'economic nationalist,' would place prohibitive tariffs on a range of imports in order to protect American jobs and wages. Unfortunately, whatever the alleged benefits of protectionism, the costs would outweigh them for most workers, and national income would certainly fall. Protectionism would lead to higher prices for all products, both foreign and domestic, resulting in lower consumption and an economic slowdown. Furthermore, America's trading partners could not be expected to sit passively while they were victimized; they too would erect higher trade barriers in response, eliminating markets for U.S. exports and the high-wage jobs that go with them. Since exports are the fastest-growing segment of the economy, policies that lead to their restriction deserve condemnation. In short, protectionism is a remedy that is worse than the disease.

Increased spending on education and training appears to be the only policy intervention that meets with universal approval across the political spectrum. Over a generation, unskilled workers will respond to the economic signals and opt for more education and training. Historical evidence suggests that this process occurs in most industrial countries undergoing significant economic change.fl But the benefits of training for dislocated workers are uncertain, and the costs of universal training would be prohibitive. Clearly, the expansion of educational opportunities should play a central role in any democratic society and should be financed--it makes for good politics and good economics. It cannot, however, provide anything resembling a near-term solution to the structural problems of unemployment and inequality.

The third approach is to increase the number of jobs through public works programs or, perhaps more effectively, employment subsidies to the private sector. Few Western countries have pursued this tack as an explicit policy since the Great Depression, but it should be remembered that the New Deal was successful in creating jobs and reducing misery. Public job creation is relatively efficient and socially productive--since it provides younger workers with needed job experience--and it can be done fairly quickly. If the government subsidizes jobs, it will get more of them. Such policies, however, must be designed carefully to avoid an unproductive substitution of subsidized for unsubsidized workers.

This approach becomes all the more compelling in light of the sharp defense drawdowns among the member states of NATO. In the United States, for example, the size of the military force has shrunk by nearly one million since 1986, closing a once-promising route to education, training, experience, and responsibility for thousands of young adults. France will soon end military conscription. Alternative paths must be forged to help this population enter the workforce. Moreover, public works spending would counteract the fiscal drag of these defense cuts.

Finally, it is clear that tax policy and income transfers must play a key role in any serious effort to help working people and to finance new programs. One possible approach, combining in a sense the best of candidate Steve Forbes' flat tax and Senator Jeff Bingaman's (D-N.M.) proposal to tax financial transactions, would be to lower overall federal income tax rates--perhaps eliminating income taxes altogether for a large number of the working poor--while making them sharply more progressive up the income ladder.

In the United States, the fiscal gap that resulted could then be covered by introducing a national value-added tax, at least on luxury goods. Most industrial countries already have a vat. In principle, workers would still pay less in overall taxes, since their vat payments would be lower than their income taxes under the current system, while the rich, who now enjoy a variety of tax loopholes, could not escape paying their fair share of the vat. Most important, more job-related services could be provided than is now the case.

In Europe, unemployment rather than income distribution is the key problem. Additional reforms are needed there if the goal is to increase labor market flexibility, the hiring of new workers, and small business creation. Again, the policies are not a mystery, and inaction reflects a lack of political will rather than of economic knowledge. Among these reforms, reductions in employer social charges such as health care costs and greater flexibility in hiring, firing, and setting work hours are absolute necessities. Small and medium-sized enterprises in particular, which are important generators of new jobs, are being stymied by these onerous charges. Furthermore, unemployment and other benefits in most European countries are simply out of proportion, and they give the jobless little incentive to seek work. Here, the Europeans probably could learn something from the United States. Savings in these areas could provide funds for programs that create employment. Unfortunately, Europe's technocratic leaders have done a poor job of explaining the economic situation to voters and have lacked imagination in promoting new ideas.

A recent Brookings Institution study of the policies needed to restore growth in the U.S. economy, including funds for education and training and adding spending for research and development, estimates annual expenditures on the order of $80 billion, a large but not Himalayan sum. In Europe with its far higher levels of unemployment, the costs would likely be greater. To pay for this program, the authors call for higher taxes on upper income groups, coupled with spending cuts in other areas, presumably defense. While one can disagree with the specifics, the cost estimate suggests the magnitude of the task that confronts decision-makers.

One of the main arguments against an expansionary strategy, of course, is that it is inflationary. In the current climate, inflation can be avoided if monetary discipline is maintained. But in the event, some inflation overseas, as in the Japanese case, might well suit American interests. For Europe, it may be time to reassess the costs associated with the doctrinaire German approach to monetary policy. While inflation is a scourge, so is double-digit unemployment, with its dangers to the global economy.

HANGING TOGETHER

No single formula would produce an optimal set of policy reforms. Each industrial country must find its own mix, given its particular political and economic circumstances. But these efforts will be more effective if pursued as part of an international effort. Without such policy coordination countries will either be penalized by financial markets for adopting growth-oriented policies or they will aggressively pursue beggar-thy-neighbor currency devaluations.

Effective coordination in the G-7 is not impossible; the global economy could not have been built without it. Nor is there a risk that such growth-oriented coordination would be undermined by massive capital flight to East Asia or other regions, since the United States and other Western countries still dominate the global financial marketplace. According to the OECD, in 1994 member countries were home to 90 percent of world stock market capitalization and bond issues.

A precedent for cooperation during hard times is the Bonn Summit of 1978. As the world economy was recovering from the oil crisis of 1973-74, the OECD called on governments to stimulate their economies to ensure that the growth prospects became a reality--remarkable in light of today's deflationary bias. The member countries agreed to a package of national measures that would collectively spur global growth. These included a reduction in U.S. oil imports, which led to a fall in world oil prices, and the implementation of expansionary policies in Germany and Japan. Unfortunately, the second oil crisis, caused by the Iranian Revolution, undercut most of these initiatives.

Why have Western countries eschewed this type of coordination in recent years? If they truly believe in globalization, they must accept that the economic performance of trading partners is converging. They should see such variables as growth rates, interest rates, and workers' wages approaching some common values. But instead, there are profound divergences in national economic performance, even in Western Europe, suggesting the continuing importance of domestic politics. This internecine competitiveness makes policy coordination difficult to achieve in the best of circumstances, but all the more so when growth is sluggish.

During the postwar decades, American leadership has time and again played a crucial role in leading the industrial countries out of the doldrums. The United States has assumed this burden not because it is magnanimous, but out of enlightened self-interest. Prosperous allies are needed for both economic and security reasons, and the OECD countries still generate by far the largest share of world trade. Today that leadership is absent. The president, perhaps pushed by Congress, seems to believe that domestic economic problems can be solved through domestic economic policies. The administration's singular focus on the international front has been export promotion. But American exports can increase only if the world economy continues to liberalize and grow.

This is an age of widespread economic insecurity, brought about by profound changes in trade, finance, and technology. For globalization to proceed, public officials in every country must give the lie to those who assert that it is anathema to workers' interests. The best way to make this case is by restoring growth and opportunity. Restrictive economic policies may have been necessary when first conceived in the 1980s to bring stability to financial markets, but they have failed too many people too long.

While the world stands at a critical time in postwar history, it has a group of leaders who appear unwilling, like their predecessors in the 1930s, to provide the international leadership to meet economic dislocations. Worse, many of them and their economic advisers do not seem to recognize the profound troubles affecting their societies. Like the German elite in Weimar, they dismiss mounting worker dissatisfaction, fringe political movements, and the plight of the unemployed and working poor as marginal concerns compared with the unquestioned importance of a sound currency and balanced budget. Leaders need to recognize the policy failures of the last 20 years and respond accordingly. If they do not, there are others waiting in the wings who will, perhaps on less pleasant terms.

Û Melvin Reder and Lloyd Ulman, 'Unionism and Unification,' in Labor and an Integrated Europe, ed. Lloyd Ulman, Barry Eichengreen, and William T. Dickens, Washington: The Brookings Institution, 1993, p. 24.

Ü Adrian Wood, North-South Trade, Employment and Inequality: Changing Futures in a Skill-driven World, New York: Oxford University Press, 1994.

ﬁ Yolanda K. Kodrzycki, 'The Costs of Defense-Related Layoffs in New England,' New England Economic Review, March/April 1995, p. 16.

ﬂ Jeffrey G. Williamson, Inequality, Poverty, and History, Cambridge: Blackwell, 1991.

Ethan B. Kapstein is Director of Studies at the Council on Foreign Relations. His most recent book is Governing the Global Economy: International Finance and the State.

Trade Policy for a Networked World

Charlene Barshefsky

REUTERS

NEW ERA, NEW CHALLENGES

Trade policy has been a notable and bipartisan success of postwar American foreign policy. Across 10 administrations and 26 Congresses, Washington has guided the world's economies toward freer trade and higher levels of development -- from the foundation of the General Agreement on Tariffs and Trade (GATT) in 1947; through the U.S. Trade Expansion Act of 1962 and the Kennedy, Tokyo, and Uruguay Rounds of GATT negotiations; to the U.S.-Canada Free Trade Agreement, the North American Free Trade Agreement

(NAFTA), recent trade agreements with China, Vietnam, and Jordan, and legislation liberalizing trade with Africa and the Caribbean. Current challenges along these lines include completing negotiations on free trade agreements with Singapore and Chile, inaugurating a new round of the World Trade Organization (WTO) and negotiating Russia's entry into it, and moving forward on a Free Trade Area of the Americas.

Trade agreements have grown in complexity and scope over time, but the landmark achievements of earlier years all dealt with essentially similar problems. They catalogued and reduced tariffs, quotas, and other trade barriers. As a new century opens, however, trade policy is taking on a fundamentally new set of challenges -- ensuring an open, competitive, well-regulated information economy. One of the principal achievements of the Clinton administration was to begin rethinking trade policy to fit this new economy. And one of the great opportunities for the new Bush administration is to build on the foundational agreements of the Clinton years and fully adapt trade policy to the information age.

SETTING STANDARDS AND PROTECTING IDEAS

Trade has typically involved goods one can see crossing the border: beef, steel, semiconductors, cars, or bottles of wine. Postwar administrations thus initially focused on such tangibles by trying to persuade other governments to remove their import tariffs. As tariffs fell, the focus shifted to eliminating import quotas, which distort market behavior and the allocation of resources. As these formal barriers began to diminish, trade negotiations moved into more arcane fields such as harmonizing technical standards -- so that a semiconductor chip built in Costa Rica and a hard drive assembled in Southeast Asia, for example, can run programs written in India for a computer designed in North Carolina.

As President Bill Clinton took office, the development of a networked world added a new set of questions to these familiar issues. Trade policy in the 1990s had to address not just tangible goods traveling by plane or boat, but also weightless products that move instantaneously around the world by wire or satellite beam. Whereas previous negotiations catalogued and reduced a set of existing trade barriers, now policymakers had to anticipate and prevent the creation of new types of barriers.

This adaptation was a high-stakes challenge with potentially enormous payoffs. History had shown that trade barriers take little time to impose but decades to remove. The newly created information networks, however, had no formal trade barriers. The emerging information economy thus offered two great opportunities: a far-sighted and multilateral U.S. trade policy could help preserve open commerce in cyberspace while creating a legal framework to give all trading nations the maximum incentives for creativity, growth, and development.

The Clinton administration, aware of its great responsibility to help shepherd the emerging global information economy, began with a set of cautionary principles designed to prevent precipitous actions and policy mistakes. Information technology (it) industries are still in their infancy, and policies made now will have enormous effect on the course of their development. And of course, policies are most beneficial and easiest to enforce when they arrive through consensus. So Washington and governments abroad need to develop policies through cooperation and discussion with industry, consumers, and others affected by electronic transmissions. Finally, because the Internet has no natural borders, any one country's policies on Internet services will affect the high-tech economies in the United States and around the world -- so domestic policies must proceed in tandem with the international system.

With these principles in mind, the Clinton administration worked carefully to develop a basic set of standards that, if adopted by foreign governments and international trade organizations, could replicate worldwide the United States' rapid development of a networked economy: strong intellectual-property standards that encourage investment, open it markets that will bring in capital and create economies of scale, competition in the telecommunications industry, open markets in services, and caution about policies that would limit development of the Internet.

The intellectual-property-rights program, dating to the Omnibus Trade and Competitiveness Act of 1988, is perhaps the oldest U.S. initiative designed to foster a worldwide information economy. At the time the act was passed, many countries had no copyright, trademark, or patent laws. Some saw intellectual-property rights -- especially when applied to pharmaceuticals or high-tech products such as computer software -- as obstacles to development. But without laws in place to protect these industries, piracy and counterfeiting were not just common but often nearly universal.

To address this problem, Washington began bilateral negotiations with countries where these practices were most egregious. These negotiations were aided by the "Special 301" law of 1988, which required the U.S. trade representative to investigate countries that denied adequate protection to intellectual property. The talks were difficult; at times, as with China in 1995 and 1996, U.S. negotiators had to threaten sanctions on billions of dollars in trade. But the efforts significantly raised the standards by which foreign countries agreed to uphold intellectual-property rights, spurring passage of internationally compatible copyright, patent, and trademark laws around the world.

A bilateral approach remains necessary in many regions today, but the United States can now go beyond adversarial tactics to more cooperative methods. Having strengthened their legal and enforcement regimes, many U.S. trading partners now enjoy increased foreign investment, which in turn enhances access to technology at home, and have thus concluded that strong intellectual-property standards could speed up their economic development. This consensus allowed for the negotiation of a landmark global agreement on intellectual-property protection (trips), implemented when the WTO was created in 1995. Through trips, all WTO members committed themselves to enact and enforce modern copyright, patent, and trademark laws.

OPENING HIGH-TECH MARKETS AND BUILDING THE NETWORK

Having secured this far-reaching agreement on intellectual-property protection, the administration set out to eliminate trade barriers in high-tech goods. Free trade benefits both consumers and producers of technology: it reduces the costs of goods and enables innovative industries to take advantage of economies of scale, thus recouping their investments in research more rapidly by selling to larger markets. As with intellectual-property protection, international technology trade has evolved from a difficult and confrontational environment toward one in which U.S. trading partners see shared benefits in open markets.

Many countries had long preferred using tariffs, subsidies, or a combination of the two to nurture their high-tech industries. The Clinton administration thus focused its initial negotiations on countries where these trade-distorting practices were especially common -- principally Japan, but also some European countries, South Korea, and other advanced trading partners. The result was a series of market-opening bilateral agreements in specific sectors, such as semiconductors, satellites, computers, supercomputers, and mobile phones.

The success of these agreements helped build an international understanding that tariffs on high-tech goods are extremely short-sighted. They weaken all parts of an economy, from manufacturing to finance, telecommunications to computer services, and countless other fields. So the United States developed a worldwide approach to fighting such barriers. This effort began by broadening the Semiconductor Agreement with Japan to include the world's other major semiconductor producers: Europe, Taiwan, and South Korea. The agreement was also expanded to address a wider array of issues, including research and development, private-sector cooperation with government, and basic market access.

These building blocks in turn allowed the Clinton administration to initiate and negotiate the WTO's 1997 Information Technology Agreement (ita). By 2004, this agreement will have eliminated the tariffs on $600 billion worth of goods, including 95 percent of the world's production of semiconductors, computers, telecommunications equipment, integrated circuits, and other goods associated with the information superhighway. The opportunities thus created -- not only for trade, but also for economic development and long-term growth -- are extraordinary. High-tech manufacturers can now sell to wider markets, develop new economies of scale, and grow. Last year, the United States produced $13 billion in semiconductor manufacturing equipment and exported $8 billion of it; U.S. makers of semiconductor chips likewise exported nearly half of all their production. For consumers overseas, the removal of tariffs has proven equally important, since it has reduced the cost of the equipment and materials that businesses need to make factories more productive, reach the Internet, find customers, and work in real time with overseas partners.

For the global economy to reap the benefits of free trade in information hardware, producers and consumers need affordable access to advanced telecommunications systems. This is the goal of the third major high-tech trade achievement of the 1990s: the WTO's 1997 Basic Telecommunications Agreement. This pact brought to the world the procompetition principles of the 1996 U.S. Telecommunications Act. The agreement now covers 102 WTO members, 95 percent of the nearly $1 trillion a year in international telecommunications trade, and services and technologies from submarine cables to satellites, broadband networks to cellular phones, and business intranets to wireless connections for rural and underserved regions.

The agreement has three substantive dimensions. First, it guarantees market access for telecommunications providers, guaranteeing them the right to offer local, long-distance, and international service through any means of network technology, including the Internet. Next, the agreement ensures that the most efficient and innovative companies can acquire, establish, or hold significant stakes in telecommunications companies around the world. And finally, the agreement commits all participants to a procompetitive regulatory structure, so that former monopoly providers cannot undermine their governments' market-access commitments.

Implementation of the agreement over the last three years has shown its benefits for both developed and developing countries. A global, competitive telecommunications industry is immensely important to some of America's leading exporters. It also helps provide a source of new technologies and modern infrastructure for countries in the developing world.

Moreover, consumers enjoy lower prices as dominant overseas carriers lose their ability to keep rates artificially high. Indeed, rates for international calls have fallen sharply to levels approximating domestic long-distance rates -- as low as 5 to 10 cents per minute for calls to Canada and the United Kingdom, or 15 cents a minute for calls to Japan.

The agreement also supports the development of a global telecommunications infrastructure. With broader market access and increased investor stability provided by WTO commitments, new investment in undersea fiber-optic cables may spark a 50-fold increase in capacity by the end of 2001, from levels of mid-1999. Already, in the last five years, traffic flowing over global telecommunications networks has increased tenfold, and with Internet traffic continuing to double every 100 days, the rate of growth is rising.

LIBERALIZING SERVICES AND DIGITIZING TRADE

These three agreements -- TRIPS, the ITA, and the Basic Telecommunications Agreement -- provide a foundation in law and policy for a sophisticated international information network. The next step is to make sure that consumers and industries can use this network to their best advantage. This goal implies, above all, the liberalization of consumer services on a broad scale, to include the sectors that can gain the most efficiency from the Internet: financial services, the professions (law, medicine, accounting, architecture, and engineering), audiovisual and media services, retailing, express delivery, and many others. Liberalizing these services will help exporters take advantage of the opportunities created by an increasingly networked global economy; a more open services industry will also create new demand that can itself accelerate investment in and improvement of the information network.

In this regard, the Clinton administration's next priority was negotiation of the WTO's Agreement on Financial Services, finally signed in late 1997. This agreement -- covering securities, banking, and insurance services in 102 countries -- is fostering the development of financial markets, especially in emerging and developing economies. Many nations had previously begun the process of financial-services liberalization; the 1997 agreement binds these improvements under the WTO's 1994 General Agreement on Trade in Services (GATS), providing secure market access to exporters and choice to consumers. At the same time, through a series of commitments to open markets, the pact has created new opportunities for competitive U.S. financial-services suppliers, who have thus been able to help emerging markets modernize their financial-services systems and improve their infrastructure for trade in goods and services.

The Internet's development perhaps best symbolizes the economic boom of the Clinton era. From fewer than 3 million users in 1994, an estimated 300 million people had gone online by the time President Clinton left office. Web-based commerce grew even faster, with the potential to improve productivity in the national economy, make existing industries more efficient, and even create new industries we have not yet imagined.

The initial goal of Internet trade policy was to prevent tariffs from being imposed on electronic transmissions over the Internet. Success came rapidly, with all WTO members making a political commitment to maintaining duty-free cyberspace at the WTO's second ministerial conference in Geneva in 1998. U.S. trade policymakers have since turned to a broader and longer-term program, whose goals include ensuring that our trading partners do not unduly restrict the development of electronic commerce, guaranteeing that WTO rules do not discriminate against new technologies and methods of trade, according proper application of WTO rules to trade in digital products, and ensuring full protection of intellectual-property rights on the Internet.

By autumn 2000, then, most of the world's governments had committed themselves through a network of WTO agreements to strong intellectual-property protections, open markets for it products, a sophisticated and competitive telecommunications network, more open services markets, and an Internet free to develop as a medium for commerce. These initiatives addressed each of the Clinton administration's basic trade concerns. But the work remained incomplete. The Clinton team therefore inaugurated in October 2000 a second-generation approach to high-tech trade: the "Networked World" initiative, a six-part effort designed to adapt the international trading system to the digital age. Completing this initiative should be one of the principal trade priorities of the Bush administration.

The "Networked World" program began with the observation that current WTO provisions do not address electronic commerce directly in any meaningful way. E-commerce is still so new that only one free trade pact in the world -- the U.S.Jordan Free Trade Agreement -- includes provisions for it. And apart from the 1998 duty-free cyberspace commitment, the WTO is largely a void in this area: although it has held extensive discussions on electronic commerce, no formal rules prevent its members from discriminating against products traveling by wire or satellite.

The WTO should therefore find global consensus on a set of general principles for Internet trade. First, WTO members should commit to technological neutrality, which means ensuring that current WTO agreements and basic WTO concepts of nondiscrimination, national treatment, and most-favored-nation status apply to e-commerce as well as to conventional trade. Next, the treatment of digital products must embody a similar principle. The WTO has correctly avoided making a decision on whether to classify products delivered in digital form as services or goods or to create a new category for them. Whatever the ultimate decision, it should not disadvantage digital products in favor of identical, physically delivered goods. For example, a software program, whether downloaded from a Web site or bought on a compact disc in a store, should not be subject to any greater trade restrictions. Finally, WTO member states should commit to regulatory forbearance, so that they avoid regulatory and oversight policies that would constitute trade barriers. The first option should thus be market-based self-regulation. This is not always possible: governments will always have to enforce laws and protect consumers. But the rapid pace of change in technology also means that effective pursuit of legitimate government responsibilities depends on working closely with the private sector.

In the field of intellectual property, the development of the Internet has both heightened the urgency of familiar questions and raised new issues. The Internet enables users to make unlimited copies of all sorts of materials -- music, film, multimedia, text, and software -- and send them instantaneously to thousands or ultimately even millions of people worldwide. This creates obvious new opportunities for artists, scholars, and innovators; it also raises obvious concerns about potential problems, ranging from massive piracy to hacking into Web sites and altering published work on-line.

These concerns can be addressed effectively only on a global basis. At the least, the response must apply existing international agreements to the Internet, but ultimately it should develop new standards for the on-line environment. Two critical treaties negotiated at the World Intellectual Property Organization are a good starting point. The first agreement addresses computer software and databases, the distribution of copyrighted materials over networks and in tangible formats, legal protections for antipiracy technology, and guarantees for new means of on-line licensing of copyrighted material. The other brings protection for sound recordings into closer accord with the protection available for other creative works, such as books, movies, and computer software. The treaties' ratifiers include the United States, most industrialized countries, and some in the developing world. This group still includes only a minority of WTO members, however, and the Bush administration should make universal ratification an early priority.

TAKING THE NEXT STEPS

The liberalization of trade in high-tech goods is also incomplete. The ITA itself misses several important categories of goods, such as radar-navigation equipment and circuit boards, which have long been proposed for inclusion in an ITA II. Furthermore, the agreement as a whole will need to be updated in the coming years as new technologies emerge and as older categories of goods begin to fuse through the development of multimedia technologies.

Today's home computers routinely perform a broad range of tasks beyond the realm of data entry and data processing -- functions that include telephone answering, electronic translation, video reproduction, stereo sound, still and video camera input, scanning and copying, faxing, playing DVDS and CD-ROMS, and providing global positioning system data. Similarly, a wide array of peripheral goods is acquiring the capacity to perform tasks for which people used to rely on computers. These devices include personal organizers, phones that convey information about weather, traffic, and news, and even "smart" washing machines and refrigerators.

This transformation raises long-term questions about how to classify technology goods for tariff purposes. Classification is already complex and somewhat arbitrary -- the Pentium III microprocessor, for example, is an essential component of many computer systems, but the World Customs Organization has an ongoing debate over whether to classify it as a semiconductor or as a "part" of an "automatic data processing machine." Classification will become even more difficult as new products continue to flood the market. Given that many countries maintain high tariffs on products considered to be consumer electronics, the ita will need to be widened to include new categories of products and ensure that existing high-tech products do not slip out of the duty-free category.

Trade policymakers must reexamine the Basic Telecommunications Agreement, which is now almost four years old. The telecommunications industry must first and foremost aim to ensure that its regulators remain committed to the agreement's procompetitive principles. Historic monopolies -- such as Nippon Telegraph and Telephone (NTT) in Japan, Telmex in Mexico, China Telecom, British Telecom, and Telkom in South Africa -- remain entrenched and powerful in many countries. As the Clinton administration came to an end, U.S. negotiators were engaged in talks with Japan and Mexico, with some important successes, to ensure that the dominant local carriers, NTT and Telmex, did not attempt to evade their WTO responsibilities. Monopoly service providers are not the only impediments to telecommunications liberalization, however. While negotiating with U.S. trading partners, the Clinton administration was also fending off short-sighted proposals in the U.S. Congress to evade commitments on openness to international investment in the American telecommunications sector.

After ensuring a competitive market, the second goal is broader participation in the Basic Telecommunications Agreement. Some WTO members are not participating at all; others have made a highly limited set of commitments, particularly concerning foreign investment. Canada, Malaysia, India, Thailand, Mexico, South Korea, Indonesia, and others still do not permit majority foreign ownership of telecommunications companies.

Beyond telecommunications, many service sectors worldwide remain protected and closed. The GATS itself implies that market-opening commitments in services are exceptions to a general rule of closed markets. With respect to trade in physical goods, ever since the Kennedy administration, international negotiating rounds have typically begun with an overall commitment to reduce tariffs; governments then seek exceptions for especially sensitive products. By contrast, in services trade negotiations, governments offer liberalization in selected areas but remain free to keep the vast bulk of services sectors off-limits. Services negotiations are now underway at the WTO, with trade proposals under consideration in sectors as varied as financial services, travel and tourism, distribution and express delivery, and the professions. GATS should ultimately move from this policy of occasional and limited market-opening to a presumption that open markets are generally desired, with exceptions to be negotiated and noted in the resulting agreements.

Closely linked to the liberalization of technology-related services is the need to reconsider policies that will encourage investment in telecommunications network development. As technological advances lower costs, surging demand strains networks' existing capacities. As a result, there is a long-term need for enormous investment to build networks with broadband capacity and the versatility to respond to increases in market demand.

A central role for the WTO is to encourage an environment conducive to investment in and use of such networks. Useful American precedents are policies that have avoided giving preference to any particular technology or means of delivering services and have promoted competition through enforcement of antitrust laws and the 1996 Telecommunications Act. Trade policy can contribute to creating this international environment, in part by encouraging foreign governments to privatize telecommunications services and open the sector to foreign investment.

OVERCOMING THE DIGITAL DIVIDE

Outside the trade policy context as strictly defined, new U.S. policies and international agreements must be complemented by practical work to prevent an international digital divide. This work should begin with a sustained commitment to technical assistance and capacity-building. This assistance would help those governments that have committed themselves to competition and market-based economics develop the regulatory capacity and civil service expertise necessary for modern telecommunications policies. It would also help ensure that WTO members can participate fully in the Basic Telecommunications Agreement, the Agreement on Financial Services, and prospective future services liberalization. Finally, assistance would achieve effective intellectual-property protection. These goals are fundamental to the capacity-building programs begun during the Clinton administration, which help developing countries gain expertise in it skills, develop Internet capability, and otherwise take advantage of the opportunities that the networked world offers.

At the same time, the United States can encourage its trading partners to help themselves. Governments in the developing world, for example, can be quick to adopt information technology and thus help spread it skills and computer literacy throughout their economies. In the commercial field, nations can unilaterally facilitate trade by making greater use of electronic networks for customs clearance, licensing, government procurement, and dissemination of regulations; similar possibilities will emerge for tax regimes, financial policy, environmental monitoring, the law, and other fields.

In this context, the direction of high-tech trade policy in the decades ahead becomes clear. Just as the shape of today's trading system was implied in the first major multilateral trade agreement -- the establishment of GATT in 1947 -- the Clinton administration's foundational high-tech agreements and Networked World initiative have laid a path for a series of further negotiations. This path leads to a highly sophisticated, competitive, and innovative worldwide information economy. Few initiatives are so demanding, but few have such promise.

Charlene Barshefsky served as U.S. Trade Representative from 1996 until the end of the Clinton administration. She is now a Public Policy Scholar at the Woodrow Wilson International Center for Scholars in Washington, D.C.

Toughest on the Poor: America's Flawed Tariff System

Edward Gresser

REUTERS

The Bush administration's decision last March to impose tariffs of 8-30 percent on steel has been called everything from hypocrisy and stupidity to Machiavellian political brilliance. The reaction has been a remarkable demonstration of the strength of free-trade opinion in the United States -- but it has also been a bit puzzling.

The steel tariffs, even if one believes they are bad policy, are just temporary aberrations from the norm; they will be lifted in a couple of years. But for dozens of other products -- sneakers, spoons, bicycles, underwear, suitcases, drinking glasses, T-shirts, plates, and more -- tariffs of 8-30 percent are neither aberrant nor temporary. In fact, they are normal and permanent parts of U.S. trade policy. Barring a deliberate change in policy, they will never be lifted -- and no one seems to care.

The reason is not simply that people care more about steel than about underwear. Rather, it is that the tariff system has become an obscure, little-studied topic. Those who debate trade and globalization view tariff policy as boring and out of date. Career trade negotiators who set tariff rates have little contact with the customs officers who collect the money. Journalists cover political debate and international disputes rather than the functioning of permanent policy. And government officials, aware that tariffs are generally low and raise little money compared to domestic taxes, rarely think about the system as a whole.

But if these groups were to look more closely, they would find a remarkable situation. Tariff policy, without any deliberate intent, has evolved into something astonishingly tough on the poor. Young single mothers buying cheap clothes and shoes now pay tariff rates five to ten times higher than middle-class or rich families pay in elite stores. Very poor countries such as Cambodia or Bangladesh face tariffs 15 times those applied to wealthy nations and oil exporters. Despite this dismal situation, however, fixing the system would be easier than many imagine.

MALIGN NEGLECT

The problem arises more from neglect than from malice. No U.S. administration since the 1970s, or perhaps even since John Kennedy's, has had a specific vision for tariff policy. Regardless of party, administrations have instead seen tariffs as a series of discrete issues that are useful in building domestic support for, and coopting potential opposition to, larger trade agreements.

In past trade negotiations, some domestic interests -- manufacturers of semiconductors, chemicals, capital goods, and so on -- sought export opportunities by advocating the elimination of overseas trade barriers and were willing to give up tariffs at home in exchange. Other industries -- shoes, textiles, cutlery, glassware -- feared foreign competition and fought to keep tariffs high. In the three big multilateral trade agreements since 1970 that have focused on manufactured goods -- the Tokyo and Uruguay Rounds of the General Agreement on Tariffs and Trade, and the Information Technology Agreement of the World Trade Organization (WTO) -- U.S. administrations tried to satisfy both groups, and largely succeeded.

These accords, combined with free trade agreements with Canada, Mexico, Israel, and Jordan, and four duty-free programs for developing countries, have brought overall U.S. tariffs to a historic low. In July, Robert Zoellick, the U.S. trade representative, told the Bundestag Forum that "the average trade-weighted tariff for the United States is now under 2 percent."

In making this point, Zoellick was not just accurate but modest. Last year, the U.S. Customs Service collected $18.6 billion in tariff revenue on $1.1 trillion in goods imports -- meaning the effective U.S. tariff rate is 1.6 percent. But the low overall average masks something more troubling.

Tariffs on industrial imports are not just low but extremely low. For expensive consumer goods such as cars, appliances, and televisions, rates are also generally low and are further reduced in practice by trade agreements with Mexico and Canada. But for light consumer goods, the story is different. Tariffs on these products (with a few exceptions, such as toys and furniture) remain at levels other industries last saw in the 1960s and 1970s: for instance, 8.7 percent for cutlery and tableware, 13.8 percent for suitcases and handbags, 10 percent for bicycles, and 11.4 percent for shoes and clothes, the largest category of consumer imports for the United States.

In effect, the United States now has two tariff systems. One, for low-tech consumer goods, has an average rate of 10.5 percent. The other, for everything else, has an average rate of 0.8 percent. As a result, most tariff revenue now comes from a very small number of goods. Shoes and clothes in particular, as Table 1 shows, make up less than 7 percent of imports but bring in nearly half of all tariff revenues.

Finally, tariffs also vary from one consumer good to the next.

Most notably, they are much higher on cheap goods than on luxuries. This disparity occurs because elite firms, selling image and brand name, find small price advantages relatively unimportant. They have not pressed the government to keep tariffs high, and tariffs on luxury goods such as silk lingerie, silver-handled cutlery, leaded-glass beer mugs, and snakeskin handbags are now very low. But makers of nylon lingerie, stainless steel cutlery, cheap water glasses, and plastic purses benefit by adding a few percentage points to their competitors' prices. So on the cheapest goods, as Table 2 shows, tariffs are even higher than overall averages for consumer goods suggest.

IF THE SHOE FITS

So the structure of the tariff system is simple: tariffs are low overall, high on consumer goods, and especially high on cheap goods. How does it work in real life? A convenient place to begin is with the justification for the tariff system: preservation of jobs in light manufacturing.

Here, the system seems ineffective. Employment in high-tariff industries now accounts for only about three percent of U.S. manufacturing jobs. It has fallen by half since 1990, and the plunge is fastest in some of the most protected industries. In 1992, for example, 20,000 Americans worked making women's shoes. No shoe tariffs have been cut since the 1970s, but since 1992 employment in women's shoes has fallen by 90 percent, to only 2,000 workers. Likewise, the number of workers making children's clothes is down from 44,000 to fewer than 7,000. For the manufacture of goods such as watches, bicycles, and drinking glasses, job totals are even lower.

In such fields, tariffs are evidently not preserving jobs. Instead they are operating more like large wholesale taxes. And although their effects are minor for domestic producers, they are considerable for people who buy and make such goods: poor families in the United States, and workers and businesses in poor countries.

One type of shoe provides an instructive example. Cheap sneakers valued at $3 or less per pair carry tariffs of 48 percent (a rate, incidentally, far above that of any product on the administration's steel list). Virtually none of these shoes is made in the United States. Last year, the United States imported 16 million pairs of these sneakers, at a total cost of $35 million. Thus the average price at the border was $2.20 per pair. The Treasury Department then collected $17 million in tariffs, adding another $1.06 per pair to the buyers' cost. The extra dollar and change is then magnified by retail markups of around 40 percent and state sales taxes of about 5 percent to raise the final consumer price of the sneakers from about $3.25 (without tariffs) to $4.80 per pair (with tariffs).

Such tariff-based overpricing exists, though at less dramatic levels, in store aisles stocking baby clothes, T-shirts, silverware, and other typical family products. Because it is most pronounced on the cheapest shoes and clothes, its effect falls most heavily on single-parent families.

Incomes for these families are very low: at an average of about $25,100 per year, they are about 40 percent of a typical two-parent family's income. But single-parent families face shoe and clothing bills nearly as high as those of wealthier families. In total, the average single-parent family spends nearly $2,000 a year on clothes and shoes. Depending on the mix of purchases, as much as $400 of this total may simply be price inflation due to tariffs. Budgets for other tariffed goods, though smaller, are still a larger expense relative to income for poor families than for rich families. And so single-parent families lose much more of their income to tariffs than do other families.

PUNISHING THE POOR

Beyond U.S. shores, the tariff system operates in a similar fashion. It hits countries that specialize in the cheapest goods, in particular very poor countries in Asia, much harder than others.

Average tariffs on European exports to the United States -- primarily cars, power equipment, computers, and chemicals -- now barely exceed one percent. Developing countries such as Malaysia, which specialize in information-technology products, get rates just as low. So do natural-resource exporters such as Saudi Arabia and Nigeria. Middle-income exporters that ship a broader variety of goods, such as China, Thailand, and Brazil, face rates typically between two percent and four percent -- above average but still not exorbitant. The least-developed Asian countries, however, take it on the chin.

For Bangladesh, Cambodia, Nepal, Mongolia, and a few others, clothes make up 90 percent of all exports to the United States. So they face average tariff rates of 14.6 percent -- nearly 10 times the world average, and 15 times the rate for wealthy Western countries. Translated into real dollars, the disparities can be remarkable.

As Table 3 notes, the U.S. now collects more tariff revenue from Bangladeshi goods than from French goods, even though Bangladesh exports $2 billion in goods a year to the United States and France $30 billion. Cambodia's exports to the United States total $900 million and Singapore's usually reach $15-$20 billion -- but the U.S. government collects nearly twice as much revenue from Cambodian goods as from Singaporean goods. And struggling Nepal faces tariff rates on its skirts, scarves, and suits fully 60 times higher than those applied to Ireland's chemicals, pacemakers, and silicon chips.

In fairness, such disparities are not universal, and some attempts to ease tariff burdens have been successful. The African Growth and Opportunity Act, set up under the Clinton administration, is the best example. Since it was enacted two years ago, African clothing exports to the United States have nearly doubled, but tariff collection on African goods has dropped by more than half. The results of the Caribbean Basin Initiative are less dramatic, but Haiti, Honduras, and several other beneficiaries also face fairly low rates.

The U.S. system is not uniquely bad. Europe's tariffs on clothes and shoes -- not to mention food -- are also high, and European Union tariff collection is far less transparent and accessible than America's. Some developing countries would also do well to look in the mirror.

Recent World Bank studies, in fact, indicate that the poorest countries would gain most from tariff reform in large developing economies. India is a case in point: as dispiriting as U.S. treatment of Nepali goods may be, Nepal still exports more each year to the United States than to its giant southern neighbor, where clothing imports are often simply banned and tariffs on other goods regularly reach 40 percent.

DO THE RIGHT THING

The fact that others have bad policies is no excuse for Americans to adopt them too. U.S. trade policies should be defended on their own merits. And a system that hits the poor harder than anyone else is quite hard to defend.

Tariffs, especially on clothes, have tenacious advocates. But in fact, this system that protects so few and hurts so many can be fixed without much dislocation. The International Trade Commission's July 2002 study finds that employment in high-tariff industries is already so low that eliminating all U.S. trade barriers would mean a net gain of about 35,000 jobs rather than a loss. And so, if the problems with the system were better understood, the solutions might be fairly simple.

One option, of course, would be simply to scrap tariffs on consumer goods for domestic policy reasons. Considered as a form of taxation, they are offensive to the principles of both parties -- Republicans always being enthusiastic for tax cuts, and Democrats being opposed to regressive taxation. A $10 billion annual tax cut would be substantial, but it seems moderate when compared to recent tax legislation.

Alternatively, with U.S. trade credibility needing a boost after the steel and farm bill decisions (and since the tariff policies of U.S. trading partners also need change), the administration could suggest a worldwide goal of zero tariffs on clothes, shoes, and other consumer goods. This would recapture whatever moral high ground on trade was lost in the past year and also create a powerful incentive for developing nations to seek a successful conclusion to the WTO negotiations begun at Doha last year.

But one point seems quite clear. A system that makes maids pay higher rates than corporate vice presidents, and hits Cambodians 15 times harder than Germans, is an ethical scandal and a problem far bigger than any temporary steel policy. The facts are plain, and reform is only a question of political will.

Edward Gresser is Director of the Project on Trade and Global Markets at the Progressive Policy Institute.

Offshoring: The Next Industrial Revolution?

Alan S. Blinder

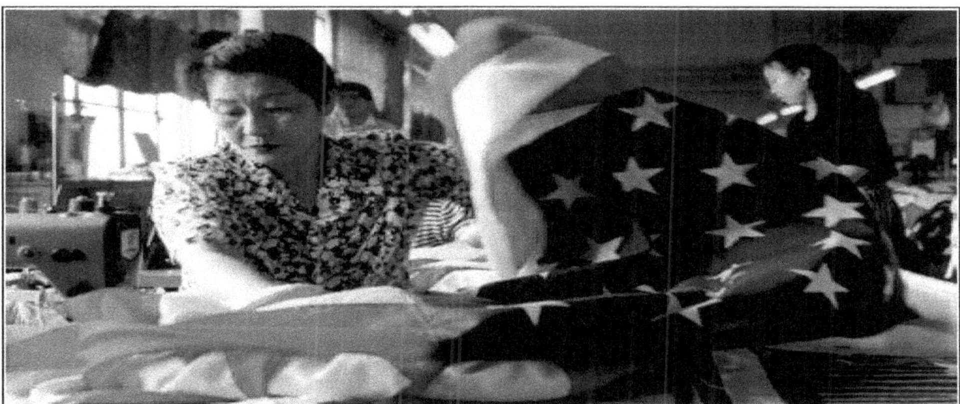

COURTESY REUTERS

A CONTROVERSY RECONSIDERED

In February 2004, when N. Gregory Mankiw, a Harvard professor then serving as chairman of the White House Council of Economic Advisers, caused a national uproar with a "textbook" statement about trade, economists rushed to his defense. Mankiw was commenting on the phenomenon that has been clumsily dubbed "offshoring" (or "offshore outsourcing") -- the migration of jobs, but not the people who perform them, from rich countries to poor ones. Offshoring, Mankiw said, is only "the latest manifestation of the gains from trade that economists have talked about at least since Adam Smith. ... More things are tradable than were tradable in the past, and that's a good thing." Although Democratic and Republican politicians alike excoriated Mankiw for his callous attitude toward American jobs, economists lined up to support his claim that offshoring is simply international business as usual.

Their economics were basically sound: the well-known principle of comparative advantage implies that trade in new kinds of products will bring overall improvements in productivity and well-being. But Mankiw and his defenders underestimated both the importance of offshoring and its disruptive effect on wealthy countries. Sometimes a quantitative change is so large that it brings about qualitative changes, as offshoring likely will. We have so far barely seen the tip of the offshoring iceberg, the eventual dimensions of which may be staggering.

To be sure, the furor over Mankiw's remark was grotesquely out of proportion to the current importance of offshoring, which is still largely a prospective phenomenon. Although there are no reliable national data, fragmentary studies indicate that well under a million service-sector jobs in the United States have been lost to offshoring to date. (A million seems impressive, but in the gigantic and rapidly churning U.S. labor market, a million jobs is less than two weeks' worth of normal gross job losses.) However, constant improvements in technology and global communications virtually guarantee that the future will bring much more offshoring of "impersonal services" -- that is, services that can be delivered electronically over long distances with little or no degradation in quality.

That said, we should not view the coming wave of offshoring as an impending catastrophe. Nor should we try to stop it. The normal gains from trade mean that the world as a whole cannot lose from increases in productivity, and the United States and other industrial countries have not only weathered but also benefited from comparable changes in the past. But in order to do so again, the governments and societies of the developed world must face up to the massive, complex, and multifaceted challenges that offshoring will bring. National data systems, trade policies, educational systems, social welfare programs, and politics all must adapt to new realities. Unfortunately, none of this is happening now.

MODERNIZING COMPARATIVE ADVANTAGE

Countries trade with one another for the same reasons that individuals, businesses, and regions do: to exploit their comparative advantages. Some advantages are "natural": Texas and Saudi Arabia sit atop massive deposits of oil that are entirely lacking in New York and Japan, and nature has conspired to make Hawaii a more attractive tourist destination than Greenland. There is not much anyone can do about such natural advantages.

But in modern economies, nature's whimsy is far less important than it was in the past. Today, much comparative advantage derives from human effort rather than natural conditions. The concentration of computer companies around Silicon Valley, for example, has nothing to do with bountiful natural deposits of silicon; it has to do with Xerox's fabled Palo Alto Research Center, the proximity of Stanford University, and the arrival of two young men named Hewlett and Packard. Silicon Valley could have sprouted up elsewhere.

One important aspect of this modern reality is that patterns of man-made comparative advantage can and do change over time. The economist Jagdish Bhagwati has labeled this phenomenon "kaleidoscopic comparative advantage," and it is critical to understanding offshoring. Once upon a time, the United Kingdom had a comparative advantage in textile manufacturing. Then that advantage shifted to New England, and so jobs were moved from the United Kingdom to the United States. Then the comparative advantage shifted once again -- this time to the Carolinas -- and jobs migrated south within the United States. Now the comparative advantage in textile manufacturing resides in China and other low-wage countries, and what many are wont to call "American jobs" have been moved there as a result.

Of course, not everything can be traded across long distances. At any point in time, the available technology -- especially in transportation and communications -- largely determines what can be traded internationally and what cannot. Economic theorists accordingly divide the world's goods and services into two bins: tradable and nontradable. Traditionally, any item that could be put in a box and shipped (roughly, manufactured goods) was considered tradable, and anything that could not be put in a box (such as services) or was too heavy to ship (such as houses) was thought of as nontradable. But because technology is always improving and transportation is becoming cheaper and easier, the boundary between what is tradable and what is not is constantly shifting. And unlike comparative advantage, this change is not kaleidoscopic; it moves in only one direction, with more and more items becoming tradable.

The old assumption that if you cannot put it in a box, you cannot trade it is thus hopelessly obsolete. Because packets of digitized information play the role that boxes used to play, many more services are now tradable and many more will surely become so. In the future, and to a great extent already, the key distinction will no longer be between things that can be put in a box and things that cannot. Rather, it will be between services that can be delivered electronically and those that cannot.

THE THREE INDUSTRIAL REVOLUTIONS

Adam Smith wrote The Wealth of Nations in 1776, at the beginning of the first Industrial Revolution. Although Smith's vision was extraordinary, even he did not imagine what was to come. As workers in the industrializing countries migrated from farm to factory, societies were transformed beyond recognition. The shift was massive. It has been estimated that in 1810, 84 percent of the U.S. work force was engaged in agriculture, compared to a paltry 3 percent in manufacturing. By 1960, manufacturing's share had risen to almost 25 percent and agriculture's had dwindled to just 8 percent. (Today, agriculture's share is under 2 percent.) How and where people lived, how they educated their children, the organization of businesses, the forms and practices of government -- all changed dramatically in order to accommodate this new reality.

Then came the second Industrial Revolution, and jobs shifted once again -- this time away from manufacturing and toward services. The shift to services is still viewed with alarm in the United States and many other rich countries, where people bemoan rather than welcome the resulting loss of manufacturing jobs. But in reality, new service-sector jobs have been created far more rapidly than old manufacturing jobs have disappeared. In 1960, about 35 percent of nonagricultural workers in the United States produced goods and 65 percent produced services. By 2004, only about one-sixth of the United States' nonagricultural jobs were in goods-producing industries, while five-sixths produced services. This trend is worldwide and continuing. Between 1967 and 2003, according to the Organization for Economic Cooperation and Development, the service sector's share of total jobs increased by about 19 percentage points in the United States, 21 points in Japan, and roughly 25 points in France, Italy, and the United Kingdom.

We are now in the early stages of a third Industrial Revolution -- the information age. The cheap and easy flow of information around the globe has vastly expanded the scope of tradable services, and there is much more to come. Industrial revolutions are big deals. And just like the previous two, the third Industrial Revolution will require vast and unsettling adjustments in the way Americans and residents of other developed countries work, live, and educate their children.

But a bit of historical perspective should help temper fears of offshoring. The first Industrial Revolution did not spell the end of agriculture, or even the end of food production, in the United States. It just meant that a much smaller percentage of Americans had to work on farms to feed the population. (By charming historical coincidence, the actual number of Americans working on farms today -- around 2 million -- is about what it was in 1810.) The main reason for this shift was not foreign trade, but soaring farm productivity. And most important, the massive movement of labor off the farms did not result in mass unemployment. Rather, it led to a large-scale reallocation of labor to factories.

Similarly, the second Industrial Revolution has not meant the end of manufacturing, even in the United States, which is running ahead of the rest of the world in the shift toward services. The share of the U.S. work force engaged in manufacturing has fallen dramatically since 1960, but the number of manufacturing workers has declined only modestly. Three main forces have driven this change. First, rising productivity in the manufacturing sector has enabled the production of more and more goods with less and less labor. Second, as people around the world have gotten richer, consumer tastes have changed, with consumers choosing to spend a greater share of their incomes on services (such as restaurant meals and vacations) and a smaller share on goods (such as clothing and refrigerators). Third, the United States now imports a much larger share of the manufactured goods it consumes than it did 50 years ago. All told, the share of manufacturing in U.S. GDP declined from a peak near 30 percent in 1953 to under 13 percent in 2004. That may be the simplest quantitative indicator of the massive extent of the second Industrial Revolution to date. But as with the first Industrial Revolution, the shift has not caused widespread unemployment.

The third Industrial Revolution will play out similarly over the next several decades. The kinds of jobs that can be moved offshore will not disappear entirely from the United States or other rich countries, but their shares of the work force will shrink dramatically. And this reduction will transform societies in many ways, most of them hard to foresee, as workers in rich countries find other things to do. But just as with the first two industrial revolutions, massive offshoring will not lead to massive unemployment. In fact, the world gained enormously from the first two industrial revolutions, and it is likely to do so from the third -- so long as it makes the necessary economic and social adjustments.

THIS TIME IT'S PERSONAL

What sorts of jobs are at risk of being offshored? In the old days, when tradable goods were things that could be put in a box, the key distinction was between manufacturing and nonmanufacturing jobs. Consistent with that, manufacturing workers in the rich countries have grown accustomed to the idea that they compete with foreign labor. But as the domain of tradable services expands, many service workers will also have to accept the new, and not very pleasant, reality that they too must compete with workers in other countries. And there are many more service than manufacturing workers.

Many people blithely assume that the critical labor-market distinction is, and will remain, between highly educated (or highly skilled) people and less-educated (or less-skilled) people -- doctors versus call-center operators, for example. The supposed remedy for the rich countries, accordingly, is more education and a general "upskilling" of the work force. But this view may be mistaken. Other things being equal, education and skills are, of course, good things; education yields higher returns in advanced societies, and more schooling probably makes workers more flexible and more adaptable to change. But the problem with relying on education as the remedy for potential job losses is that "other things" are not remotely close to equal. The critical divide in the future may instead be between those types of work that are easily deliverable through a wire (or via wireless connections) with little or no diminution in quality and those that are not. And this unconventional divide does not correspond well to traditional distinctions between jobs that require high levels of education and jobs that do not.

A few disparate examples will illustrate just how complex -- or, rather, how untraditional -- the new divide is. It is unlikely that the services of either taxi drivers or airline pilots will ever be delivered electronically over long distances. The first is a "bad job" with negligible educational requirements; the second is quite the reverse. On the other hand, typing services (a low-skill job) and security analysis (a high-skill job) are already being delivered electronically from India -- albeit on a small scale so far. Most physicians need not fear that their jobs will be moved offshore, but radiologists are beginning to see this happening already. Police officers will not be replaced by electronic monitoring, but some security guards will be. Janitors and crane operators are probably immune to foreign competition; accountants and computer programmers are not. In short, the dividing line between the jobs that produce services that are suitable for electronic delivery (and are thus threatened by offshoring) and those that do not does not correspond to traditional distinctions between high-end and low-end work.

The fraction of service jobs in the United States and other rich countries that can potentially be moved offshore is certain to rise as technology improves and as countries such as China and India continue to modernize, prosper, and educate their work forces. Eventually, the number of service-sector jobs that will be vulnerable to competition from abroad will likely exceed the total number of manufacturing jobs. Thus, coping with foreign competition, currently a concern for only a minority of workers in rich countries, will become a major concern for many more.

There is currently not even a vocabulary, much less any systematic data, to help society come to grips with the coming labor-market reality. So here is some suggested nomenclature. Services that cannot be delivered electronically, or that are notably inferior when so delivered, have one essential characteristic: personal, face-to-face contact is either imperative or highly desirable. Think of the waiter who serves you dinner, the doctor who gives you your annual physical, or the cop on the beat. Now think of any of those tasks being performed by robots controlled from India -- not quite the same. But such face-to-face human contact is not necessary in the relationship you have with the telephone operator who arranges your conference call or the clerk who takes your airline reservation over the phone. He or she may be in India already.

The first group of tasks can be called personally delivered services, or simply personal services, and the second group impersonally delivered services, or impersonal services. In the brave new world of globalized electronic commerce, impersonal services have more in common with manufactured goods that can be put in boxes than they do with personal services. Thus, many impersonal services are destined to become tradable and therefore vulnerable to offshoring. By contrast, most personal services have attributes that cannot be transmitted through a wire. Some require face-to-face contact (child care), some are inherently "high-touch" (nursing), some involve high levels of personal trust (psychotherapy), and some depend on location-specific attributes (lobbying).

However, the dividing line between personal and impersonal services will move over time. As information technology improves, more and more personal services will become impersonal services. No one knows how far this process will go. Forrester Research caused a media stir a few years ago by estimating that 3.3 million U.S. service-sector jobs will move offshore by 2015, a rate of about 300,000 jobs per year. That figure sounds like a lot until you realize that average gross job losses in the U.S. labor market are more than 500,000 in the average week. In fact, given the ample possibilities for technological change in the next decade, 3.3 million seems low. So do the results of a 2003 Berkeley study and a recent McKinsey study, both of which estimated that 11 percent of U.S. jobs are at risk of being offshored. The Berkeley estimate came from tallying up workers in "occupations where at least some [offshoring] has already taken place or is being planned," which means the researchers considered only the currently visible tip of the offshoring iceberg. The future will reveal much more.

To obtain a ballpark figure of the number of U.S. jobs threatened by offshoring, consider the composition of the U.S. labor market at the end of 2004. There were 14.3 million manufacturing jobs. The vast majority of those workers produced items that could be put in a box, and so virtually all of their jobs were potentially movable offshore. About 7.6 million Americans worked in construction and mining. Even though these people produced goods, not services, their jobs were not in danger of moving offshore. (You can't hammer a nail over the Internet.) Next, there were 22 million local, state, and federal government jobs. Even though many of these jobs provide impersonal services that need not be delivered face to face, hardly any are candidates for offshoring -- for obvious political reasons. Retail trade employed 15.6 million Americans. Most of these jobs require physical presence, although online retailing is increasing its share of the market, making a growing share of retail jobs vulnerable to offshoring as well.

Those are the easy cases. But the classification so far leaves out the majority of private-service jobs -- some 73.6 million at the end of 2004. This extremely heterogeneous group breaks down into educational and health services (17.3 million), professional and business services (16.7 million), leisure and hospitality services (12.3 million), financial services (8.1 million), wholesale trade (5.7 million), transportation (4.3 million), information services (3.2 million), utilities (0.6 million), and "other services" (5.4 million). It is hard to divide such broad job categories into personal and impersonal services, and it is even more difficult to know what possibilities for long-distance electronic delivery the future will bring. Still, it is possible to get a rough sense of which of these jobs may be vulnerable to offshoring.

The health sector is currently about five times as large as the educational sector, and the vast majority of services in the health sector seem destined to be delivered in person for a very long time (if not forever). But there are exceptions, such as radiology. More generally, laboratory tests are already outsourced by most physicians. Why not out of the country rather than just out of town? And with a little imagination, one can envision other medical procedures being performed by doctors who are thousands of miles away. Indeed, some surgery has already been performed by robots controlled by doctors via fiber-optic links.

Educational services are also best delivered face to face, but they are becoming increasingly expensive. Electronic delivery will probably never replace personal contact in K-12 education, which is where the vast majority of the educational jobs are. But college teaching is more vulnerable. As college tuition grows ever more expensive, cheap electronic delivery will start looking more and more sensible, if not imperative.

The range of professional- and business-service jobs includes everything from CEOs and architects to typists and janitors -- a heterogeneous lot. That said, in scanning the list of detailed subcategories, it appears that many of these jobs are at least potentially offshorable. For example, future technological developments may dictate how much accounting stays onshore and how much comes to be delivered electronically from countries with much lower wages.

The leisure and hospitality industries seem much safer. If you vacation in Florida, you do not want the beachboy or the maid to be in China. Reservation clerks can be (and are) located anywhere. But on balance, only a few of these jobs can be moved offshore.

Financial services, a sector that includes many highly paid jobs, is another area where the future may look very different from the present. Today, the United States "onshores" more financial jobs (by selling financial services to foreigners) than it offshores. Perhaps that will remain true for years. But improvements in telecommunications and rising educational levels in countries such as China and, especially, India (where many people speak English) may change the status quo dramatically.

Wholesale trade is much like retail trade, but with a bit less personal contact and thus somewhat greater potential for offshoring. The same holds true for transportation and utilities. Information-service jobs, however, are the quintessential types of jobs that can be delivered electronically with ease. The majority of these jobs are at risk. Finally, the phrase "other services" is not very informative, but detailed scrutiny of the list (repair and laundry workers appear, for example) reveals that most of these services require personal delivery.

The overall picture defies generalization, but a rough estimate, based on the preceding numbers, is that the total number of current U.S. service-sector jobs that will be susceptible to offshoring in the electronic future is two to three times the total number of current manufacturing jobs (which is about 14 million). That said, large swaths of the U.S. labor market look to be immune. But, of course, no one knows exactly what technological changes the future will bring.

A DISEASE WITHOUT A CURE

One additional piece of economic analysis will complete the story, and in a somewhat worrisome way. Economists refer to the "cost disease" of the personal services as Baumol's disease, after the economist who discovered it, William Baumol. The problem stems from the fact that in many personal services, productivity improvements are either impossible or highly undesirable. In the "impossible" category, think of how many musician hours it took to play one of Mozart's string quartets in 1790 versus in 1990, or how many bus drivers it takes to get children to school today versus a generation ago. In the "undesirable" category, think of school teachers. Their productivity can be increased rather easily: by raising class size, which squeezes more student output from the same teacher input. But most people view such "productivity improvements" as deteriorations in educational quality, a view that is well supported by research findings. With little room for genuine productivity improvements, and with the general level of real wages rising all the time, personal services are condemned to grow ever more expensive (relative to other items) over time. That is the essence of Baumol's disease.

No such problem besets manufacturing. Over the years, automakers, to take one example, have drastically reduced the number of labor hours it takes to build a car -- a gain in productivity that has not come at the expense of quality. Here once again, impersonal services are more like manufactured goods than personal services. Thanks to stunning advances in telecommunications technology, for example, your telephone company now handles vastly more calls with many fewer human operators than it needed a generation ago. And the quality of telephony has improved, not declined, as its relative price has plummeted.

The prediction of Baumol's disease -- that the prices of personal services (such as education and entertainment) will rise relative to the prices of manufactured goods and impersonal services (such as cars and telephone calls) -- is borne out by history. For example, the theory goes a long way toward explaining why the prices of health care and college tuition have risen faster than the consumer price index for decades.

Constantly rising relative prices have predictable consequences. Demand curves slope downward -- meaning that the demand for an item declines as its relative price rises. Applied in this context, this should mean decreasing relative demand for many personal services and increasing relative demand for many goods and impersonal services over time. The main exceptions are personal services that are strong "luxury goods" (as people get richer, they want relatively more of them) and those few goods and impersonal services that economists call "inferior" (as people get richer, they want fewer of them).

Baumol's disease connects to the offshoring problem in a rather disconcerting way. Changing trade patterns will keep most personal-service jobs at home while many jobs producing goods and impersonal services migrate to the developing world. When you add to that the likelihood that the demand for many of the increasingly costly personal services is destined to shrink relative to the demand for ever-cheaper impersonal services and manufactured goods, rich countries are likely to have some major readjustments to make. One of the adjustments will involve reallocating labor from one industry to another. But another will show up in real wages. As more and more rich-country workers seek employment in personal services, real wages for those jobs are likely to decline, unless the offset from rising demand is strong enough. Thus, the wage prognosis is brighter for luxury personal-service jobs (such as plastic surgery and chauffeuring) than for ordinary personal-service jobs (such as cutting hair and teaching elementary school).

IS FOREWARNED FOREARMED?

What is to be done about all of this? It is easier to describe the broad contours of a solution than to prescribe specific remedies. Indeed, this essay is intended to get as many smart people as possible thinking creatively about the problem.

Most obvious is what to avoid: protectionist barriers against offshoring. Building walls against conventional trade in physical goods is hard enough. Humankind's natural propensity to truck and barter, plus the power of comparative advantage, tends to undermine such efforts -- which not only end in failure but also cause wide-ranging collateral damage. But it is vastly harder (read "impossible") to stop electronic trade. There are just too many "ports" to monitor. The Coast Guard cannot interdict "shipments" of electronic services delivered via the Internet. Governments could probably do a great deal of harm by trying to block such trade, but in the end they would not succeed in repealing the laws of economics, nor in holding back the forces of history. What, then, are some more constructive -- and promising -- approaches to limiting the disruption?

In the first place, rich countries such as the United States will have to reorganize the nature of work to exploit their big advantage in nontradable services: that they are close to where the money is. That will mean, in part, specializing more in the delivery of services where personal presence is either imperative or highly beneficial. Thus, the U.S. work force of the future will likely have more divorce lawyers and fewer attorneys who write routine contracts, more internists and fewer radiologists, more salespeople and fewer typists. The market system is very good at making adjustments like these, even massive ones. It has done so before and will do so again. But it takes time and can move in unpredictable ways. Furthermore, massive transformations in the nature of work tend to bring wrenching social changes in their wake.

In the second place, the United States and other rich nations will have to transform their educational systems so as to prepare workers for the jobs that will actually exist in their societies. Basically, that requires training more workers for personal services and fewer for many impersonal services and manufacturing. But what does that mean, concretely, for how children should be educated? Simply providing more education is probably a good thing on balance, especially if a more educated labor force is a more flexible labor force, one that can cope more readily with nonroutine tasks and occupational change. However, education is far from a panacea, and the examples given earlier show that the rich countries will retain many jobs that require little education. In the future, how children are educated may prove to be more important than how much. But educational specialists have not even begun to think about this problem. They should start right now.

Contrary to what many have come to believe in recent years, people skills may become more valuable than computer skills. The geeks may not inherit the earth after all -- at least not the highly paid geeks in the rich countries. Creativity will be prized. Thomas Friedman has rightly emphasized that it is necessary to steer youth away from tasks that are routine or prone to routinization into work that requires real imagination. Unfortunately, creativity and imagination are notoriously difficult to teach in schools -- although, in this respect, the United States does seem to have a leg up on countries such as Germany and Japan. Moreover, it is hard to imagine that truly creative positions will ever constitute anything close to the majority of jobs. What will everyone else do?

One other important step for rich countries is to rethink the currently inadequate programs for trade adjustment assistance. Up to now, the performance of trade adjustment assistance has been disappointing. As more and more Americans -- and Britons, and Germans, and Japanese -- are faced with the necessity of adjusting to the dislocations caused by offshoring, these programs must become both bigger and better.

Thinking about adjustment assistance more broadly, the United States may have to repair and thicken the tattered safety net that supports workers who fall off the labor-market trapeze -- improving programs ranging from unemployment insurance to job retraining, health insurance, pensions, and right down to public assistance. At present, the United States has one of the thinnest social safety nets in the industrialized world, and there seems to be little if any political force seeking to improve it. But this may change if a larger fraction of the population starts falling into the safety net more often. The corresponding problem for western Europe is different. By U.S. standards, the social safety nets there are broad and deep. The question is, are they affordable, even now? And if so, will they remain affordable if they come to be utilized more heavily?

To repeat, none of this is to suggest that there will be massive unemployment; rather, there will be a massive transition. An effective safety net would ease the pain and, by so doing, speed up the adjustment.

IMPERFECT VISION

Despite all the political sound and fury, little service-sector offshoring has happened to date. But it may eventually amount to a third Industrial Revolution, and industrial revolutions have a way of transforming societies.

That said, the "threat" from offshoring should not be exaggerated. Just as the first Industrial Revolution did not banish agriculture from the rich countries, and the second Industrial Revolution has not banished manufacturing, so the third Industrial Revolution will not drive all impersonal services offshore. Nor will it lead to mass unemployment. But the necessary adjustments will put strains on the societies of the rich countries, which seem completely unprepared for the coming industrial transformation.

Perhaps the most acute need, given the long lead-times, is to figure out how to educate children now for the jobs that will actually be available to them 10 and 20 years from now. Unfortunately, since the distinction between personal services (likely to remain in rich countries) and impersonal services (likely to go) does not correspond to the traditional distinction between high-skilled and low-skilled work, simply providing more education cannot be the whole answer.

As the transition unfolds, the number of people in the rich countries who will feel threatened by foreign job competition will grow enormously. It is predictable that they will become a potent political force in each of their countries. In the United States, job-market stress up to now has been particularly acute for the uneducated and the unskilled, who are less inclined to exercise their political voice and less adept at doing so. But the new cadres of displaced workers, especially those who are drawn from the upper educational reaches, will be neither as passive nor as quiet. They will also be numerous. Open trade may therefore be under great strain.

Large-scale offshoring of impersonal-service jobs from rich countries to poor countries may also bear on the relative economic positions of the United States and Europe. The more flexible, fluid American labor market will probably adapt more quickly and more successfully to dramatic workplace and educational changes than the more rigid European labor markets will.

Contrary to current thinking, Americans, and residents of other English-speaking countries, should be less concerned about the challenge from China, which comes largely in manufacturing, and more concerned about the challenge from India, which comes in services. India is learning to exploit its already strong comparative advantage in English, and that process will continue. The economists Jagdish Bhagwati, Arvind Panagariya, and T. N. Srinivasan meant to reassure Americans when they wrote, "Adding 300 million to the pool of skilled workers in India and China will take some decades." They were probably right. But decades is precisely the time frame that people should be thinking about -- and 300 million people is roughly twice the size of the U.S. work force.

Many other effects of the coming industrial transformation are difficult to predict, or even to imagine. Take one possibility: for decades, it has seemed that modern economic life is characterized by the ever more dehumanized workplace parodied by Charlie Chaplin in Modern Times. The shift to personal services could well reverse that trend for rich countries -- bringing less alienation and greater overall job satisfaction. Alas, the future retains its mystery. But in any case, offshoring will likely prove to be much more than just business as usual.

Alan S. Blinder is Gordon S. Rentschler Memorial Professor of Economics at Princeton University. He served on the White House Council of Economic Advisers from 1993 to 1994 and as Vice Chairman of the Board of Governors of the Federal Reserve from 1994 to 1996.

Globalization and Unemployment

The Downside of Integrating Markets

Michael Spence

REUTERS

Globalization is the process by which markets integrate worldwide. Over the past 60 years, it has accelerated steadily as new technologies and management expertise have reduced transportation and transaction costs and as tariffs and other man-made barriers to international trade have been lowered. The impact has been stunning. More and more developing countries have been experiencing sustained growth rates of 7-10 percent; 13 countries, including China, have grown by more than 7 percent per year for 25 years or more. Although this was unclear at the outset, the world now finds itself just past the midpoint in a century-long process in which income levels in developing countries have been converging toward those in developed countries. Now, the emerging economies' impact on the global economy and the advanced economies is rising rapidly.

Until about a decade ago, the effects of globalization on the distribution of wealth and jobs were largely benign. On average, advanced economies were growing at a respectable rate of 2.5 percent, and in most of them, the breadth and variety of employment opportunities at various levels of education seemed to be increasing. With external help, even the countries ravaged by World War II recovered. Imported goods became cheaper as emerging markets engaged with the global economy, benefiting consumers in both developed and developing countries.

But as the developing countries became larger and richer, their economic structures changed in response to the forces of comparative advantage: they moved up the value-added chain. Now, developing countries increasingly produce the kind of high-value-added components that 30 years ago were the exclusive purview of advanced economies. This climb is a permanent, irreversible change. With China and India -- which together account for almost 40 percent of the world's population -- resolutely moving up this ladder, structural economic changes in emerging countries will only have more impact on the rest of the world in the future.

By relocating some parts of international supply chains, globalization has been affecting the price of goods, job patterns, and wages almost everywhere. It is changing the structure of individual economies in ways that affect different groups within those countries differently. In the advanced economies, it is redistributing employment opportunities and incomes.

For most of the postwar period, U.S. policymakers assumed that growth and employment went hand in hand, and the U.S. economy's performance largely confirmed that assumption. But the structural evolution of the global economy today and its effects on the U.S. economy mean that, for the first time, growth and employment in the United States are starting to diverge. The major emerging economies are becoming more competitive in areas in which the U.S. economy has historically been dominant, such as the design and manufacture of semiconductors, pharmaceuticals, and information technology services.

At the same time, many job opportunities in the United States are shifting away from the sectors that are experiencing the most growth and to those that are experiencing less. The result is growing disparities in income and employment across the U.S. economy, with highly educated workers enjoying more opportunities and workers with less education facing declining employment prospects and stagnant incomes. The U.S. government must urgently develop a long-term policy to address these distributional effects and their structural underpinnings and restore competitiveness and growth to the U.S. economy.

JOBLESS IN THE U.S.

Between 1990 and 2008, the number of employed workers in the United States grew from about 122 million to about 149 million. Of the roughly 27 million jobs created during that period, 98 percent were in the so-called nontradable sector of the economy, the sector that produces goods and services that must be consumed domestically. The largest employers in the U.S. nontradable sector were the government (with 22 million jobs in 2008) and the health-care industry (with 16 million jobs in 2008). Together, the two industries created ten million new jobs between 1990 and 2008, or just under 40 percent of total additions. (The retail, construction, and hotel and restaurant industries also contributed significantly to job growth.) Meanwhile, employment barely grew in the tradable sector of the U.S. economy, the sector that produces goods and services that can be consumed anywhere, such as manufactured products, engineering, and consulting services. That sector, which accounted for more than 34 million jobs in 1990, grew by a negligible 600,000 jobs between 1990 and 2008.

Dramatic, new labor-saving technologies in information services eliminated some jobs across the whole U.S. economy. But employment in the United States has been affected even more by the fact that many manufacturing activities, principally their lower-value-added components, have been moving to emerging economies. This trend is causing employment to fall in virtually all of the U.S. manufacturing sector, except at the high end of the value-added chain. Employment is growing, however, in other parts of the tradable sector -- most prominently, finance, computer design and engineering, and top management at multinational enterprises. Like the top end of the manufacturing chain, these expanding industries and positions generally employ highly educated people, and they are the areas in which the U.S. economy continues to have a comparative advantage and can successfully compete in the global economy.

In other words, the employment structure of the U.S. economy has been shifting away from the tradable sector, except for the upper end of the value-added chain, and toward the nontradable sector. This is a problem, because the nontradable sector is likely to generate fewer jobs than is expected of it in the future. Moreover, the range of employment opportunities available in the tradable sector is declining, which is limiting choices for U.S. workers in the middle-income bracket. It would be unwise to assume that under present circumstances, employment in the government and health care in the United States will continue to grow as much as it had been growing before the recent economic crisis. If anything, it is remarkable that the U.S. economy did not have much of an employment problem until the recent economic crisis. If the nontradable sector continues to lose its capacity to absorb labor, as it has in recent years, and the tradable sector does not become an employment engine, the United States should brace itself for a long period of high unemployment.

FOR WHAT IT'S WORTH

One way to measure the size of a company, industry, or economy is to determine its output. But a better way is to determine its added value -- namely, the difference between the value of its outputs, that is, the goods and services it produces, and the costs of its inputs, such as the raw materials and energy it consumes. (Value added comes from the capital and labor that turn the inputs into outputs.) Goods and services themselves are often purchased as intermediate inputs by other companies or industries, legal services purchased by a corporation being one example. The value added produced by all the industries in all the sectors of an economy adds up to that country's GDP.

Unlike employment, value added in the tradable and nontradable parts of the U.S. economy has increased at a similar rate since 1990. In the nontradable sector, which experienced rapid employment growth, this means that value added grew slightly faster than employment: value added per employee increased modestly, by an annual average of 0.7 percent since 1990. On the tradable side of the U.S. economy, where employment levels barely increased, both value added overall and value added per employee rose very swiftly as the U.S. tradable sector moved up the value-added chain and grew in sync with the global economy. Whereas in the nontradable sector, value added per employee grew from $72,000 to over $80,000 between 1990 and 2008, in the tradable sector it grew from $79,000 to $120,000 -- in other words, it grew by just about 12 percent in the nontradable sector but by close to 52 percent in the tradable sector.

Most striking are the trends within the tradable sector. Value added rose across that sector, including in finance, where employment increased, and in manufacturing industries, where employment mostly declined. In fact, at the upper end of the manufacturing chain, value added increased so much that it outweighed the losses at the lower end caused by the movement of economic activity from the United States to other countries.

Value added represents income for someone. For employed people, it means personal income; for shareholders and other owners of capital, profit or returns on investment; for the government, tax revenues. Generally, the incomes of workers are closely correlated with value added per employee (this is not the case in the mining industry and utilities, however, where value added per employee is much higher than wages because these activities are very capital intensive and most value added is a return on capital). Since value added in the nontradable part of the U.S. economy did not rise much, neither did average incomes in that sector. In the tradable sector, on the other hand, incomes rose rapidly along with value added per employee thanks both to rising productivity gains in some industries and the movement of lower-income jobs to other countries. And since most new jobs were created in the nontradable part of the economy, in which wages grew little, the distribution of income in the U.S. economy became more uneven.

The overall picture is clear: employment opportunities and incomes are high, and rising, for the highly educated people at the upper end of the tradable sector of the U.S. economy, but they are diminishing at the lower end. And there is every reason to believe that these trends will continue. As emerging economies continue to move up the value-added chain -- and they must in order to keep growing -- the tradable sectors of advanced economies will require less labor and the more labor-intensive tasks will shift to emerging economies.

Highly educated U.S. workers are already gravitating toward the high-value-added parts of the U.S. economy, particularly in the tradable sector. As labor economists have noted, the return on education is rising. The highly educated, and only them, are enjoying more job opportunities and higher incomes. Competition for highly educated workers in the tradable sector spills over to the nontradable sector, raising incomes in the high-value-added part of that sector as well. But with fewer jobs in the lower-value-added part of the tradable sector, competition for similar jobs in the nontradable sector is increasing. This, in turn, further depresses income growth in the lower-value-added part of the nontradable sector.

Thus, the evolving structure of the global economy has diverse effects on different groups of people in the United States. Opportunities are expanding for the highly educated throughout the economy: they are expanding in the tradable sector because the global economy is growing and in the nontradable sector because that job market must remain competitive with the tradable sector. But opportunities are shrinking for the less well educated.

Faced with an undesirable economic outcome, economists tend to assume that its cause is a market failure. Market failures come in many forms, from inefficiencies caused by information gaps to the unpriced impacts of externalities such as the environment. But the effects on the U.S. economy of the global economy's structural evolution is not a market failure: it is not an economically inefficient outcome. (If anything, the global economy is generally becoming more efficient.) But it is nonetheless a cause for concern in that it is creating a distributional problem in the advanced economies. Not everyone is gaining in those countries, and some may be losing.

Although everyone does benefit from lower-priced goods and services, people also care greatly about the chance to be productively employed and the quality of their work. Declining employment opportunities feel real and immediate; the rise in real incomes brought by lower prices does not. For example, according to recent surveys, a substantial number of Americans believe that their children will have fewer opportunities than they have had. The slow recovery from the recent economic crisis may be affecting these perceptions, which means that they might dissipate as the situation improves and growth returns. But the long-term structural evolution of the U.S. and global economies suggests that distributional issues will remain. These must be taken seriously.

MAKING IT WORK

Analysts have been quick to point out that not all the structural changes under way in the U.S. economy should be attributed to greater openness in the global economy. Some important changes in employment patterns and income distribution are the result of labor-saving information technology and the automation of transactions. Automation has undoubtedly cut jobs in the information- and transaction-intensive parts of value-added chains throughout the U.S. economy, in both the tradable and the nontradable sectors. But if that were the only trend, why would employment decline so much more in manufacturing than in other industries?

One answer might be that information processing and automation occupy a more significant fraction of the value-added chain in manufacturing. But this is not true.

Information-processing technology, for example, has eliminated jobs throughout the U.S. economy, including in finance, retail, and the government -- all areas in which employment has grown. The structural trends affecting the U.S. economy cannot be explained by changes in technology alone. To think otherwise tends to yield the misleading conclusions that technology, not the global economy, is the principal cause of the United States' employment challenge and that the most important forces operating on the structure of the U.S. economy are internal, not external. In fact, all these factors are relevant, with some more significant in some sectors of the economy than in others.

If giving technology as the preferred explanation for the U.S. economy's distributional problems is a way to ignore the structural changes of the global economy, invoking multinational companies (MNCs) as the preferred explanation is a way to overstate their impact. MNCs are said to underpay and otherwise exploit poor people in developing countries, exporting jobs that should have stayed in the United States.

MNCs do, indeed, play a central role in managing the evolution of the global economy. They are the principal architects of global supply chains, and they move the production of goods and services around the world in response to supply-chain and market opportunities that are constantly changing. MNCs have generated growth and jobs in developing countries, and by moving to those countries some lower-value-added parts of their supply chains, they have increased growth and competitiveness in advanced economies such as the United States. A June 2010 report by the McKinsey Global Institute estimated that U.S.-based MNCs accounted for 31 percent of GDP growth in the United States since 1990.

With ample labor available in various skill and educational categories throughout the tradable sector globally, companies have little incentive to invest in technologies that save on labor or otherwise increase the competitiveness of the labor-intensive value-added activities in advanced economies. In short, companies' private interest (profit) and the public's interest (employment) do not align perfectly. These conditions might not last: if growth continues to be high in emerging economies, in two or three decades there will be less cheap labor available there. But two or three decades is a long time.

In the meantime, even though public and private interests are not perfectly aligned today, they are not perfectly opposed either. Relatively modest shifts at the margin could bring them back in sync. Given the enormous size of the global labor force, the dial would not need to be moved very much to restore employment growth in the tradable sector of the U.S. economy. Specifically, the right combination of productivity-enhancing technology and competitive wage levels could keep some manufacturing industries, or at least some value-added pieces of their production chains, in the United States and other advanced countries. But accomplishing this will require more than a decision from the market; it must also involve labor, business, and governments. Germany, for one, has managed to retain its advanced manufacturing activities in industrial machinery by removing rigidities in the labor market and making a conscious effort to privilege employment over rapid rises in incomes. Wages may have increased only modestly in Germany over the past decade, but income inequality is markedly flatter there than in the United States, where it is higher than in most other industrial countries and rising steadily.

Conditioning access to the domestic market on domestic production is a form of protectionism and a way to try to limit the movement out of the country of jobs and of value-added components in the supply chain. This is more common than might be supposed. It exists in the aerospace industry; and in the 1970s and 1980s, in the car industry, quotas on Japanese imports to the United States led to an expansion of the manufacture of Japanese cars in the United States. However, if the large economies -- such as China, the European Union, Japan, or the United States -- pursue protectionist measures on a broad front, the global economy will be undermined. Yet that may be exactly what happens if employment challenges such as the ones affecting the United States are not tackled differently. With pressure on government budgets at all levels, rapidly rising health-care costs, a fragile housing market, the postcrisis effort to curb excess consumption and boost savings, and the risk of a second economic downturn, it is highly unlikely that net employment in the nontradable sector of the U.S. economy will continue to grow as rapidly as it has been.

The drop in domestic consumption in the United States has left the country with a shortage of aggregate demand. More public-sector investment would help, but the fiscal consolidation currently under way may make expanding government investment difficult. Meanwhile, because private-sector investment responds to demand and currently there is a shortfall in demand caused by the economic crisis and increased savings by households, such investment will not return until domestic consumption or exports increase. Therefore, the United States will need to focus on increasing job growth in the tradable sector. Some growth will naturally come from the high-value-added part of that sector. The question is whether there will be enough growth and whether the educational attainment of U.S. workers will keep pace with rising job requirements at that level. There are reasons to be skeptical.

THE BIG TRADEOFF

It is a common view that the market will solve the disparities in employment and incomes once the economic crisis recedes and growth is restored. Warren Buffet and other very smart, experienced, and influential opinion-makers say so clearly. But as this analysis suggests, they may not be right. And as long as their view dominates U.S. public policy and opinion, it will be difficult to address the issues related to structural change and employment in the United States in a systematic way.

What is needed instead of benign neglect is, first, an agreement that restoring rewarding employment opportunities for a full spectrum of Americans should be a fundamental goal. With that objective as a starting point, it will then be necessary to develop ways to increase both the competitiveness and the inclusiveness of the U.S. economy. This is largely uncharted territory: distributional issues are difficult to solve because they require correcting outcomes on the global market without doing too much damage to its efficiency and openness. But admitting that not all the answers are known is a good place to begin.

With considerable uncertainty about the efficacy of various policy options, a multistakeholder, multipronged approach to addressing these distributional problems is best. The relevant knowledge about promising new technologies and market opportunities is dispersed among business, the government, labor, and universities, and it needs to be assembled and turned into initiatives. President Barack Obama has already appointed a commission, led by Jeffrey Immelt, the CEO of General Electric, to focus on competitiveness and employment issues in the U.S. economy. This is an important step forward. But it will be hugely difficult to invest in human capital, technology, and infrastructure as much as is necessary at a time of fiscal distress and declining government employment. And yet restoring opportunities for future generations requires making sacrifices in the present.

Given the structural changes under way in the U.S. economy - - especially the growing premium on highly educated workers at the top end of the value-added chain -- education should be boosted. As many people as possible should be able to compete in that part of the economy. But if this goal is clear, the ways to achieve it are less so. Improving the performance of the educational system has been a priority for some years, yet the results are in doubt. For example, the Organization for Economic Cooperation and Development administers a set of standardized tests, the Program for International Student Assessment, across more than 60 countries, advanced and developing, to measure the cognitive skills of teenage students. The United States ranks close to the average in reading and science and well behind most countries in math.

The problems in the quality and effectiveness of parts of the U.S. educational system have been recognized for some time. Numerous attempts to improve matters, including administering national standardized tests and providing merit-based compensation, have thus far yielded inconclusive results. And the problem extends beyond the school system. A lack of commitment to education in families and in communities makes the entire field of education seem unattractive, demoralizing dedicated teachers and turning off talented students from teaching. That, in turn, reduces the incentives of communities to value the primacy of education. To break this pattern, it will be necessary to shift communities' -- and the country's -- values about education through moral leadership, at both the community and the national levels. Creating attractive employment opportunities conditional on educational success is another important incentive. One comes full circle, in other words: increased educational effectiveness is needed for the United States to be competitive, and the promise of rewarding employment is a necessary incentive for committing to improving education.

As important as education is, it cannot be the whole solution; the United States will not educate its way out of its problems. Both the federal and state governments must pursue complementary lines of attack. They should invest in infrastructure, which would create jobs in the short term and raise the return on private-sector investment in the medium to longer term. They should also invest in technologies that could expand employment opportunities in the tradable sector of the U.S.

economy at income levels other than the very top. The private sector will have to help guide these investments because it has much of the relevant knowledge about where these opportunities might lie. But this effort will also require the participation of the public sector. The U.S. government already invests heavily in science and technology but not with job creation as its primary focus; that has generally been viewed only as a beneficial side effect. It is time to devote public funding to developing infrastructure and the technological base of the U.S. economy with the specific goal of restoring competitiveness and expanding employment in the tradable sector.

The tax structure also needs to be reformed. It should be simplified and reconfigured to promote competitiveness, investment, and employment. And both loopholes and distorting incentives should be eliminated. For example, corporate tax rates and tax rates on investment returns should be lowered in order to make the United States more attractive for business and investment. MNCs with earnings outside the United States currently have a strong incentive to keep their earnings abroad and reinvest them abroad because earnings are taxed both where they are earned and also in the United States if they are repatriated. Lower tax rates would mean a loss in revenue for the U.S. government, but that could be replaced by taxes on consumption, which would have the added benefit of helping shift the composition of demand from domestic to foreign -- a necessary move if the United States wants to avoid high unemployment and an unsustainable current account deficit.

But even these measures may not be sufficient. Globalization has redefined the competition for employment and incomes in the United States. Tradeoffs will have to be made between the two. Germany clearly chose to protect employment in the industries of its tradable sector that came under competitive threat. Now, U.S. policymakers must choose, too.

Some will argue that global market forces should simply be allowed to operate without interference. Tampering with market outcomes, the argument goes, risks distorting incentives and reducing efficiency and innovation. But this is not the only approach, nor is it the best one. The distribution of income across many advanced economies (and major emerging economies) differs markedly. For example, the ratio of the average income of the top 20 percent of the population to the average income of the bottom 20 percent is four to one in Germany and eight to one in the United States. Many other advanced countries have flatter income distributions than the United States, suggesting that tradeoffs between market forces and equity are possible. The U.S. government needs to face up to them.

EXPERIMENTING THE WAY FORWARD

The massive changes in the global economy since World War II have had overwhelmingly positive effects. Hundreds of millions of people in the developing world have escaped poverty, and more will in the future. The global economy will continue to grow -- probably at least threefold over the next 30 years. One person's gain is not necessarily another's loss; global growth is not even close to a zero-sum game. But globalization hurts some subgroups within some countries, including the advanced economies.

The late American economist Paul Samuelson once said, "Every good cause is worth some inefficiency." Surely, equity and social cohesion are among them. The challenge for the U.S. economy will be to find a place in the rapidly evolving global economy that retains its dynamism and openness while providing all Americans with rewarding employment opportunities and a reasonable degree of equity. This is not a problem to which there are easy answers. As the issue becomes more pressing, ideology and orthodoxy must be set aside, and creativity, flexibility, and pragmatism must be encouraged. The United States will not be able to deduce its way toward the solutions; it will have to experiment its way forward.

MICHAEL SPENCE is Distinguished Visiting Fellow at the Council on Foreign Relations and the author of The Next Convergence: The Future of Economic Growth in a Multispeed World. He received the Nobel Prize in Economics in 2001. His Web site is www.thenextconvergence.com.

After Doha

Why the Negotiations Are Doomed and What We Should Do About It

Susan C. Schwab

COURTESY REUTERS

It is time for the international community to recognize that the Doha Round is doomed. Started in November 2001 as the ninth multilateral trade negotiation under the auspices of the General Agreement on Tariffs and Trade and its successor, the World Trade Organization (WTO), the talks have sought to promote economic growth and improve living standards across the globe -- especially in developing countries -- through trade liberalization and reforms. Yet after countless attempts to achieve a resolution, the talks have dragged on into their tenth year, with no end in sight.

To be sure, world leaders, negotiators, and commentators have expressed their unanimous support for a successful outcome -- the "balanced" and "ambitious" agreement called for by so many summit statements. But concluding a trade agreement is like pole-vaulting. Everything must come together at once -- after the extensive preparation and the building of momentum, there is that one giant leap -- with the hope that the entire body will sail over the bar. Most trade agreements survive several failed attempts before success is achieved. But the Doha Round keeps crashing into the bar.

To a significant degree, Doha's failure can be traced to its outdated structure and negotiating dynamic: even the best of intentions are stymied when every negotiator's concessions are more clear than their potential gains and when the bipolar division between developed and developing countries shortchanges most in the developing world. More fundamental, however, has been the Doha Round's failure to address the central question facing international economic governance today: What are the relative roles and responsibilities of advanced (or developed), emerging, and developing countries? (Although there are no universally recognized definitions, advanced countries are generally mature economies that have industrialized and attained high levels of per capita income. Emerging-market economies are those that are undergoing rapid rates of growth and industrialization but have not yet reached developed status. Developing countries have not yet experienced these transitions.) World leaders are frustrated that their mandates to negotiators have failed to translate into a successful conclusion to the round. Meanwhile, the negotiators either cannot or prefer not to admit that Doha's flaws will prevent them from closing the deal, let alone ever addressing that fundamental question.

What this means, simply, is that it is time to give up on trying to "save" Doha. For years, the threat of being blamed for the Doha Round's collapse has made it too risky for governments to suggest that the talks are dead. Negotiators obsess over how to keep the dead cat from landing on their doorstep. But the pretense that the deal will somehow come together at long last is now a greater threat to the multilateral trading system than acknowledging the truth: prolonging the Doha process will only jeopardize the multilateral trading system and threaten future prospects for WTO-led liberalization and reform.

To avoid that outcome, negotiators should salvage any partial agreements they can from the round and walk away from the rest. World leaders and trade policymakers should then immediately redirect all the energy, initiative, and frequent-flier miles devoted to Doha into launching new multilateral initiatives to restore trust in the WTO and preserve it as a dynamic venue for both improving and enforcing the rules governing international trade.

DEFINING SUCCESS

The initial meetings that led to the Doha Round stumbled before the process could get started, signified by the failed 1999 WTO ministerial summit in Seattle. When the Doha Round finally began in the wake of September 11, 2001, negotiators continued to disagree over its objectives and how to achieve them.

The use of trade liberalization and reform to generate economic growth and help alleviate poverty formed the core of the initiative. Negotiators initially identified 21 subjects for negotiation, including reductions in agricultural trade barriers, the elimination of agricultural export subsidies, cuts in trade-distorting domestic subsidies, major improvements in market access for manufactured goods, and more open trade in services. Although economists have shown that countries would benefit from undertaking such actions unilaterally, most political leaders and negotiators would prefer to trade their own country's market reforms for better access elsewhere.

Participants originally scheduled the Doha talks to end by early 2005, in time for the Bush administration to use trade promotion authority (TPA), which was set to expire in June 2007, to gain approval of the agreement. TPA is a fast-track mechanism for trade agreements, under which the executive branch commits to extensive consultations with Congress and the range of relevant U.S. constituencies during trade negotiations in exchange for Congress' agreement to employ procedural rules that move bills through the process faster, ban potentially deal-killing amendments, and mandate timely up-or-down votes. But the talks collapsed in 2003 in Cancún, Mexico, when a bloc of emerging and developing countries expressed their displeasure over a perceived European Union and U.S. effort to impose excessive burdens on them in the form of new issues and obligations. Revived with the 2004 Framework Agreement, which finally established the round's negotiating parameters, the talks stumbled through a December 2005 ministerial meeting in Hong Kong and suffered further breakdowns at gatherings of trade ministers in 2006, 2007, and 2008.

As the many summits and negotiating sessions held over the last decade can attest, Doha's failure does not owe to any lack of effort. Former U.S. President George W. Bush attended easily over a hundred such gatherings with foreign leaders and his advisers during the second half of his tenure alone. He made concluding the Doha Round his top trade priority, capping an active and successful trade agenda that secured comprehensive free-trade agreements with 17 countries in Asia, Latin America, and the Middle East.

The Bush administration identified three criteria to define success in the Doha Round. First and foremost, any outcome had to contribute to global economic growth and development through the generation of new trade flows, especially between and among emerging and developing economies. With these economies together representing close to half the world's GDP and registering twice the growth rate of the developed world, the administration decided that negotiators could not meet Doha's growth and poverty-alleviation objectives without reducing emerging-market tariffs and nontariff barriers.

Second, the administration resolved that the final agreement should increase market opportunities for U.S. exports of farm products, manufactured goods, and services -- particularly in high-potential, high-growth markets such as Brazil, China, and India. Finally, the administration believed that any Doha agreement should avoid contributing to the growth of economic isolationism, whether in the United States or elsewhere.

ELEPHANTS HIDING BEHIND MICE

When the negotiations collapsed again in the summer of 2008, none of the administration's criteria had been met. From almost the start of the negotiations, the rapidly evolving nature of the global economy had rendered Doha's dichotomy between developed and developing countries outdated and its negotiating structure obsolete. And even as it became obvious over the decade that emerging economies had become a dominant force in global economic growth and trade, those nations' perceptions of their consequent needs and responsibilities had failed to keep pace.

As they currently stand, Doha's negotiating texts create two main categories of obligations -- one applying to the developed economies and another applying to those characterized as developing countries, which make up the majority of the WTO's members. In fact, over two-thirds of the countries in the "developing" category have special breaks built into their obligations, so that their obligations are dramatically less than even those of the countries meeting the official developing-country criteria. These include groups such as those designated as "least-developed countries" and "small and vulnerable economies." To the extent that nations such as Brazil, China, India, and South Africa have taken positions against further market opening in the name of developing countries, they are actually taking positions that go against the group's interests.

At Doha, these emerging economies have minimized their own difficult market-opening decisions by seeking maximum flexibility for developing countries. And they have found it easier to avoid confronting their own needs for greater access to one another's markets by focusing on what they can all agree on -- namely, the market-opening obligations of developed countries. The result is what one African ambassador to the WTO once described as "the elephants hiding behind the mice."

A number of emerging and developing economies -- among them Chile, Colombia, Costa Rica, Hong Kong, Malaysia, Pakistan, and Singapore -- have attempted to advocate for more ambitious emerging-market contributions. Yet these countries have been either ignored or harshly criticized by their peers, particularly Brazil, India, and South Africa. Even when Brazil attempted to break with other developing countries to save the Doha Round in the summer of 2008, it found itself the target of the same kind of criticism it periodically levels against others.

The dilemma facing China's negotiators has been particularly acute. China's manufacturing prowess and export drive are a phenomenon never before encountered in a major trade round, and fear of increased imports from China may be the most unacknowledged reason behind Doha's continued failures. Although Beijing stands to gain tremendously from a successful Doha Round, internal critics resist liberalization by pointing to the significant market opening that the country undertook when it joined the WTO in 2001 as yet another unequal treaty imposed by foreign powers. Combined, these factors have made it difficult for Beijing to break with the other major emerging markets in Doha -- even if it might have meant saving the round.

The developed-versus-developing-country framework itself is increasingly anachronistic. China's GDP has already overtaken that of Japan and will likely have exceeded that of the United States before any Doha agreement can be fully implemented. Meanwhile, the International Monetary Fund predicts that by mid-decade, in terms of GDP, India will have exceeded Germany, Brazil will have outpaced France and the United Kingdom, Mexico will have passed Canada, and Indonesia and Turkey will have superseded Australia.

To be sure, advanced economies should shoulder a somewhat heavier share of the burden of any multilateral economic agreement, making their contributions consistent with their more dominant positions in the global economy. After all, even when China's GDP reaches U.S. levels, Chinese citizens will still have just about a third of the yearly income of their U.S. counterparts, and Indians are likely to have one third of that. But the size and growth trajectories of the emerging economies, combined with the fact that some are now leading producers and exporters in key sectors, such as chemicals, information technology, car parts, pharmaceuticals, and environmental goods, set them apart. The inability of Doha's structure and negotiating dynamic to reflect this evolution has helped ensure its downfall.

DOHA'S OBSTACLES

The lumping together of all emerging and developing economies in the Doha negotiating structure, and the associated peer pressure, has given leverage in the talks to those emerging economies disinclined to open their markets and taken it away from those advanced, emerging, and developing countries that might have backed a more ambitious outcome to the round.

In addition, the negotiations' heavy emphasis on rigid formulas for tariff cuts, rather than a looser combination of targets and negotiations over specific openings, has generated "formula and flex" models that undermine both the negotiating dynamic and any potential outcome. This is most evident in the proposed texts associated with the failed July 2008 ministerial gathering in Geneva. Although the formulas appropriately target the highest tariffs for the greatest cuts and place the most significant burden on the developed countries, the developing countries enjoy far shallower cuts and slower implementation. Also, the developing countries have significant flexibilities in the form of exclusions from the formula cuts that they insist on selecting themselves rather than negotiating.

For manufactured goods, these proposals would, by the end of the Doha implementation period, allow the tariffs of most emerging economies, other than China and South Africa, to remain largely unchanged from those in place when the Doha Round began. Based on 2008 calculations, this would result in the developed economies' delivering over three-quarters of the Doha Round's market-opening results, well beyond their current 53 percent (and shrinking) share of global GDP.

The framework has also posed problems when it comes to agricultural trade. The current proposals task the developed countries with eliminating export subsidies, cutting trade-distorting domestic subsidies, and reducing tariff and nontariff barriers to imports. The developing countries are also obligated to reduce trade barriers, albeit to a lesser extent. But although exceptions to the formula cuts enable both the developed and the developing countries to protect some items, the extreme flexibilities given to the developing economies will again enable the emerging economies to negate the bulk of their formula cuts. The 2008 package, for example, would allow India to shield close to 90 percent of its current agricultural trade from tariff cuts and permit China to exclude from the cuts commodities of keen interest to both developing and developed countries, including corn, cotton, sugar, rice, and wheat. Moreover, a proposed new agricultural safeguard for the emerging and developing countries anticipated in the agreement raises the prospect that trade barriers in those countries could actually end up being higher than before the Doha talks started.

In an effort to move the Doha Round forward, the WTO leadership has worked to establish key agreement parameters through draft texts. These texts have progressively narrowed and in some cases precluded the negotiation of specific and substantive product concessions -- trapping participants in almost a decade of negotiations about negotiations. In fact, the combination in the framework of rigid formulas and ill-defined, largely nonnegotiable flexibilities put all the negotiators in a defensive posture from the outset, left to assume that their own import-sensitive constituencies would face severe tariff cuts but unable to point to the kind of concrete gains in market access necessary to build domestic support for the trade talks. Finally, the dramatic imbalance in the negotiating flexibilities available to the emerging economies as opposed to the advanced economies has left both sides with little room to maneuver. Even if the emerging countries wanted to put more on the table, their offers today would look like unilateral concessions, since the developed countries have nothing of perceived value left to concede in return.

The uneven negotiating field is not the only structural roadblock that has undermined the negotiations. Multilateral trade talks have traditionally called for the United States and fellow developed countries to take the lead in offering concessions to jump-start flagging negotiations -- the idea being that a significant unilateral initiative by a large economy will encourage others to reciprocate, thus paying dividends to all. Yet during the Doha Round, such efforts by the United States -- even those explicitly conditioned on a meaningful response -- have not been met in kind. And as time has passed, U.S. and EU compromises have effectively been pocketed, forming the base line for the next set of demands.

The challenges posed by the negotiating structure are compounded by the fact that Doha mandates a single undertaking. This means that nothing is considered agreed until everything is agreed. This rule was designed to encourage countries to make tough calls in one sector knowing that they would be able to show gains in other sectors. However, in the context of Doha, the rule has enabled individual countries to play the spoiler and seek lowest-common-denominator outcomes or to free-ride on others' concessions.

The passage of time has also defeated the Doha Round. Over the years, political and economic windows for a deal have opened and closed. The 2007 expiration of TPA undermined the willingness of U.S. trading partners to take risks because they no longer knew whether the U.S. Congress would attempt to amend the negotiated commitments. Domestic political concerns in India prior to the country's 2009 elections likely destroyed any potential for a deal in 2008. Brazil has retreated to a defensive crouch when it comes to market access for industrial goods, citing the threat of currency appreciation and Chinese imports. Japan's frequent shifts in government this past decade have undermined its ability to negotiate. EU member states continue to expend the bulk of their negotiating capital on internal debates about reform, leaving little room for dealing at Doha. And China faces a 2012 leadership transition that appears to have solidified its unwillingness to take risks.

RISKS TO THE MULTILATERAL SYSTEM

Despite all these problems, it is far too soon to give up on multilateral agreements and the global trading system. If any more evidence were needed to demonstrate the WTO's critical importance to the world economy, one need look no further than the recent global financial crisis. Although countries took protectionist measures in the wake of the crisis, the international community avoided a quick deterioration into a spiral of beggar-thy-neighbor actions to block imports. Previous multilateral agreements that reduced permitted tariff levels, WTO-consistent escape valves and enforcement opportunities, and a high-profile G-20 commitment to avoid discriminatory trade actions helped ensure this outcome. The fact that the independent policy research think tank Global Trade Alert began publishing lists of G-20 trade-pledge violations certainly helped as well.

But with the exception of limiting some of the WTO-consistent tariff increases by emerging countries, the Doha Round agreement currently under negotiation would not have precluded most of the discriminatory actions taken. Similarly, the fact that the Doha Round is still officially in progress has failed to stem the proliferation of low-quality bilateral and regional trade agreements. The number of such agreements in place has doubled to over 200 worldwide since the Doha talks began, with hundreds still in negotiation. They are of uneven quality. Some, such as those negotiated by the Bush administration, eliminate virtually all barriers between signatory countries, while others exclude whole swaths of commerce. Yet they all exclude, and therefore discriminate against, the vast majority of other trading nations, including most developing countries. And they skew commerce and global supply chains through complex rules that dictate how much of a product must be made in a given location to qualify for duty-free treatment.

Although the countries with which the United States has negotiated bilateral and regional trade agreements have almost uniformly advocated for an ambitious conclusion to the Doha talks, the negotiation of often lower-quality bilateral and regional trade agreements has eroded support and political will for the pursuit of a strong multilateral deal among other countries. A robust multilateral trade agreement, involving the vast majority of trading countries, can contribute far more to global economic growth and welfare than even the best bilateral and regional trade agreements. Such an agreement can better address systemic challenges such as subsidies and enjoy the potential to achieve significantly more international market opening, as countries can point to a whole world of new market opportunities gained in exchange for their own concessions.

Granted, the phenomenon of bilateral and regional trade agreements has been the result in part of a vicious cycle. Countries have pursued these agreements because Doha is faltering and bilateral and regional agreements can deliver commercial results; Doha is faltering in part because some countries think they can avoid difficult decisions by opting for easier bilateral or regional talks instead. But as the Doha talks meander, the international community may be reaching a tipping point, where the pursuit of these lesser agreements becomes the preferred option.

ONE LAST TRY?

Even if, in the interest of saving the Doha Round, key emerging economies were inclined to liberalize their markets well beyond what the 2008 proposals explicitly mandate, the current negotiating structure and peer pressure would make doing so exceedingly difficult, if not impossible. But any attempt to salvage Doha on the basis of those proposals would still raise questions about its ultimate benefit -- both in absolute terms and in terms of opportunity costs -- if this is the deal that is to set the global terms of trade for the next two decades or more.

Gary Hufbauer, Jeffrey Schott, and Woan Foong Wong of the Peterson Institute for International Economics estimated in June 2010 that implementing the formula cuts under consideration when the talks collapsed in July 2008 would increase world GDP by $63 billion, or 0.1 percent. This would result from an increase in global trade of $183 billion, an amount less than half the value of U.S. trade with Canada in a single year. The Peterson Institute study then calculated the potential value of a major boost to the 2008 proposals, including additional tariff cuts in certain key industrial sectors, a ten percent reduction in barriers to services trade, and a successful conclusion of the trade facilitation negotiation. The study estimated that these measures -- unlikely to occur in the first place -- would raise global GDP by around $283 billion, or 0.5 percent. The trade gains, slightly higher than the value of U.S. trade with Canada and Mexico in 2009, would require at least a decade to be phased in.

In fact, the only readily measurable benefits of the plan currently on the table come from developed-country tariff cuts, since it remains unclear how emerging economies would choose to allocate their flexibilities. Indeed, the 2008 proposals' potential commercial benefits would come primarily from tariff savings in mature-country markets, rather than from any meaningful increase in new trade flows in the fastest-growing economies.

To even approach the more optimistic projections of what a successful Doha agreement might contain would require upending the present structure to generate negotiations based on substance and specifics. Not all 153 WTO members would have to increase their commitments. But ultimately, to generate real value for all participants, greater concessions from a dozen or so emerging countries would make a difference.

In the case of manufactured goods, creating a negotiation in which the advanced and the emerging countries both had greater flexibility to cut their tariffs more or less than the levels currently dictated by the formulas would move the process forward. In agriculture, the negotiations should only permit new safeguards if they are limited to temporary responses to damaging import surges. And with regard to market access, the emerging economies would have to accept fewer flexibilities. The developed countries could improve their offers on domestic farm support, but the past ten years have made it clear that cuts to agricultural subsidies deliver little in the way of new agricultural- or industrial-market access. Finally, participants would need to engage in a far more serious negotiation about services than anything contemplated to date.

Variations on these and other ideas, designed to prompt real negotiations over specific trade barriers so as to build momentum and pro-agreement constituencies, have thus far failed to gain traction. As long as the current negotiating dynamic remains, there is little reason for influential countries such as Brazil, China, India, Indonesia, and South Africa to surrender their favorable negotiating positions and risk attack from one another for breaking developing-country solidarity.

HOW TO MOVE FORWARD

The only way for world leaders to advance a healthy multilateral trading system now is to liberate themselves from the stranglehold of the Doha Round. Another series of draft proposals is not the answer.

Participants must close out the Doha Round in 2011. With leadership and goodwill, several smaller agreements could be salvaged from the existing negotiations. A top candidate for rescue is the trade facilitation package, the subject of a serious negotiation among the advanced, emerging, and developing economies. The package would reduce the costs associated with moving goods across borders, and the Peterson Institute has estimated that it could contribute over $100 billion to global GDP.

Other areas that might potentially be saved include the largely completed agricultural-export pillar, comprising proposed agreements on export credits, food aid, state-trading firms, and the elimination of export subsidies. Negotiators should also endeavor to complete two environment-related agreements, one cutting subsidies to industrial fishing fleets guilty of overfishing the world's oceans and the other ending tariff and nontariff barriers to "green" technologies in major producing and consuming countries.

These smaller elements of the Doha undertaking would deliver tangible near-term results. In theory, world leaders could instruct that they be spun off and concluded this year. In practice, it is possible that in the current environment, not even these smaller deals can be achieved. But it is worth trying, because the Doha Round certainly has not delivered them. And if the effort is made and then blocked, at least the media can shine a spotlight on the spoilers.

Above all, world leaders should not wait to determine whether they can conclude these before laying the groundwork to launch a new series of multilateral negotiations under WTO auspices. The large multilateral trade round format epitomized by Doha's predecessors need not be obsolete, but WTO members will need a clean break from the current round to reestablish trust and regain momentum before attempting that model again. More narrowly drawn negotiations and small deals with some commercial value may offer the best near-term approach.

One obvious avenue would be to expand the product coverage in the plurilateral Information Technology Agreement, through which every major producer and consumer in the world of information technology products, save for Brazil, has eliminated their tariffs. Nations could initiate a similar multiparty accord for a package that includes pharmaceuticals, medical equipment, and health-care services, designed to reduce the cost of delivering health care. Such negotiations would have to follow WTO rules, and the outcome would have to apply equally to all WTO members, regardless of whether they took part in the negotiations. Yet veto power over any given deal would be granted only to those members who chose to negotiate and contribute, improving the chances of constructive engagement by most interested parties.

The international community could also draw from some of the more practical or innovative elements of existing bilateral or multiparty agreements and seek to multilateralize them. These might include provisions governing investment, transparency, e-commerce, services that contribute to entrepreneurial infrastructure, or even enhanced WTO intellectual property protections. WTO members could also commit to results-based business practice reforms, addressing such international indices as the World Bank's Ease of Doing Business Index and Transparency International's Corruption Perceptions Index.

To reduce some of the negative effects of bilateral and regional trade deals, WTO members might consider guidelines to ensure that such agreements have built-in docking provisions that allow like-minded countries to join them. Meanwhile, interested members should consider using focused WTO cases and dispute settlements to target poor-quality bilateral and regional trade agreements that fail to meet the letter and spirit of the WTO's requirement that such agreements cover "substantially all trade." This would help reassert the fundamental principles of an open trading system, curb the proliferation of inadequate bilateral and regional trade agreements, and lay the foundation for devising better agreements in the future.

The most significant contribution the United States could make to reestablishing WTO negotiations as a viable enterprise -- and offering a serious new deadline for action -- would be to obtain a renewal of TPA from Congress, even if limited to plurilateral and multilateral trade agreements. Along with an Obama administration push to achieve congressional approval of pending free-trade agreements with Colombia, Panama, and South Korea, a renewed TPA would provide needed credibility and make trading partners far more willing to listen to U.S. proposals and take risks in any future trade talks.

Meanwhile, the United States and other developed countries may want to review whether their trade-preference programs for developing countries are benefiting the developing countries that need the most assistance and not creating a disincentive to swap trade concessions for access.

Once the dust has settled on the Doha Round, the United States and the other WTO members should dispassionately study Doha's successes and failures to prepare for the next major negotiating exercise. They should explore simpler formulas that can lead to real negotiations on tariffs, nontariff barriers, subsidies, and services, with give-and-take that builds momentum and ignites enthusiasm from pro-trade constituencies. Participants should also begin to address new issues, such as food security and the damaging use of export bans.

No future multilateral negotiation will succeed, however, without addressing the very real differences in economic strength, prospects, and capabilities within the so-called developing world. It is worth recalling that one of the WTO's most important characteristics is the inclusion of these developing economies in governance and decision-making from its origins as the General Agreement on Tariffs and Trade in 1948. In private, most emerging and developing countries acknowledge that it is in their interest to bridge the increasingly artificial divide between developed and developing nations when it comes to global issues such as trade, international finance, and climate change. Escaping the confines of the Doha Round could hasten the emergence of new models. These might include multilateral negotiations designed to offer a better balance between benefits and obligations, or they could include plurilateral deals that set a high bar but enable like-minded countries to participate.

Doha may be dead, but by accepting what everyone knows and no one wants to admit, the world can actually reinvigorate and strengthen the multilateral trading system. The WTO has served the world well, but it risks losing its relevance as the Doha Round continues to drain its credibility and resources. Now is the time to liberate the would-be trade liberalizers and move on.

SUSAN C. SCHWAB served as U.S. Trade Representative from 2006 to 2009.

The Truth About Trade

What Critics Get Wrong About the Global Economy

Douglas A. Irwin

LUCAS JACKSON / REUTERS

A container ship enters New York Harbor, November 2015.

Just because a U.S. presidential candidate bashes free trade on the campaign trail does not mean that he or she cannot embrace it once elected. After all, Barack Obama voted against the Central American Free Trade Agreement as a U.S. senator and disparaged the North American Free Trade Agreement (NAFTA) as a presidential candidate. In office, however, he came to champion the Trans-Pacific Partnership (TPP), a giant trade deal with 11 other Pacific Rim countries.

Yet in the current election cycle, the rhetorical attacks on U.S. trade policy have grown so fiery that it is difficult to imagine similar transformations. The Democratic candidate Bernie Sanders has railed against "disastrous" trade agreements, which he claims have cost jobs and hurt the middle class. The Republican Donald Trump complains that China, Japan, and Mexico are "killing" the United States on trade thanks to the bad deals struck by "stupid" negotiators. Even Hillary Clinton, the expected Democratic nominee, who favored the TPP as secretary of state, has been forced to join the chorus and now says she opposes that agreement.

Blaming other countries for the United States' economic woes is an age-old tradition in American politics; if truth is the first casualty of war, then support for free trade is often an early casualty of an election campaign. But the bipartisan bombardment has been so intense this time, and has been so unopposed, that it raises real questions about the future of U.S. global economic leadership.

The anti-trade rhetoric paints a grossly distorted picture of trade's role in the U.S. economy. Trade still benefits the United States enormously, and striking back at other countries by imposing new barriers or ripping up existing agreements would be self-destructive. The badmouthing of trade agreements has even jeopardized the ratification of the TPP in Congress. Backing out of that deal would signal a major U.S. retreat from Asia and mark a historic error.

Still, it would be a mistake to dismiss all of the anti-trade talk as ill-informed bombast. Today's electorate harbors legitimate, deep-seated frustrations about the state of the U.S. economy and labor markets in particular, and addressing these complaints will require changing government policies. The solution, however, lies not in turning away from trade promotion but in strengthening worker protections.

By and large, the United States has no major difficulties with respect to trade, nor does it suffer from problems that could be solved by trade barriers. What it does face, however, is a much larger problem, one that lies at the root of anxieties over trade: the economic ladder that allowed previous generations of lower-skilled Americans to reach the middle class is broken.

SCAPEGOATING TRADE

Campaign attacks on trade leave an unfortunate impression on the American public and the world at large. In saying that some countries "win" and other countries "lose" as a result of trade, for example, Trump portrays it as a zero-sum game. That's an understandable perspective for a casino owner and businessman: gambling is the quintessential zero-sum game, and competition is a win-lose proposition for firms (if not for their customers). But it is dead wrong as a way to think about the role of trade in an economy. Trade is actually a two-way street—the exchange of exports for imports—that makes efficient use of a country's resources to increase its material welfare. The United States sells to other countries the goods and services that it produces relatively efficiently (from aircraft to soybeans to legal advice) and buys those goods and services that other countries produce relatively efficiently (from T-shirts to bananas to electronics assembly). In the aggregate, both sides benefit.

To make their case that trade isn't working for the United States, critics invoke long-discredited indicators, such as the country's negative balance of trade. "Our trade deficit with China is like having a business that continues to lose money every single year," Trump once said. "Who would do business like that?" In fact, a nation's trade balance is nothing like a firm's bottom line. Whereas a company cannot lose money indefinitely, a country—particularly one, such as the United States, with a reserve currency—can run a trade deficit indefinitely without compromising its well-being. Australia has run current account deficits even longer than the United States has, and its economy is flourishing.

One way to define a country's trade balance is the difference between its domestic savings and its domestic investment. The United States has run a deficit in its current account—the broadest measure of trade in goods and services—every year except one since 1981. Why? Because as a low-saving, high-consuming country, the United States has long been the recipient of capital inflows from abroad. Reducing the current account deficit would require foreigners to purchase fewer U.S assets. That, in turn, would require increasing domestic savings or, to put it in less popular terms, reducing consumption. One way to accomplish that would be to change the tax system—for example, by instituting a consumption tax. But discouraging spending and rewarding savings is not easy, and critics of the trade deficit do not fully appreciate the difficulty involved in reversing it. (And if a current account surplus were to appear, critics would no doubt complain, as they did in the 1960s, that the United States was investing too much abroad and not enough at home.)

Trade still benefits the United States enormously.

Critics also point to the trade deficit to suggest that the United States is losing more jobs as a result of imports than it gains due to exports. In fact, the trade deficit usually increases when the economy is growing and creating jobs and decreases when it is contracting and losing jobs. The U.S. current account deficit shrank from 5.8 percent of GDP in 2006 to 2.7 percent in 2009, but that didn't stop the economy from hemorrhaging jobs. And if there is any doubt that a current account surplus is no economic panacea, one need only look at Japan, which has endured three decades of economic stagnation despite running consistent current account surpluses.

And yet these basic fallacies—many of which Adam Smith debunked more than two centuries ago—have found a new life in contemporary American politics. In some ways, it is odd that anti-trade sentiment has blossomed in 2016, of all years. For one thing, although the post-recession recovery has been disappointing, it has hardly been awful: the U.S. economy has experienced seven years of slow but steady growth, and the unemployment rate has fallen to just five percent. For another thing, imports have not swamped the country and caused problems for domestic producers and their workers; over the past seven years, the current account deficit has remained roughly unchanged at about two to three percent of GDP, much lower than its level from 2000 to 2007. The pace of globalization, meanwhile, has slowed in recent years. The World Trade Organization (WTO) forecasts that the volume of world trade will grow by just 2.8 percent in 2016, the fifth consecutive year that it has grown by less than three percent, down significantly from previous decades.

REBECCA COOK / REUTERS

Nice work if you can get it: at a Ford plant in Michigan, November 2012.

What's more, despite what one might infer from the crowds at campaign rallies, Americans actually support foreign trade in general and even trade agreements such as the TPP in particular. After a decade of viewing trade with skepticism, since 2013, Americans have seen it positively. A February 2016 Gallup poll found that 58 percent of Americans consider foreign trade an opportunity for economic growth, and only 34 percent viewed it as a threat.

THE VIEW FROM THE BOTTOM

So why has trade come under such strident attack now? The most important reason is that workers are still suffering from the aftermath of the Great Recession, which left many unemployed and indebted. Between 2007 and 2009, the United States lost nearly nine million jobs, pushing the unemployment rate up to ten percent. Seven years later, the economy is still recovering from this devastating blow. Many workers have left the labor force, reducing the employment-to-population ratio sharply. Real wages have remained flat. For many Americans, the recession isn't over.

For many Americans, the recession isn't over.

Thus, even as trade commands broad public support, a significant minority of the electorate—about a third, according to various polls—decidedly opposes it. These critics come from both sides of the political divide, but they tend to be lower-income, blue-collar workers, who are the most vulnerable to economic change. They believe that economic elites and the political establishment have looked out only for themselves over the past few decades. As they see it, the government bailed out banks during the financial crisis, but no one came to their aid.

For these workers, neither political party has taken their concerns seriously, and both parties have struck trade deals that the workers think have cost jobs. Labor unions that support the Democrats still feel betrayed by President Bill Clinton, who, over their strong objections, secured congressional passage of NAFTA in 1993 and normalized trade relations with China in 2000. Blue-collar Republican voters, for their part, supported the anti-NAFTA presidential campaigns of Pat Buchanan and Ross Perot in 1992. They felt betrayed by President George W. Bush, who pushed Congress to pass many bilateral trade agreements. Today, they back Trump.

Among this demographic, a narrative has taken hold that trade has cost Americans their jobs, squeezed the middle class, and kept wages low. The truth is more complicated. Although imports have put some people out of work, trade is far from the most important factor behind the loss of manufacturing jobs. The main culprit is technology. Automation and other technologies have enabled vast productivity and efficiency improvements, but they have also made many blue-collar jobs obsolete. One representative study, by the Center for Business and Economic Research at Ball State University, found that productivity growth accounted for more than 85 percent of the job loss in manufacturing between 2000 and 2010, a period when employment in that sector fell by 5.6 million. Just 13 percent of the overall job loss resulted from trade, although in two sectors, apparel and furniture, it accounted for 40 percent.

This finding is consistent with research by the economists David Autor, David Dorn, and Gordon Hanson, who have estimated that imports from China displaced as many as 982,000 workers in manufacturing from 2000 to 2007. These layoffs also depressed local labor markets in communities that produced goods facing Chinese competition, such as textiles, apparel, and furniture. The number of jobs lost is large, but it should be put in perspective: while Chinese imports may have cost nearly one million manufacturing jobs over almost a decade, the normal churn of U.S. labor markets results in roughly 1.7 million layoffs every month.

DAVE KAUP / REUTERS

Robotic arms work on the chassis of a Ford Transit Van at the Ford Claycomo Assembly Plant in Claycomo, Missouri, April 2014.

Research into the effect of Chinese imports on U.S. employment has been widely misinterpreted to imply that the United States has gotten a raw deal from trade with China. In fact, such studies do not evaluate the gains from trade, since they make no attempt to quantify the benefits to consumers from lower-priced goods. Rather, they serve as a reminder that a rapid increase in imports can harm communities that produce substitute goods—as happened in the U.S. automotive and steel sectors in the 1980s.

Furthermore, the shock of Chinese goods was a one-time event that occurred under special circumstances. Imports from China increased from 1.0 percent of U.S. GDP in 2000 to 2.6 percent in 2011, but for the past five years, the share has stayed roughly constant. There is no reason to believe it will rise further. China's once-rapid economic growth has slowed. Its working-age population has begun to shrink, and the migration of its rural workers to coastal urban manufacturing areas has largely run its course.

The influx of Chinese imports was also unusual in that much of it occurred from 2001 to 2007, when China's current account surplus soared, reaching ten percent of GDP in 2007. The country's export boom was partly facilitated by China's policy of preventing the appreciation of the yuan, which lowered the price of Chinese goods. Beginning around 2000, the Chinese central bank engaged in a large-scale, persistent, and one-way intervention in the foreign exchange market—buying dollars and selling yuan. As a result, its foreign exchange reserves rose from less than $300 million in 2000 to $3.25 trillion in 2011. Critics rightly groused that this effort constituted currency manipulation and violated International Monetary Fund rules. Yet such complaints are now moot: over the past year, China's foreign exchange reserves have fallen rapidly as its central bank has sought to prop up the value of the yuan. Punishing China for past bad behavior would accomplish nothing.

THE RIGHT—AND WRONG—SOLUTIONS

The real problem is not trade but diminished domestic opportunity and social mobility. Although the United States boasts a highly skilled work force and a solid technological base, it is still the case that only one in three American adults has a college education. In past decades, the two-thirds of Americans with no postsecondary degree often found work in manufacturing, construction, or the armed forces. These parts of the economy stood ready to absorb large numbers of people with limited education, give them productive work, and help them build skills. Over time, however, these opportunities have disappeared. Technology has shrunk manufacturing as a source of large-scale employment: even though U.S. manufacturing output continues to grow, it does so with many fewer workers than in the past. Construction work has not recovered from the bursting of the housing bubble. And the military turns away 80 percent of applicants due to stringent fitness and intelligence requirements. There are no comparable sectors of the economy that can employ large numbers of high-school-educated workers.

The anti-trade rhetoric of the campaign has made it difficult for even pro-trade members of Congress to support new agreements.

This is a deep problem for American society. The unemployment rate for college-educated workers is 2.4 percent, but it is more than 7.4 percent for those without a high school diploma—and even higher when counting discouraged workers who have left the labor force but wish to work. These are the people who have been left behind in the twenty-first-century economy—again, not primarily because of trade but because of structural changes in the economy. Helping these workers and ensuring that the economy delivers benefits to everyone should rank as urgent priorities.

But here is where the focus on trade is a diversion. Since trade is not the underlying problem in terms of job loss, neither is protectionism a solution. While the gains from trade can seem abstract, the costs of trade restrictions are concrete. For example, the United States has some 135,000 workers employed in the apparel industry, but there are more than 45 million Americans who live below the poverty line, stretching every dollar they have. Can one really justify increasing the price of clothing for 45 million low-income Americans (and everyone else as well) in an effort to save the jobs of just some of the 135,000 low-wage workers in the apparel industry?

Like undoing trade agreements, imposing selective import duties to punish specific countries would also fail. If the United States were to slap 45 percent tariffs on imports from China, as Trump has proposed, U.S. companies would not start producing more apparel and footwear in the United States, nor would they start assembling consumer electronics domestically. Instead, production would shift from China to other low-wage developing countries in Asia, such as Vietnam. That's the lesson of past trade sanctions directed against China alone: in 2009, when the Obama administration imposed duties on automobile tires from China in an effort to save American jobs, other suppliers, principally Indonesia and Thailand, filled the void, resulting in little impact on U.S. production or jobs.

And if restrictions were levied against all foreign imports to prevent such trade diversion, those barriers would hit innocent bystanders: Canada, Japan, Mexico, the EU, and many others. Any number of these would use WTO procedures to retaliate against the United States, threatening the livelihoods of the millions of Americans with jobs that depend on exports of manufactured goods. Trade wars produce no winners. There are good reasons why the very mention of the 1930 Smoot-Hawley Tariff Act still conjures up memories of the Great Depression.

Ripping up NAFTA would do immense damage.

If protectionism is an ineffectual and counterproductive response to the economic problems of much of the work force, so, too, are existing programs designed to help workers displaced by trade. The standard package of Trade Adjustment Assistance, a federal program begun in the 1960s, consists of extended unemployment compensation and retraining programs. But because these benefits are limited to workers who lost their jobs due to trade, they miss the millions more who are unemployed on account of technological change. Furthermore, the program is fraught with bad incentives. Extended unemployment compensation pays workers for prolonged periods of joblessness, but their job prospects usually deteriorate the longer they stay out of the labor force, since they have lost experience in the interim.

And although the idea behind retraining is a good one—helping laid-off textile or steel workers become nurses or technicians—the actual program is a failure. A 2012 external review commissioned by the Department of Labor found that the government retraining programs were a net loss for society, to the tune of about $54,000 per participant. Half of that fell on the participants themselves, who, on average, earned $27,000 less over the four years of the study than similar workers who did not find jobs through the program, and half fell on the government, which footed the bill for the program. Sadly, these programs appear to do more harm than good.

A better way to help all low-income workers would be to expand the Earned Income Tax Credit. The EITC supplements the incomes of workers in all low-income households, not just those the Department of Labor designates as having been adversely affected by trade. What's more, the EITC is tied to employment, thereby rewarding work and keeping people in the labor market, where they can gain experience and build skills. A large enough EITC could ensure that every American was able to earn the equivalent of $15 or more per hour. And it could do so without any of the job loss that a minimum-wage hike can cause. Of all the potential assistance programs, the EITC also enjoys the most bipartisan support, having been endorsed by both the Obama administration and Paul Ryan, the Republican Speaker of the House. A higher EITC would not be a cure-all, but it would provide income security for those seeking to climb the ladder to the middle class.

The main complaint about expanding the EITC concerns the cost. Yet taxpayers are already bearing the burden of supporting workers who leave the labor force, many of whom start receiving disability payments. On disability, people are paid—permanently—to drop out of the labor force and not work. In lieu of this federal program, the cost of which has surged in recent years, it would be better to help people remain in the work force through the EITC, in the hope that they can eventually become taxpayers themselves.

THE FUTURE OF FREE TRADE

Despite all the evidence of the benefits of trade, many of this year's crop of presidential candidates have still invoked it as a bogeyman. Sanders deplores past agreements but has yet to clarify whether he believes that better ones could have been negotiated or no such agreements should be reached at all. His vote against the U.S.-Australian free-trade agreement in 2004 suggests that he opposes all trade deals, even one with a country that has high labor standards and with which the United States runs a sizable balance of trade surplus. Trump professes to believe in free trade, but he insists that the United States has been outnegotiated by its trade partners, hence his threat to impose 45 percent tariffs on imports from China to get "a better deal"—

whatever that means. He has attacked Japan's barriers against imports of U.S. agricultural goods, even though that is exactly the type of protectionism the TPP has tried to undo. Meanwhile, Clinton's position against the TPP has hardened as the campaign has gone on.

The response from economists has tended to be either meek defenses of trade or outright silence, with some even criticizing parts of the TPP. It's time for supporters of free trade to engage in a full-throated championing of the many achievements of U.S. trade agreements. Indeed, because other countries' trade barriers tend to be higher than those of the United States, trade agreements open foreign markets to U.S. exports more than they open the U.S. market to foreign imports.

ATHIT PERAWONGMETHA / REUTERS

A worker stands next to shipping containers on a ship at a port in Bangkok, Thailand, March 2016.

That was true of NAFTA, which remains a favored punching bag on the campaign trail. In fact, NAFTA has been a big economic and foreign policy success. Since the agreement entered into force in 1994, bilateral trade between the United States and Mexico has boomed. For all the fear about Mexican imports flooding the U.S. market, it is worth noting that about 40 percent of the value of imports from Mexico consists of content originally made in the United States—for example, auto parts produced in the United States but assembled in Mexico. It is precisely such trade in component parts that makes standard measures of bilateral trade balances so misleading.

NAFTA has also furthered the United States' long-term political, diplomatic, and economic interest in a flourishing, democratic Mexico, which not only reduces immigration pressures on border states but also increases Mexican demand for U.S. goods and services. Far from exploiting Third World labor, as critics have charged, NAFTA has promoted the growth of a middle class in Mexico that now includes nearly half of all households. And since 2009, more Mexicans have left the United States than have come in. In the two decades since NAFTA went into effect, Mexico has been transformed from a clientelistic one-party state with widespread anti-

American sentiment into a functional multiparty democracy with a generally pro-American public. Although it has suffered from drug wars in recent years (a spillover effect from problems that are largely made in America), the overall story is one of rising prosperity thanks in part to NAFTA.

Ripping up NAFTA would do immense damage. In its foreign relations, the United States would prove itself to be an unreliable partner. And economically, getting rid of the agreement would disrupt production chains across North America, harming both Mexico and the United States. It would add to border tensions while shifting trade to Asia without bringing back any U.S. manufacturing jobs. The American public seems to understand this: in an October 2015 Gallup poll, only 18 percent of respondents agreed that leaving NAFTA or the Central American Free Trade Agreement would be very effective in helping the economy.

A more moderate option would be for the United States to take a pause and simply stop negotiating any more trade agreements, as Obama did during his first term. The problem with this approach, however, is that the rest of the world would continue to reach trade agreements without the United States, and so U.S. exporters would find themselves at a disadvantage compared with their foreign competitors. Glimpses of that future can already be seen. In 2012, the car manufacturer Audi chose southeastern Mexico over Tennessee for the site of a new plant because it could save thousands of dollars per car exported thanks to Mexico's many more free-trade agreements, including one with the EU. Australia has reached trade deals with China and Japan that give Australian farmers preferential access in those markets, cutting into U.S. beef exports.

If Washington opted out of the TPP, it would forgo an opportunity to shape the rules of international trade in the twenty-first century. The Uruguay Round, the last round of international trade negotiations completed by the General Agreement on Tariffs and Trade, ended in 1994, before the Internet had fully emerged. Now, the United States' high-tech firms and other exporters face foreign regulations that are not transparent and impede market access. Meanwhile, other countries are already moving ahead with their own trade agreements, increasingly taking market share from U.S. exporters in the dynamic Asia-Pacific region. Staying out of the TPP would not lead to the creation of good jobs in the United States. And despite populist claims to the contrary, the TPP's provisions for settling disputes between investors and governments and dealing with intellectual property rights are reasonable. (In the early 1990s, similar fears about such provisions in the WTO were just as exaggerated and ultimately proved baseless.)

The United States should proceed with passage of the TPP and continue to negotiate other deals with its trading partners. So-called plurilateral trade agreements, that is, deals among relatively small numbers of like-minded countries, offer the only viable way to pick up more gains from reducing trade barriers. The current climate on Capitol Hill means that the era of small bilateral agreements, such as those pursued during the George W. Bush administration, has ended. And the collapse of the Doha Round at the WTO likely marks the end of giant multilateral trade negotiations.

Free trade has always been a hard sell. But the anti-trade rhetoric of the 2016 campaign has made it difficult for even pro-trade members of Congress to support new agreements. Past experience suggests that Washington will lead the charge for reducing trade barriers only when there is a major trade problem to be solved—namely, when U.S. exporters face severe discrimination in foreign markets. Such was the case when the United States helped form the General Agreement on Tariffs and Trade in 1947, when it started the Kennedy Round of trade negotiations in the 1960s, and when it initiated the Uruguay Round in the 1980s. Until the United States feels the pain of getting cut out of major foreign markets, its leadership on global trade may wane. That would represent just one casualty of the current campaign.

DOUGLAS A. IRWIN is John Sloan Dickey Third Century Professor in the Social Sciences in the Department of Economics at Dartmouth College and the author of *Free Trade Under Fire*. Follow him on Twitter @D_A_Irwin.

Nafta's Economic Upsides

The View From the United States

Carla A. Hills

WIN MCNAMEE / COURTESY REUTERS

U.S. President Bill Clinton signs side deals to the North American Free Trade Agreement, September 1993.

In the 20 years since it entered into force, the North American Free Trade Agreement has been both lauded and attacked in the United States. But to properly assess NAFTA's record, it is important to first be clear about what the agreement has actually done. Economically speaking, the answer is a lot. By uniting the economies of Canada, Mexico, and the United States, NAFTA created what is today a $19 trillion regional market with some 470 million consumers. The U.S. Chamber of Commerce figures that some six million U.S. jobs depend on trade with Mexico and another eight million on trade with Canada. NAFTA was the first comprehensive free-trade agreement to join developed and developing nations, and it achieved broader and deeper market openings than any trade agreement had before.

NAFTA did that by eliminating tariffs on all industrial goods, guaranteeing unrestricted agricultural trade between the United States and Mexico, opening up a broad range of service sectors, and instituting national treatment for cross-border service providers. It also set high standards of protection for patents, trademarks, copyrights, and trade secrets. To preserve the rights of investors, it prohibited barriers such as local-content and import-substitution rules, which require producers to ensure that specified inputs are produced domestically.

For the United States, the economic consequences of these reforms -- which have also had social, political, and cultural impacts -- have been dramatic. If North America is to remain a uniquely competitive region, however, it will need to build on NAFTA's success by opening markets beyond its borders.

TRADE AND GROWTH

NAFTA ignited an explosion in cross-border economic activity. Today, Canada ranks as the United States' largest single export market, and it sends 98 percent of its total energy exports to the United States, making Canada the United States' largest supplier of energy products and services. Mexico is the United States' second-largest single export market. Over the past two decades, a highly efficient and integrated supply chain has developed among the three North American economies. Intraregional trade flows have increased by roughly 400 percent, from around $290 billion in 1993 to over $1.1 trillion in 2012. Every day, nearly $2 billion in goods and services cross the United States' northern border and roughly $1 billion worth cross its southern border.

Today, thanks to NAFTA, North Americans not only sell more things to one another; they also make more things together. About half of U.S. trade with Canada and Mexico takes place between related companies, and the resulting specialization has boosted productivity in all three economies. For every dollar of goods that Canada and Mexico export to the United States, there are 25 cents' worth of U.S. inputs in the Canadian goods and 40 cents' worth in the Mexican goods. By way of comparison, there are four cents' worth of U.S. inputs in Chinese goods going to the American market and two cents' worth for Japanese goods.

NAFTA has also caused cross-border investment to soar. Since the treaty was signed, the United States, Canada's largest source of foreign capital, has invested more than $310 billion in Canada, and Canada, the United States' fifth-largest source of foreign capital, has invested over $200 billion in the United States. Mexico has also made major investments north of its border since NAFTA was signed, especially in the cement, bread, dairy, and retail sectors, thereby contributing to U.S. jobs and tax revenues. Similarly, U.S. investment in Mexico has grown substantially, with about half of it going to the manufacturing sector and much of that share flowing to the automotive industry. The United States derives a unique benefit from its investments in Canada and Mexico because a large percentage of that output returns home as imports of intermediate goods, which allows U.S. firms to focus on the higher-end task of assembling finished products.

The United States' expanded economic collaboration has created another economic benefit: a boom in intraregional travel by businesspeople, tourists, and students. According to the U.S. Department of Commerce, in 2011, Americans made nearly 12 million trips to Canada and spent almost $8 billion there, and they made 20 million trips to Mexico (the top destination for U.S. tourists) and spent over $9 billion there. The United States' neighbors returned the favor, with Canadians making 21 million trips to the United States and spending $24 billion there and Mexicans making more than 13 million trips and spending almost $8 billion.

In spite of this impressive economic record, NAFTA has its critics. Most of those who attack it on economic grounds focus on Mexico, not Canada, and claim that the partnership is one-sided: that NAFTA is Mexico's gain and America's pain. But the economic data prove otherwise. Last year, roughly 14 percent of U.S. exports went to Mexico -- more than went to Brazil, Russia, India, and China combined. Indeed, Mexico buys more U.S. goods than the rest of Latin America combined, and more than France, Germany, the Netherlands, and the United Kingdom combined. Although economists still debate whether NAFTA has caused a net gain or a net loss in U.S. jobs, they agree that the market openings it created have generated more export-related jobs in the United States, which pay an average of 15 to 20 percent more than those focused purely on domestic production.

With 116 million consumers who have a combined purchasing power of more than $1 trillion, Mexico represents a major market opportunity for U.S. entrepreneurs large and small. But small U.S. enterprises, lacking the global reach of major corporations, benefit in particular from Mexico's proximity and openness. Mexicans purchase about 11 percent of the exports of small and medium-size U.S. companies, which account for more than half of all job creation in the United States. Even Mexican exports worldwide benefit the U.S. economy, because of their high percentage of U.S. content. And making the picture even brighter, for every dollar that Mexico earns from its exports, it spends 50 cents on U.S. goods.

MOVING NORTH AND SOUTH

Another of NAFTA's positive effects has been the increased sharing of talent. Today, Canadians constitute about three percent of the United States' total foreign-born population, and Mexicans constitute about 30 percent. Americans make up about four percent of Canada's foreign-born population and roughly 70 percent of Mexico's. The Canadians and Mexicans who live in the United States are younger than the overall U.S. population. And according to a study conducted by the Kauffman Foundation, immigrants in the United States are almost twice as likely to start a new business as native-born Americans.

Complaints about U.S. immigration policy focus primarily on concerns about Mexico. What are the facts? According to the Pew Hispanic Center, 34 million Hispanics of Mexican origin live in the United States, roughly two-thirds of whom were born there. Of those born in Mexico, the majority arrived in the United States after 1990, encouraged by the growth of cross-border travel, trade, investment, and business collaboration that NAFTA stimulated. About half of them reside in the United States legally. In recent years, however, as the Mexican economy has expanded and created more jobs, both illegal and legal immigration from Mexico to the United States has plummeted. Compared with 1990, today, as a result of higher-than-average birthrates, the number of U.S.-born people of Mexican origin has more than doubled. Also, compared with their predecessors from that year, today's Mexican immigrants tend to be older, with an average age of 38, versus 29, and better educated, with 41 percent holding at least a high school degree, versus 25 percent. Their numbers have had a cultural impact, too. Holidays such as Cinco de Mayo are widely celebrated across America. As a nation of immigrants, the United States celebrates its cultural diversity.

In addition to contributing youth, talent, and cultural diversity, these immigrants are having an impact on politics. In the 2012 presidential election, Hispanic voters composed ten percent of the electorate, up from eight percent in 2004. They lean Democratic and tend to hold more liberal views on immigration policy. An exit poll conducted during the 2012 election asked voters what should happen to unauthorized immigrants working in the United States, and 77 percent of Hispanic respondents, compared with 65 percent overall, said that these immigrants should be given a chance to apply for legal status.

Hispanics' growing numbers have contributed to a shift in the balance of political power in some battleground states. In 2012, President Barack Obama carried 75 percent of the Hispanic vote in Colorado and 70 percent in Nevada, winning both states. As Hispanics' share of the U.S. population increases, their political voice should only grow stronger. Increasingly, they are joining politically interested civic groups; the United States now has 2.3 million Hispanic business owners and 1.2 million Hispanic military veterans.

BEYOND NAFTA

The economic, political, and social integration that has taken place in North America since NAFTA went into effect has made the region one of the most competitive on the planet. But the rest of the world has not stood still. Supply chains encircle the globe, and bilateral and regional trade agreements to which the United States is not a party are giving other countries preferential access to key markets.

To ensure that the U.S. economy continues to grow and remain competitive, the United States needs to keep North America's supply chains working at maximum efficiency and global markets open to North American products, services, investment, and ideas. There are a number of actions the United States could take, building on the NAFTA platform, to create new commercial opportunities. For example, when the U.S. government evaluates a potential trade arrangement, it should assess the benefits not only on a national basis but also on a regional basis. In that regard, it was encouraging to see Canada and Mexico join the negotiations of the Trans-Pacific Partnership, a proposed free-trade agreement among 12 countries in Asia and the Americas.

Similarly, as the United States negotiates the Transatlantic Trade and Investment Partnership with the 28 countries that compose the EU, it would benefit immensely by including Canada and Mexico, which would add 150 million consumers and $3 trillion in GDP, making an even stronger agreement. Doing so would reduce needless complexity, too, since Mexico has had a free-trade agreement with the EU since 2000 and Canada just concluded one in October 2013. For entrepreneurs on both sides of the Atlantic, having to deal with three separate agreements with different rules of origin and different customs measures would add unnecessary costs and regulatory headaches. It would also erode the hugely beneficial economic integration North America has achieved thanks to NAFTA. A single agreement among the three countries of North America and the EU would bring badly needed regulatory coherence to more than half of the world's trading volume.

In addition, having all three North American governments participate in the negotiations would give them an opportunity to upgrade the provisions of NAFTA that were not especially relevant 20 years ago, such as those dealing with digital data flows. Finally, such a deal could facilitate the economic reforms of Mexican President Enrique Peña Nieto, who is seeking to open up Mexico's energy sector to foreign investment. Pointing to the benefits that Mexico could obtain from a mega-agreement that involved half of global GDP could help Peña Nieto build political support for his energy reforms, which the United States strongly supports.

In just 20 years, NAFTA has succeeded in spurring an enormous amount of economic activity throughout Canada, the United States, and Mexico. But in order to maximize future growth, North American universities, think tanks, and business organizations will need to better educate the public about the tremendous gains that can come from increased regional economic integration. Given how closely NAFTA has drawn the nations of North America together -- not just economically but also politically, culturally, and socially -- this is a goal they can and should strive to achieve.

CARLA A. HILLS is **Co-Chair of the Council on Foreign Relations** and Chair and CEO of Hills & Company. From 1989 to 1993, she served as U.S. Trade Representative.

Inequality and Globalization

How the Rich Get Richer as The Poor Catch Up

François Bourguignon

VIVEK PRAKASH / REUTERS

A farmer in Narayangaon, India, September 2012.

When it comes to wealth and income, people tend to compare themselves to the people they see around them rather than to those who live on the other side of the world. The average Frenchman, for example, probably does not care how many Chinese exceed his own standard of living, but that Frenchman surely would pay attention if he started lagging behind his fellow citizens. Yet when thinking about inequality, it also makes sense to approach the world as a single community: accounting, for example, not only for the differences in living standards within France but also for those between rich French people and poor Chinese (and poor French and rich Chinese).

When looking at the world through this lens, some notable trends stand out. The first is that global inequality greatly exceeds inequality within any individual country. This observation should come as no surprise, since global inequality reflects the enormous differences in wealth between the world's richest and the world's poorest countries, not just the differences within them. Much more striking is the fact that, in a dramatic reversal of the trend that prevailed for most of the twentieth century, global inequality has declined markedly since 2000 (following a slower decline during the 1990s). This trend has been due in large part to the rising fortunes of the developing world, particularly China and India. And as the economies of these countries continue to converge with those of the developed world, global inequality will continue to fall for some time.

Even as global inequality has declined, however, inequality within individual countries has crept upward. There is some disagreement about the size of this increase among economists, largely owing to the underrepresentation of wealthy people in national income surveys. But whatever its extent, increased inequality within individual countries has partially offset the decline in inequality among countries. To counteract this trend, states should pursue policies aimed at redistributing income, strengthen the regulation of the labor and financial markets, and develop international arrangements that prevent firms from avoiding taxes by shifting their assets or operations overseas.

THE GREAT SUBSTITUTION

Economists typically measure income inequality using the Gini coefficient, which ranges from zero in cases of perfect equality (a theoretical country in which everyone earns the same income) to one in cases of perfect inequality (a state in which a single individual earns all the income and everyone else gets nothing). In continental Europe, Gini coefficients tend to fall between 0.25 and 0.30. In the United States, the figure is around 0.40. And in the world's most unequal countries, such as South Africa, it exceeds 0.60. When considering the world's population as a whole, the Gini coefficient comes to 0.70—a figure so high that no country is known to have ever reached it.

PASCAL FLETCHER / REUTERS

A Nigerian family walks past a newly opened supermarket in Kano, Nigeria, April 2014.

Determining the Gini coefficient for global inequality requires making a number of simplifications and assumptions. Economists must accommodate gaps in domestic data—in Mexico, an extreme case, surveys of income and expenditures miss about half of all households. They need to come up with estimates for years in which national surveys are not available. They need to convert local incomes into a common currency, usually the U.S. dollar, and correct for differences in purchasing power. And they need to adjust for discrepancies in data collection among countries, such as those that arise when one state measures living standards by income and another by consumption per person or when a state does not collect data at all.

Such inexactitudes and the different ways of compensating for them explain why estimates of just how much global inequality has declined over the past two-plus decades tend to vary—from around two percentage points to up to five, depending on the study. No matter how steep this decline, however, economists generally agree that the end result has been a global Gini coefficient of around 0.70 in the years between 2008 and 2010.

The decline in global inequality is largely the product of the convergence of the economies of developing countries, particularly China and India, with those of the developed world. In the first decade of this century, booming economies in Latin America and sub-Saharan Africa also helped accelerate this trend. Remarkably, this decline followed a nearly uninterrupted rise in inequality from the advent of the Industrial Revolution in the early nineteenth century until the 1970s. What is more, the decline has been large enough to erase a substantial part of the inequality that built up over that century and a half.

Even as inequality among countries has decreased, however, inequality within individual countries has increased, gaining, on average, more than two percentage points in terms of the Gini coefficient between 1990 and 2010. The countries with the biggest economies are especially responsible for this trend—particularly the United Sates, where the Gini coefficient rose by five percentage points between 1990 and 2013, but also China and India and, to a lesser extent, most European countries, among them Germany and the Scandinavian states. Still, inequality within countries is not rising fast enough to offset the rapid decline in inequality among countries.

In a dramatic reversal of the trend that prevailed for most of the twentieth century, global inequality has declined markedly since 2000.

The good news is that the current decline in global inequality will probably persist. Despite the current global slowdown, China and India have such huge domestic markets that they retain an enormous amount of potential for growth. And even if their growth rates decline significantly in the next decade, so long as they remain higher than those of the advanced industrial economies, as is likely, global inequality will continue to fall. The prospects for growth are less favorable for the smaller economies in Latin America and sub-Saharan Africa that depend primarily on commodity exports, since world commodity prices may remain low for some time. All told, then, global inequality will likely keep falling in the coming decades—but probably at the slow pace seen during the 1990s rather than the rapid one enjoyed during the following decade.

STR / AFP / GETTY IMAGES
Scavenging in a garbage dump in Hefei, China, December 2012.

The bad news, however, is that economists might have underestimated inequality within individual countries and the extent to which it has increased since the 1990s, because national surveys tend to underrepresent the wealthy and underreport income derived from property, which disproportionately accrues to the rich. Indeed, tax data from many developed states suggest that national surveys fail to account for a substantial portion of the incomes of the very highest earners.

According to the most drastic corrections for such underreporting, as calculated by the economists Sudhir Anand and Paul Segal, global inequality could have remained more or less constant between 1988 and 2005. Most likely, however, this conclusion is too extreme, and the increase in national inequality has been too small to cancel out the decline in inequality among countries. Yet it still points to a disheartening trend: increased inequality within countries has offset the drop in inequality among countries. In other words, the gap between average Americans and average Chinese is being partly replaced by larger gaps between rich and poor Americans and between rich and poor Chinese.

INTERCONNECTED AND UNEQUAL

The same factor that can be credited for the decline in inequality among countries can also be blamed for the increase in inequality within them: globalization. As firms from the developed world moved production overseas during the 1990s, emerging Asian economies, particularly China, started to converge with those of the developed world. The resulting boom triggered faster growth in Africa and Latin America as demand for commodities increased. In the developed world, meanwhile, as manufacturing firms outsourced some of their production, corporate profits rose but real wages for unskilled labor fell.

Economic liberalization also played an important role in this process. In China, the market reforms initiated by Deng Xiaoping in the 1980s contributed just as much to rapid growth as did the country's opening to foreign investment and trade, and the same is true of the reforms India undertook in the early 1990s. As with globalization, such reforms didn't just enable developing countries to get closer to the developed world; they also created a new elite within those countries while leaving many citizens behind, thus increasing domestic inequality.

Economists might have underestimated inequality within individual countries and the extent to which it has increased since the 1990s.

The same drive toward economic liberalization has contributed to increasing inequality in the developed world. Reductions in income tax rates, cuts to welfare, and financial deregulation have also helped make the rich richer and, in some instances, the poor poorer. The increase in the international mobility of firms, wealth, and workers over the past two decades has compounded these problems by making it harder for governments to combat inequality: for example, companies and wealthy people have become increasingly able to shift capital to countries with low tax rates or to tax havens, allowing them to avoid paying more redistributive taxes in their home countries. And in both developed and developing countries, technological progress has exacerbated these trends by favoring skilled workers over unskilled ones and creating economies of scale that disproportionately favor corporate managers.

MAINTAINING MOMENTUM

In the near future, the greatest potential for further reductions in global inequality will lie in Africa—the region that has arguably benefited the least from the past few decades of globalization, and the one where global poverty will likely concentrate in the coming decades as countries such as India leap ahead. Perhaps most important, the population of Africa is expected to double over the next 35 years, reaching some 25 percent of the world's population, and so the extent of global inequality will increasingly depend on the extent of African growth. Assuming that the economies of sub-Saharan Africa sustain the modest growth rates they have seen in recent years, then inequality among countries should keep declining, although not as fast as it did in the first decade of this century.

ERIC THAYER / REUTERS

An Armani store in New York, February 2009.

To maintain the momentum behind declining global inequality, all countries will need to work harder to reduce inequality within their borders, or at least prevent it from growing further. In the world's major economies, failing to do so could cause disenchanted citizens to misguidedly resist further attempts to integrate the world's economies—a process that, if properly managed, can in fact benefit everyone.

In practice, then, states should seek to equalize living standards among their populations by eliminating all types of ethnic, gender, and social discrimination; regulating the financial and labor markets; and implementing progressive taxation and welfare policies. Because the mobility of capital dulls the effectiveness of progressive taxation policies, governments also need to push for international measures that improve the transparency of the financial system, such as those the G-20 and the Organization for Economic Cooperation and Development have endorsed to share information among states in order to clamp down on tax avoidance. Practical steps such as these should remind policymakers that even though global inequality and domestic inequality have moved in opposite directions for the past few decades, they need not do so forever.

URGUIGNON is Professor of Economics at the Paris School of Economics, former Chief Economist of the World Bank, and the author of *The Globalization of Inequality*.

The Strategic Logic of Trade

New Rules of the Road for the Global Market

Michael B. Froman

COURTESY REUTERS

For much of the twentieth century, leaders and policymakers around the world viewed the strategic importance of trade, and of international economic policy more generally, largely through the lens of military strength. They believed that the role of a strong economy was to act as an enabler, supporting a strong military, which they saw as the best way to project power and influence. But in recent decades, leaders have come to see the economic clout that trade produces as more than merely a purse for military prowess: they now understand prosperity to be a principal means by which countries measure and exercise power.

The strategic importance of trade is not new, but it has grown in recent years and strongly reinforces the economic case for expanding trade. Over 40 years ago, the economist Thomas Schelling observed, "Broadly defined to include investment, shipping, tourism, and the management of enterprises, trade is what most of international relations are about. For that reason trade policy is national security policy." In a world where markets can have as much influence as militaries, any tension between the United States' national security priorities and its economic goals is more apparent than real. Still, in considering new trade agreements, Washington must first and foremost evaluate their economic merits. Trade deals must promote U.S. economic growth, support jobs, and strengthen the middle class.

Trade's contribution to the U.S. economy has never been more significant than it is today. Trade supports higher-paying jobs, spurs economic growth, and enhances the competitiveness of the U.S. economy. Last year, the United States exported a record $2.3 trillion in goods and services, which in turn supported around 11.3 million American jobs. Over the last five years, the increase in U.S. exports has accounted for nearly a third of total U.S. economic growth and, during the past four years, has supported 1.6 million additional jobs. Better yet, those jobs typically pay somewhere between 13 and 18 percent more than jobs unrelated to exports.

Moreover, trade plays a major role in attracting investors and manufacturers to the United States. The country offers a massive market, strong rule of law, a skilled work force with an entrepreneurial culture, and increasingly abundant sources of affordable energy. The Obama administration's trade policy seeks to make the United States even more attractive to investors by positioning the country at the center of a web of agreements that will provide unfettered access to nearly two-thirds of the global economy. As a result, the United States is already enjoying increased investment, attracting manufacturing jobs, and establishing itself as the world's production platform of choice. Companies of all sizes once again want to make things in the United States and export them all over the world.

For nearly seven decades, the global trading system has accomplished the goals of its lead architects, including U.S. statesmen such as Dean Acheson and George Marshall. It has brought jobs to American shores and peace and prosperity to countries around the world. But no one should take that system for granted. In recent years, tectonic shifts, such as economic globalization, technological change, and the rise of emerging economies, have reshaped the international landscape. As President Barack Obama remarked earlier this year, "Just as the world has changed, this architecture must change as well."

To help achieve that change, the Obama administration's trade agenda focuses on three strategic objectives: establishing and enforcing rules of the road, strengthening U.S. partnerships with other countries, and spurring broad-based economic development. Each of these objectives serves the overarching goals of revitalizing the global trading system, allowing the United States to continue to play a leading role in it, and ensuring that it reflects both American interests and American values.

RULES OF THE ROAD

With some of the most innovative companies and productive workers in the world, the United States can compete in the global marketplace and win -- if the playing field is level. The Obama administration has made enforcement of the rules governing trade a top priority, and every time the administration has brought a dispute before the World Trade Organization and the WTO has made a decision, the United States has won. Preventing China from restricting access to rare-earth minerals and stopping Argentina from wrongly restricting imports of agricultural products -- to cite just two examples -- not only benefits U.S. workers, farmers, and businesses but also reinforces the rules-based trading system itself.

The Trans-Pacific Partnership presents an unprecedented opportunity to update the rules of the road. An ambitious and comprehensive trade agreement that the United States is currently negotiating with 11 countries in the Asia-Pacific region, the TPP represents a main pillar of the Obama administration's broader strategy of rebalancing toward Asia. Taken together, the parties negotiating the TPP represent nearly 40 percent of the world's GDP and account for roughly a third of all global trade.

This agreement would level the playing field of international trade by establishing the strongest environmental and labor standards of any trade agreement in U.S. history. For example, the United States is pressing other countries to address forced labor and child labor and to maintain acceptable working conditions. The United States has also broken new ground with proposals that would address illicit wildlife trafficking, illegal logging, and subsidies that contribute to dangerous overfishing. Rules limiting such activities would help ensure that trade remains sustainable and that its benefits are broadly shared. The TPP countries are also working to ensure fair competition between private firms and state-owned enterprises that receive subsidies or other preferences. And Washington is pushing to protect unrestricted access to the Internet and the free flow of data so that small and medium-sized businesses around the world will be able to access global markets efficiently.

As the need for new rules has grown, so, too, has the difficulty of reaching agreement on the details. Emerging economies such as China and India have pressed for a stronger voice in international matters, but they have been reluctant to take on responsibilities commensurate with their increasing role in the global economy. Earlier this year, for example, a handful of countries led by India blocked the implementation of the WTO's Trade Facilitation Agreement, which seeks to eliminate red tape in border and customs disputes and therefore contribute significantly to economic activity, especially in developing countries. In this and other areas, the United States will continue to press ahead, working with those countries willing to adopt stronger rules and, in doing so, hopefully giving new momentum to the WTO's multilateral efforts.

STRENGTHENING PARTNERS

Trade has played a leading role in many of the most important chapters of U.S. history, often as a tool for strengthening international partnerships and alliances. The best-known example of this occurred in the wake of World War II, when the United States provided more access to Western European countries and Japan than it received from them, in an attempt to speed their reconstruction and solidify their integration into an open, rules-based international order.

Trade also serves as an effective way to send signals to allies and rivals. Signaling was the primary motivation behind the United Kingdom's push for the trade agreement it signed with the United States in 1938, just before the outbreak of World War II. The British gained little economically, but the deal bolstered the appearance of Anglo-American solidarity. Similarly, signaling was as important as economics to the United States' first-ever free-trade agreement, which was concluded with Israel in 1985. If anyone doubts the strategic importance of trade, consider Russia's reaction during the past year to the prospect of Ukraine deepening its trade ties with the West.

The global trading system also provides avenues for peaceful competition and mechanisms for resolving grievances that might otherwise escalate. Over time, the habits of cooperation shaped through trade can reduce misperceptions, build trust, and increase cooperation between states on other issues -- creating "an atmosphere congenial to the preservation of peace," as U.S. President Harry Truman put it in 1947, while making the case for the creation of an early international trade organization.

Given recent developments in Asia and Europe -- tensions over the East China and South China seas, the crisis in Ukraine -- the strategic implications of U.S. trade policy have rarely been clearer. For many of the countries that would be party to the TPP, the economic benefits of the agreement are further sweetened by expectations that the United States will become more deeply embedded in the region. And just as completing the tpp would underscore Washington's commitment to development and stability in Asia during a time of flux, finalizing the Transatlantic Trade and Investment Partnership (T-TIP) would send an unmistakable signal to the world about the strength of the U.S.-European bond -- a timely reminder, as the crisis in Ukraine has triggered deep unease across the continent.

The economic ties between the United States and its European trading partners are substantial: $1 trillion in trade each year, $4 trillion in investments, and jobs for 13 million American and European workers whose employment depends on transatlantic trade and investment. T-TIP aims to strengthen those already robust ties by better aligning the regulations and standards that the United States and European countries impose on firms -- without compromising the environmental safeguards or health and safety measures that protect consumers on both sides of the Atlantic. From an economic perspective, T-TIP presents an enormous opportunity to increase trade, potentially grow the economies of the United States and its European partners by hundreds of billions of dollars, and support hundreds of thousands of additional jobs. And many in Europe believe that T-TIP will not only spur much-needed economic growth but also support efforts to reform European energy policies and create greater energy security.

KEEP ON GROWING

U.S. trade policy aims not only to update the global economic architecture but also to expand it. In the postwar era, the United States has been a leader in providing market access to developing countries. More people now benefit from the global trading system than at any time in history. Unfortunately, however, what then UN Secretary-General Kofi Annan said at the beginning of this century still remains true: "The main losers in today's very unequal world are not those who are too much exposed to globalization. They are those who have been left out." The world's poorest countries still face significant challenges, but by encouraging good governance and sustainable growth, U.S. trade policy can help alleviate poverty and promote stability.

Trade cannot solve every development challenge, but it is a necessary part of any successful and sustainable development strategy. Trade fuels faster growth, stimulates investment, and promotes competition, which results in more jobs and more income for the poor. Growth and investment, in turn, make it easier for developing countries to finance antipoverty programs and improve public services. This virtuous cycle depends on a number of factors, such as strong institutions, the rule of law, sufficient infrastructure, and quality health care and education. Foreign assistance plays a critical role in many of these areas as well, but over time, truly sustainable growth requires trade and investment.

The link between trade and development has never been stronger than in recent decades. Between 1991 and 2011, developing countries' share of world trade doubled and nearly one billion people escaped poverty. Some of the countries that were most engaged in trade, including many in Asia, saw the greatest progress in development, whereas countries that remained largely closed, including many in the Middle East and North Africa, generally saw substantially less progress. In the mid-1990s, foreign direct investment in developing countries surpassed the amount they received in foreign aid. And last year, for the first time in history, the value of trade between developing countries exceeded that between developing and developed countries.

Trade-led development serves U.S. interests by growing markets for U.S. exports and by preventing conflict. It is also an important expression of American values. U.S. trade policy supports greater competition, more participation in the market, and more rigorous labor and environmental standards. In doing so, U.S. trade policy advances broader definitions of international security, including human security and environmental security.

The United States' commitment to promoting development through trade is at the heart of the African Growth and Opportunity Act, which has opened U.S. markets to a wide array of African exports, including textiles, apparel, horticultural goods, and processed agricultural products. Adopted near the end of the Clinton administration, AGOA has become the cornerstone of U.S. trade policy with sub-Saharan Africa. From 2001 to 2013, U.S. imports covered by AGOA more than tripled, including a nearly fourfold increase in non-oil imports. During the same period, the amount of U.S. direct investment in sub-Saharan countries nearly quadrupled.

AGOA has supported hundreds of thousands of jobs in sub-Saharan Africa, creating economic opportunities that otherwise might not exist. The United States has benefited from the stability that has accompanied this increased prosperity, as well as from the market opportunities AGOA has created for U.S. firms. Since 2001, U.S. exports to the region have more than tripled, and last year, those exports supported nearly 120,000 American jobs. Africa -- home to the world's fastest-growing middle classes and several of the world's fastest-growing economies -- will likely continue to rise, economically and geopolitically, in the coming years. Still, there is much more to be done. The Obama administration has proposed not just renewing AGOA but also updating it to reflect changes within Africa and between African countries and their trading partners. Doing so would send a strong message to the world that the United States is deeply committed to Africa and to promoting broad-based development through trade.

BUYING IN TO TRADE

The Obama administration's three strategic trade objectives -- establishing and enforcing rules of the road, strengthening partnerships, and promoting development -- all serve the greater goal of revitalizing the international economic architecture. Establishing and enforcing rules of the road will ensure that tomorrow's global trading system is consistent with American values and interests. Strengthening the United States' partnerships and alliances with other countries will protect that system and lay the foundation for pursuing broader mutual interests. Promoting broad-based, inclusive development will expand that system so that its benefits are both greater and more widely shared.

The economic foundation of the Obama administration's trade agenda is sound, and the strategic stakes of following through with it could not be higher. Given the current constraints on fiscal and monetary policies, there is no better source of growth than trade. As tensions rise in Asia and on the periphery of Europe, the strategic merits of the TPP and T-TIP become even clearer.

At the same time, Washington faces unprecedented constraints in crafting trade policy. The United States no longer holds as dominant a position in the global economy as it did at the end of World War II, and it must build trade coalitions willing to work toward consensus positions. Meanwhile, the economic struggles facing many Americans have fostered a sense of insecurity and skepticism about the benefits of trade.

Such concerns are legitimate, but too often they reflect a conflation of the impact of technological change and economic globalization with the effects of trade agreements. To help address these worries and better engage Congress, the public, and other stakeholders, the Obama administration has worked to make its trade agenda the most transparent in U.S. history, closely discussing trade issues and negotiations with small-business owners, nongovernmental organizations, and labor unions and holding more than 1,400 congressional briefings on the TPP alone. The Office of the U.S. Trade Representative consults with congressional committees on every proposal the United States makes during trade negotiations, and any member of Congress can review the negotiating texts.

These efforts have given unprecedented weight to public input and congressional oversight. Congress' involvement could be further enhanced and institutionalized by the passage of trade promotion authority, which would allow Congress to guide trade policy by laying out the United States' negotiating objectives, defining how the executive branch must consult with Congress about trade agreements, and detailing the legislative procedures that will guide Congress' consideration of trade agreements. At the same time, by ensuring that Congress will consider trade agreements as they have been negotiated by the executive branch, trade promotion authority would give U.S. trading partners the necessary confidence to put their best and final offers on the table. Trade promotion authority has a long, bipartisan history -- stretching back to President Franklin Roosevelt and the U.S. Congress during the New Deal era -- of ensuring congressional oversight while also strengthening the United States' hand at the international bargaining table.

CHOOSE OR LOSE

Trade initiatives such as the TPP, T-TIP, and AGOA give Americans a chance to shape the global economy, rather than just be shaped by it. Increasingly, the rules-based, open trading system is competing with state-directed, mercantilist models. The United States is not alone in working to define the rules of the road in the Asia-Pacific, for example, and not all of the United States' competitors share Washington's commitment to raising labor and environmental standards, enforcing intellectual property rights, ensuring that state-owned enterprises compete fairly with private firms, and maintaining a free and open Internet. Failing to deliver on the Obama administration's agenda would mean missing an opportunity to create safer workplaces, a better environment, and healthier and more open societies. The failure to lead could spill into other domains as others filled the gap.

There is no doubt that it is in the interests of American workers, farmers, and ranchers; manufacturers and service providers; entrepreneurs and inventors for the United States to actively shape the global trading system and promote a race to the top, rather than engage in a race to the bottom. If the United States wants to strengthen its economic power and extend its strategic influence during uncertain times, Washington must make a decision: either lead on global trade or be left on the sidelines. There really is no choice.

MICHAEL FROMAN is the U.S Trade Representative.

Fair Trade

The TPP's Promise and Pitfalls

Rebecca Liao

DARREN WHITESIDE / REUTERS

A worker uses a blow torch to break up parts of a ship brought to shore for scrap metal near Tanjung Priok port in North Jakarta December 3, 2015.

The rebalance to Asia undertaken by the administration of U.S. President Barack Obama is perhaps the most important Western initiative in the region since U.S. President Richard Nixon went to China in the early 1970s. A linchpin for this strategy is the Trans-Pacific Partnership (TPP), a sweeping trade agreement that has been tasked with three main objectives: to bring the United States closer to Asia's sizable economic markets, to establish the world's largest free trade zone, and to challenge China's dominance in the Pacific Rim.

After the agreement's actual text was released in November, though, critics of the TPP have raised doubts about whether it can achieve any of those goals. Several influential members of Congress, including Senators Orrin Hatch (R-Utah) and Bernie Sanders (D-Vt.), have expressed their disappointment with aspects of the deal. Sanders, a U.S. presidential candidate, stated that "the disastrous Trans-Pacific Partnership trade agreement . . . will hurt consumers and cost American jobs." Industry representatives from Ford Motor Company and the Pharmaceutical Research and Manufacturers of America have expressed concerns with the lack of provisions against currency manipulation and more extensive patent protection for brand-name drugs, respectively.

The TPP's detractors all have their points, but the five years of negotiation that led to the deal should not go to waste. If the TPP is to live up to its creators' expectations, its member states must come up with solutions to the problems that its critics have identified. Long-term, innovative policies are required to make the TPP work, whether the deal is perfect or not.

WINNERS AND LOSERS IN THE UNITED STATES

The TPP does have both benefits and drawbacks for the United States. According to a widely cited report by the Peterson Institute for International Economics (PIIE), the TPP's total benefits to the global economy could reach $223 billion by 2025. That same year, U.S. income gains would hit $77 billion, or 0.1 percent of the nation's GDP. U.S. export gains are also projected to reach $54.8 billion, an increase of 1.9 percent. Foreign direct investment would similarly rise by 1.9 percent, reaching $169 billion.

But as with all trade deals, these gains will not be spread evenly. The services industry, in which the United States already runs a trade surplus, will benefit disproportionately. So too will agriculture, owing to the new export markets for staple foods such as beef, corn, and soybeans. And technology firms stand to gain ground thanks to the relaxation and elimination of protectionist policies within TPP member nations aimed at incubating domestic technology sectors. The semiconductor industry, for example, is particularly encouraged by rules that will prohibit market-access restrictions on encrypted products, measures that countries had previously put in place on cybersecurity grounds.

At the same time, however, the TPP will likely have negative consequences for employment in the United States, particularly in the manufacturing sector. The public understands that free trade deals typically lead to lower overseas labor costs, which in turn depresses domestic wages. But the dynamics are much more complex than that. In recent years, manufacturing companies have begun to bring back jobs to the United States because of rising international wages and a desire to improve quality control for their products and services. In fact, since 2010, manufacturing jobs in the United States have increased by approximately one million, according to the Bureau of Labor Statistics.

With the TPP in place, however, this trend should reverse. Approximately 650,000 more people (0.5 percent of the U.S. labor force) will find work in export-related jobs, with a smaller number winning jobs in fields that compete with imported goods. The PIIE has made the argument that export-related jobs are likely to be higher paying and would therefore raise the median U.S. wage, leading to welfare gains in the United States to the tune of $459,000 per job. Others, including the economist David Rosnick of the Center for Economic and Policy Research, are less optimistic, concluding that median wage earners will see their wages go down, while low-income workers will maintain their level of wages and high-income employees will see their pay rise even more.

ISSEI KATO / REUTERS

Campaign stickers on packages of meat meant to promote beef meat imported from Australia at a supermarket in Tokyo, Japan, November 16, 2015.

However one comes down on the TPP, U.S. employment issues are better solved by looking beyond the deal. The partnership only reinforces a nearly five-decade-long trend in the United States in which service jobs have replaced manufacturing positions. Even if the TPP yields more service positions, this trend cannot continue unchecked. To be sure, low-skilled manufacturing work may be performed at a lower cost and with greater efficiency in other TPP member countries, but high-skilled manufacturing jobs are a key driver of economic productivity and wage levels in the United States, and losing them would be devastating.

If the United States is to regain its competitiveness in the manufacturing sector, it must invest in technologies that allow workers to do their jobs more efficiently. Other sectors of the U.S. economy could provide these solutions, and as the Nobel laureate Michael Spence argues in The Next Convergence, Washington can establish public policies (particularly in infrastructure and technology, where such high-skilled manufacturing jobs may be found) to promote their development now.

WHAT THE TPP DOES AROUND THE WORLD

The TPP comes with benefits and drawbacks for other countries as well. On the one hand, the timing of the agreement's passage is not ideal, given that the World Trade Organization's Doha Round of negotiations on a comprehensive global trade regime are nearly 80 percent complete. On the other, the TPP supports the work of the Doha talks. As the North American Free Trade Agreement put pressure on the WTO Uruguay Rounds to reach a final agreement on global trading systems, the TPP could encourage countries to resume stalled Doha proceedings, lest the United States and others abandon Doha and focus their efforts on further piecemeal free trade agreements.

There is no doubt, however, that the WTO is aware of the deep fissures in its multilateral foundations, and the TPP is but the latest blow to the notion of a global trade regime. Economists such as Columbia University Professors Jagdish Bhagwati and Joseph Stiglitz have argued that the proliferation of bilateral and regional free trade agreements can lead to a "spaghetti bowl" of trade regulations that create confusion, inefficiency, and economic losses.

None of this is to suggest that Asia or the United States should rely only on Doha to achieve the urgent goal of economic integration. A global regime would, by necessity, require more lead time to take effect and be unable to take advantage of local synergies in production capacities, economic systems, geography, and even governing institutions. At the time that the TPP was being negotiated, a couple of other Asian free trade agreements were in the works. The Regional Comprehensive Economic Partnership had progressed the furthest. Encompassing all members of the Association of Southeast Asian Nations (ASEAN) and the countries with which they have free trade agreements, the RCEP trade area represents approximately 27 percent of global trade, with a combined GDP of $21 trillion. RCEP negotiations first began in November 2012 at the East Asia Summit and have steadily progressed since. At last year's Asia-Pacific Economic Cooperation summit, member countries agreed to launch a two-year study into establishing the Free Trade Area of the Asia-Pacific (FTAAP), an initiative spearheaded by China in response to the TPP that would cover all countries in the Pacific Rim.

Though there was by no means a horserace between the TPP, RCEP, and FTAAP to become the dominant trade regime in Asia, the economic dynamics in the region have changed significantly now that the TPP deal has been finalized. Given U.S. and Latin American participation, the TPP has the most heterogeneous membership roster out of the three. The TPP is betting that greater economic integration within Asia and with the rest of the world will be best achieved through convergence to an international, not local, order. It remains to be seen whether the economic relations among Asian countries can be normalized while governed by these different agreements. The rules of origin, for example, remain an area of confusion even at the WTO level and are unlikely to be harmonized with the proliferation of free trade agreements.

Edgar Su / Reuters
The central business district is seen shrouded by slight haze in Singapore, August 20, 2015.

In addition to the wrench it throws into these ongoing trade negotiations, the TPP has several drawbacks. The TPP's "gold standards" in trade and governance regulations closely align with U.S. law and may not be appropriate in emerging markets. For example, the stringent U.S. patent and copyright laws that made it into the final TPP text do more to protect larger businesses than foster innovation. The deal also includes environmental protections that may be too costly for developing industrial economies. In fact, the TPP has set forth a host of legal and economic requirements that will push developing markets to adopt reforms before they are ready to do so.

The TPP also wades into one of the world's thorniest globalization issues: the loss of national sovereignty. Under the TPP, investor-state dispute settlement (ISDS) mechanisms will allow private entities (namely, corporations) to sue countries for TPP violations. Historically, these suits have been settled in favor of the United States and other countries with lots of economic clout. The ISDS system provides little transparency about its arbitration decisions, and no appeals process exists through which incorrect decisions can be ameliorated.

Additionally—and perhaps most important—the TPP will further divide Asia between those countries that are more welcoming of U.S. regional influence and those that fear offending China by aligning with Washington on trade. In order to establish a true free trade area in Asia and unlock the economic benefits that come with it, these countries will have to come together through smaller regional agreements, such as the RCEP or the FTAAP. Now that the TPP has made it across the finish line first, Asian unity and integration have become much more complicated propositions.

WHY THE TPP IS NECESSARY

In spite of its flaws, it's hard to overstate how important the TPP is for global economic policy and for Washington's interests in Asia. The Asian Development Bank estimates that the region's developing countries will grow by 6.3 percent in both 2015 and 2016, making it one of the most dynamic regions in the world. China has made significant inroads toward becoming the dominant player in Asia's growth. In 2007, China surpassed the United States as the trade leader with ASEAN and has maintained that position ever since. Last year, China's total goods trade with ASEAN reached $480 billion, more than twice that of the United States.

Leaving aside China's interests in establishing political and economic clout in Asia, Beijing recognizes that it needs to deepen its economic engagement with its neighbors. In the last four years, China's foreign direct investment increased at a compound annual growth rate of 16 percent, twice that of the global average. However, Southeast Asia receives only four percent of China's investment. On the trade front, the region's low-cost industrial inputs are crucial to China's transition from a manufacturing to a services economy in the years ahead. So for China's own economic growth to continue, investment needs to increase.

Despite some fears about Beijing's growing economic bargaining power and military might, China remains the paramount example of successful development in Asia. The difference between the U.S. and Chinese approaches in this area could not be clearer. China has existing free trade agreements with all ten ASEAN countries, and none of them address issues that the U.S. considers non-negotiable for future trade agreements (such as intellectual property, environmental policy, and labor rights). Perhaps for that reason, until the TPP, the United States had only one free trade agreement in the area—with Singapore.

China's agnosticism about legal and governance institutions is apparent in its Asian Infrastructure Investment Bank and the "One Belt, One Road" initiative, China's marquee international economic initiatives. The AIIB pledges to spend up to $100 billion on infrastructure needs in Asia, and the "One Belt, One Road" initiative pledges $40 billion toward development in its member countries, which span from Central Asia to Europe and even Africa. The AIIB and "One Belt, One Road" both promise to invest capital first and ask questions afterward. Although China will doubtless keep an eye out for the health of its investments, it refuses to do so through mandating standards common in the Western industrialized world. Beijing maintains this perspective not only because it cannot comply with these standards itself but also because it aims to speak the same language of development as other emerging economies.

Although the TPP goes a long way in challenging China's dominance in Asia, it cannot be the only solution offered by those who are skeptical of Beijing's outsize role. The TPP will increase the growth of Asian economies: Indonesia stands to add four percent to its national income, and Vietnam will grow 14 percent by 2025. Japan, Korea, and Singapore will benefit a little less but will still see gains of two to three percent in their national incomes. However, the TPP's trade liberalization initiatives will require domestic reforms that will be very costly for developing Asian countries. Therefore, it is important that the United States join China's development initiatives in addition to passing the TPP. This strategy would allow the United States to challenge China economically, usher in long-term governance reforms that it deems central to the developing world, and prevent the country from monopolizing regional short-term development activity. More than simply a free trade agreement, then, the TPP presents the United States with a unique opportunity to adjust its long-standing global development model and lead on a new strategy.

The TPP's architects have heralded the deal as a "trade agreement for the twenty-first century" for the past five years. If the deal is to fulfill its promise, it needs to be supported by other twenty-first-century initiatives: greater support for highly skilled manufacturing jobs in the United States, harmonization with existing international economic systems, and participation in development programs that are driven by other countries. Ultimately, the TPP is on shaky ground not because it is imperfect but because it is expected to act alone.

REBECCA LIAO is an international corporate attorney, writer, and China analyst based in Silicon Valley.

How to Free Trade

And Still Protect Democracy

Petra Pinzler

FRANCOIS LENOIR / REUTERS

Anti-trade graffiti in Brussels, Belgium, July 27, 2015.

In the past, it was easy to make the case for free trade. Countries that reduced tariffs and opened their borders for new products and ideas were usually better off than those that shut their markets off. Free trade agreements seemed to create opportunities, help millions out of poverty, and generate growth. More trade, to cut a long story short, made the world a better place.

Today, a growing number of Europeans and Americans believe that the opposite is true. Free trade agreements have become increasingly unpopular. For example, last autumn, about 250,000 Germans demonstrated in Berlin against the Transatlantic Trade and Investment Partnership (TTIP), the trade pact that is currently being negotiated between the United States and the European Union. Around 3.2 million Europeans signed a petition against it, saying that the EU was "trading away our public services, consumer protection, environmental standards, and in fact, our democracy." The most prestigious association of judges, known as Deutscher Richterbund, also recently spoke out against an important component of TTIP, a clause on settling trade disputes, arguing that it had "neither a legal basis nor was necessary."

In the United States, meanwhile, there have been similar protests against the Transatlantic Partnership Agreement (TPP), which Washington signed with 11 Pacific Rim countries but that the U.S. Congress has yet to ratify. Protestors have also argued that the deal "undermines democracy" and allows corporate power to thwart environment and labor protections, as well as the right to free Internet. All the leading presidential candidates have spoken out against it: on the Democratic side, Hillary Clinton has said that she "opposes" TPP, and her party rival, Bernie Sanders, promises that he "will do all" he can to defeat it. Meanwhile, Republican Donald Trump trashes it, calling it a "horrible deal."

The foreign policy and trade elites usually regard these opinions with contempt. The German Economics Minister and Vice Chancellor Sigmar Gabriel portrayed the TTIP protesters as "hysterical." His American colleagues dismiss them as a bizarre return of anti-globalization fervor heightened by a whirlwind U.S. election. After all, hysteria often becomes the norm during election cycles. Trade elites also know that, in the last few decades, similar campaigns have almost never changed the course of trade deals, no matter who held the presidency. It stands to reason that this protest will fade away, too.

And yet, their perspective is shortsighted. Today's anti–free trade movement has gained a new relevance. It no longer appeals to only the real and self-perceived losers of globalization, such as the American Trade Union members and environmentalists who opposed the North American Free Trade Agreement in the 1990s. Today, the protest digs much deeper into mainstream society, particularly into the Western middle class. At the StopTTIP demonstration in Berlin last autumn, the streets surrounding the Brandenburg Gate were crowded by students and academics, as well as blue- and white-collar workers. These were the people who traditionally believe in cooperation, government, and global rules, but had now become concerned that modern trade policy has undermined democracy.

To understand how this shift happened, it is worth looking at how trade deals have changed. In the past, trade politics largely involved lowering duties. For example, one side offered to erase tariffs on meat if the other side did the same on cars. After some haggling behind closed doors, an agreement would be reached and governments could sign it. All this was deathly dull, but it made products cheaper and doing business across borders easier.

Marco Garcia / Reuters
The twelve Trans-Pacific Partnership (TPP) Ministers hold a press conference to discuss progress in the negotiations in Lahaina, Maui, Hawaii, July 31, 2015.

Today, traditional elements, such as eliminating tariffs, make up only a small part of trade agreements. Much more important are "non-tariff trade barriers," a technical but politically important term that restricts imports through regulations such as food safety standards, public services, or regulation of the Internet. As a result of trying to get rid of such barriers, trade agreements today reach far beyond the traditional sphere of business and into values, social norms, and social progress that have been defined and refined by decades of democratic governance. Today, trade agreements affect issues that people strongly care about and fight to make better.

Consider the example of patent protection. How long should a patent for a life-saving pill remain in place before others can copy it? If the protection is too weak, it diminishes incentives to invest in the product since no one would spend money to develop a product that can immediately be replicated by others. But if the protection is too strong, it hinders competition, harms innovation, and raises health-care costs.

The United States, as with many other developed countries, is usually well equipped to come up with a decent compromise. When democracy works, there is a public debate about an issue, after which a party or a politician might bring it before the legislature to reach a compromise and create a new law. This is what Western societies are supposed to be good at.

Modern trade agreements, however, frequently undermine this democratic process. Their job, in fact, is to create multinational rules to prevent democracies from setting and changing rules autonomously. To a certain extent this makes sense in the ever more interconnected world of business. However, once trade deals touch upon issues beyond mere logistics—when they start to affect health care and other social issues—it seems irresponsible to leave such decisions to trade experts. Unfortunately, this is exactly what is happening.

A good example is the TPP. This agreement was hashed out behind closed doors and none of its 30 chapters was ever put up for public discussion during the negotiation process. Even members of Congress faced difficulties in getting access to the TPP draft, and both they and the tiny group of civil society advisers who were given clearance still faced criminal prosecution if they discussed it with their own staff. Only after the negotiations were concluded was the text was finally made available to a broader public in November 2015. Shortly after its release, U.S. President Barack Obama asked Congress to greenlight the trade deal. At that point, the legislators could only agree to the TPP or refuse it. Rewriting is not an option. They have to decide if the pro-trade arguments—such as the lowering of some tariffs and forming an economic bloc with the 11 other Asian nations to challenge China—outweigh the disadvantages, such as the loss of jobs in some U.S. regions due to the outsourcing of cheap labor. There is also reduced access to health care in poorer countries, because new laws enabling pharmaceuticals to extend their monopolies on patented medicines restrict the availability of more affordable generic prescription drugs.

Some people argue that as long as trade deals promise growth they are fine. Others go even further and state that a bad deal is still better than no deal because it enhances cooperation. Both arguments are wrong. First, not all agreements lead to sustainable growth in all participating countries. Second, not every common boundary increases the political will to collaborate. Just look at the recent referendum in Scotland on leaving the United Kingdom after more that 400 years of common governance, or, more recently, the debate over Brexit, the British withdrawal from the EU.

FABRIZIO BENSCH / REUTERS

Consumer rights activists protest against the TTIP in Berlin, Germany, October 10, 2015.

In fact, a deal is only as good as the results it produces and this depends on the process through which it was made. A good deal requires broad participation, which not only increases the legitimacy of the agreement but also ensures protection of vulnerable populations or issues. The TPP, for example, does not mention at all the impact of trade on climate change. And it is no wonder, since there wasn't a single environmentalist on the negotiation team. Human rights is another example. One of the commonly stated aims of U.S. foreign policy is the promotion of human rights around the globe. But when the TPP was written, there was no opportunity for civil rights activists to publicly analyze its impact on partner countries and suggest workable suggestions to protect the human rights of those in the Asia-Pacific. Now, Human Rights Watch is arguing that the TTP's provisions will not adequately safeguard workers' rights.

Admittedly, there can be too many cooks. First of all, more participants often means slower deliberation. But the old-fashioned trade policy no longer delivers agreements that promote Western values. For example, in agreements that the United States or the EU signed, protections of human rights, the environment, and public health have often been treated as nuisances rather than as achievements. An unfortunate example is the U.S.- Colombia Free Trade Agreement. The text is filled with compelling language about the protection of human rights. In reality, though, the agreement has merely increased the number of goods imported to the United States that are produced under inhumane working conditions. And not a single paragraph of the agreement has stopped the murder of human rights and labor activists in Colombia.

Even worse, governments and companies have repeatedly used trade laws to undermine those very protections. In a recent ruling, the World Trade Organization struck down the country-of-origin meat labels required by the United States. Allegedly, these labels discriminate against foreign meat producers, even though consumers use them to make informed choices about their food. The TPP is likely to further erode public safeguards. For example, even though the TPP's proponents argue that the pact requires the legalization of independent labor unions in Vietnam, the legal means to enforce this through trade measures remain limited.

Credibility is easily lost and hard to rebuild. That is why the United States and the EU Commission must tread carefully. This does not mean denouncing the TTIP altogether. It still has the potential to become a model for twenty-first-century agreements, if only the negotiators take seriously what the West stands for. Europe and the United States share many values. They both believe in human rights and the protection of the planet, and appreciate innovation and competition. Why not promote a good mix of theses ambitions through the TTIP?

The way the TTIP could deal with environmental protection is a good example. In Europe today, many citizens are afraid that the TTIP will lower food standards, forcing people to eat genetically modified vegetables with high levels of pesticide residues or hormone-treated beef. Some of these fears are out of proportion, but they could also be easily calmed if this agreement was negotiated with a clearly pronounced aim to honor higher food standards. This might sound counterintuitive, as trade negotiations are traditionally about getting rid of regulations, but developing high standards is exactly what Europe and the United States have been good at.

MICHAELA REHLE / REUTERS

Environmental activists in Germany demonstrate against the TTIP, which they fear will allow "U.S. chlorine chickens" into the European market, Munich, October 1, 2014.

Higher standards can also be a boon to trade. According to the former EU trade commissioner Pascal Lamy, high safety standards are the West's competitive advantage. Standards are about not having to worry about milk formula being tainted with melamine, as has happened in China. High safety standards are what make Western products highly desirable and even enviable. In this month alone, Chinese tourists in Germany emptied supermarkets of baby milk formula. This practice is quite common across Europe, where there has been a recent growth of baby formula traffickers selling Western baby formula online. Chinese consumers appear to trust Western products more than domestically produced products. Why not use the TTIP to expand upon this effect?

With the TTIP, Europe and the United States can demonstrate to the world how to write agreements that make the world a safer place. Through trade, they can create the most prosperous and best-protected places to live. Together, they can enhance consumer protection and nature conservancy and transform the TTIP into a successful case study of how trade and Western values complement each other.

All this would be much easier, though, if trade negotiations were more open to input from various segments of society, such as regulators, ecologists, and foreign policy and human rights experts. An emphasis should be placed on new recruits to replace the outdated teams in the office of the U.S. Trade Representative and the EU's trade directorate. These new negotiators should not only support trade and globalization but also emphasize the voices of working people and those who care about democracy and the environment. Doing this would rejuvenate, broaden, and enrich the transatlantic relationship. Unfortunately, however, this can only happen if the TTIP is redesigned from scratch.

At this point, that seems unlikely to happen, as the negotiation teams on both sides of the Atlantic still prefer to continue business as usual. Yet, they are already in the third year of negotiations and have not made much progress on the issues at stake. Frustrations are rising and protests are growing more aggressive. This could reach a tipping point, which would create more pressure for a reset. Right now, delaying the TPP, which is possible because it's become so vilified during the election campaign season, could at least offer the time needed to rethink and redesign both it and the TTIP. Most important, it would offer a moment for reevaluating how the West can keep free trade while keeping its democracy free, too.

PETRA PINZLER is the author of the book *Der Unfreihandel* (*The Unfree Trade*) and is Berlin correspondent for the German weekly newspaper *Die Zeit.* Prior to that she worked for *Die Zeit* as a business editor and as a correspondent in Washington, D.C., and Brussels.

www.ingramcontent.com/pod-product-compliance
Lightning Source LLC
Chambersburg PA
CBHW081151270326
41930CB00014B/3111
* 9 7 8 0 8 7 6 0 9 6 8 1 9 *